KILLER
PSYCHOPATHS

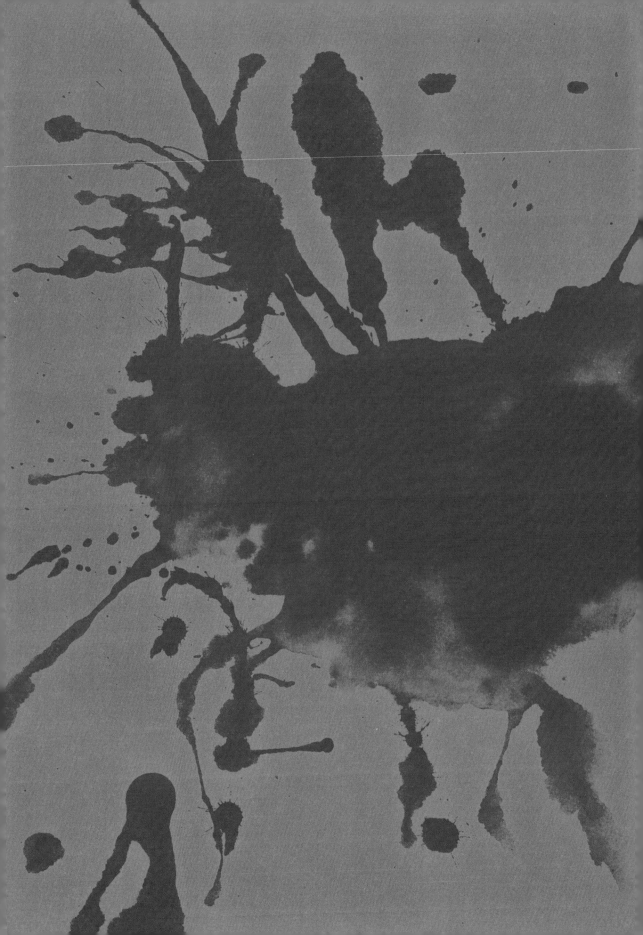

KILLER PSYCHOPATHS

**AL CIMINO, CHARLOTTE GREIG
AND JOHN MARLOWE**

SIRIUS

SIRIUS

This edition published in 2025 by Sirius Publishing, a division of
Arcturus Publishing Limited,
26/27 Bickels Yard, 151–153 Bermondsey Street,
London SE1 3HA

Copyright © Arcturus Holdings Limited

All rights reserved. No part of this publication may be reproduced, stored
in a retrieval system, or transmitted, in any form or by any means,
electronic, mechanical, photocopying, recording or otherwise, without
prior written permission in accordance with the provisions of the
Copyright Act 1956 (as amended). Any person or persons who do any
unauthorised act in relation to this publication may be liable to criminal
prosecution and civil claims for damages.

ISBN: 978-1-3988-5179-5
AD012481UK

Printed in China

CONTENTS

INTRODUCTION 6

CHAPTER 1
UNFORGIVING VIOLENCE 8
Gary Ridgway 10
Anatoly Onoprienko 18
Carl Panzram 22
Daniel Camargo Barbosa 28
Henry Lee Lucas. 32
Douglas Clark and Carol Bundy. . . .40
Charles Sobhraj 44
Paul Knowles 48
Peter Manuel. 52

CHAPTER 2
DOUBLE LIVES 58
Mikhail Popkov 60
Vlado Taneski 68
Jack Unterweger 74
Serhiy Tkach 80
Alexander Pichushkin 84

CHAPTER 3
BLOODY BUTCHERS 88
Robert Pickton 90
Katherine Knight 96
Dennis Rader 102
David Parker Ray and Cindy Hendy . . .116

CHAPTER 4
CHAMBERS OF HORROR 124
Leonard Lake and Charles Ng 126
Josef Fritzl 132
Gary Heidnik. 138
John Reginald Christie 148
Robert Berdella 154

CHAPTER 5
ANGELS OF DEATH 160
Harold Shipman. 162
Donald Harvey 168
Lainz Angels of Death 174
Beverley Allitt 178

CHAPTER 6
MASS MURDERERS 186
Anders Breivik. 188
Eric Harris and Dylan Klebold 192
Ted Kaczynski 196
Adam Lanza 200

Index 206
Picture Credits 208

Many serial killers have a warped childhood and have developed an almost overwhelming addiction to murder.

INTRODUCTION

Murder fascinates us all – whether it is the gentle slaughter written into existence by Agatha Christie or the choreographed butchery of Quentin Tarantino. Shakespeare's tragedies leave blood on the stage and in Dostoyevsky there would be no punishment if there hadn't been a crime – in *Crime and Punishment*, former law student Raskolnikov commits murder and sets in train his own downfall.

Murder in all its forms addresses unblinkingly the most fundamental question of human existence – the fact that we are going to die. So is everyone we know and love.

But murder is the thing we all fear more than anything. Somehow we must learn to come to terms with that. And as a writer, I know another thing about murder: no matter how gruesome, it always makes a good story. With serial killers – those addicted to murder – there is another element. Serial killers are the ultimate outlaws. They step outside not just the law, but any human norms. They are fascinating because they are almost impossible to understand.

But let's try. Say one night you accidentally killed someone and got away with it. Maybe it was an accident, but if you reported the incident to the authorities it would be impossible to escape the accusation of culpability.

If you went to jail, there would be terrible consequences for your family and children. So best keep quiet. The problem is, if you had killed once and got away with it, wouldn't there be a temptation to do it again? And again? If you got away with it each time, wouldn't it become addictive?

Some of the villains in this book slipped into serial killing that way, though rarely for the purest of motives. Usually the impulse is sexual and truly none of us are in our right minds when it comes to matters of the heart. Often they have had an almost pitiably warped childhood. Cranial trauma and other brain damage during their youth is sometimes a factor too. As they grow up, they find themselves gripped by an overwhelming urge to step outside the law. It may begin with small acts of vandalism or theft, then burglary, progressing to rape and finally murder.

Clearly, some of the perpetrators are purely evil and no excuses can be made for them. Others do seem to struggle with themselves. Many are relieved when they are finally caught, knowing that, if left at large, they would continue killing.

While studying serial killers gives us a powerful insight into the human condition, we must not forget their victims. Each one is a tragedy. Many are young and vulnerable and all of them are ruthlessly deprived of the possibilities and pleasures of a fulfilling life simply for the gratification of someone who is clearly, by any measure, inadequate. But there is nothing to be done. Those who have been murdered cannot be revived.

Then there are the families and friends of the victims to consider, who must go through the rest of their lives knowing that someone they loved has been snuffed out. They must deal with the urge for revenge, or somehow struggle with themselves to find a way to forgive. In most cases, I am sure that is impossible.

Some must ask how they did not see it coming. The parents of someone who kills, however blameless, must wonder whether it was something they did that sent their offspring down the road to murder. The children of killers even ask themselves whether they have inherited the murderous trait.

The people in this book are of a different order. It is clear that once they had killed they had to do it again. They got to enjoy it. Murder took over their lives, just the way crack cocaine or crystal meth takes over their users' lives. The killers in this book are quite literally addicted to murder.

CHAPTER 1

UNFORGIVING VIOLENCE

For most killers, the feelings of the victims never come into the equation. Begging and pleading only incite the killers to ever more brutal acts. The violence continues to grow as they discover that they have got away with their crimes, leading them to expand their reach and up their body counts. Some even have a gruesome fascination with their newfound notoriety.

GARY RIDGWAY

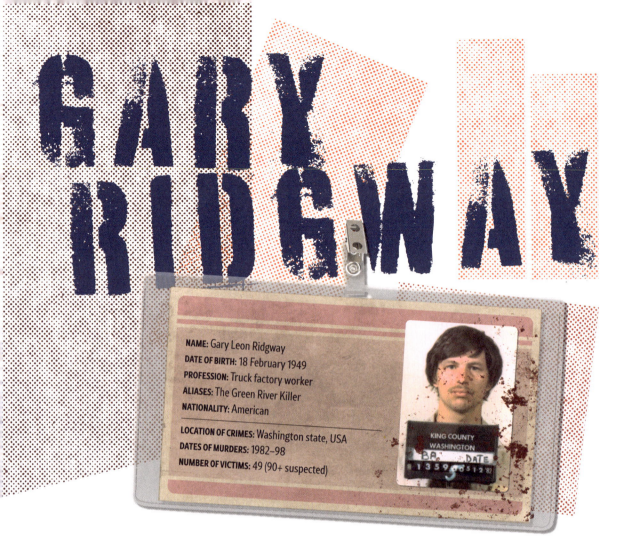

NAME: Gary Leon Ridgway
DATE OF BIRTH: 18 February 1949
PROFESSION: Truck factory worker
ALIASES: The Green River Killer
NATIONALITY: American

LOCATION OF CRIMES: Washington state, USA
DATES OF MURDERS: 1982–98
NUMBER OF VICTIMS: 49 (90+ suspected)

Gary Ridgway admitted killing 49 women between 1982 and 1984, dumping most of their bodies in or around the Green River in Washington state. There may have been many more. 'I killed so many women I have a hard time keeping them straight,' he said. The Green River Task Force worked on the case for nearly 20 years – even accepting advice at one point from notorious serial killer Ted Bundy, then on death row – until Ridgway was finally arrested in 2001.

On 15 July 1982, the body of 16-year-old Wendy Lee Coffield was found in the Green River east of Seattle. On 12 August the corpse of Debra Bonner, 23, was pulled from the same river, about half a mile upstream from where Wendy's body had been dumped. Detective Dave Reichert was assigned to the case. Three days later three more bodies – those of Marcia Faye Chapman, 31, Opal Charmaine Mills, 16, and Cynthia Jean Hinds, 17 – were found. They had all been strangled and a task force was set up to investigate what appeared to be a series of linked crimes.

Two earlier killings were not initially recognized as part of the series. On 21 January 1982, the body of 16-year-old Leann Wilcox was found in a field near Tacoma several miles from the river. A friend of Wendy Coffield, she too had been strangled. Then on 7 July 1982, 36-year-old Amina Agisheff disappeared. Her skeletal remains were not found and identified until April 1984.

The list of missing young women soon began to swell. Sixteen-year-old Kasee Ann Lee disappeared on 28 August. Ridgway admitted strangling her, but her body has never been found. Terry Rene Milligan went missing the following day. Three more teenagers disappeared in September. The killer claimed three more victims in October, and another two in December.

He killed twice the following March, five times in April and four more times in May. Between June 1983 and March 1984, Ridgway killed at least another 15. Then the murders became more sporadic.

There were murders in 1987, 1990 and 1998 that Ridgway confessed to, along with another four where he was not sure of the date. He was suspected of another ten murders which he did not confess to, or there was not enough evidence for charges to be filed.

The killings tailed off after Ridgway began dating Judith Mawson, who became his third wife in 1988. Interviewed in prison, Ridgway said that his urge to kill declined once he was in a relationship with Mawson. It did not go away completely, though. When she moved into his house while they were dating, Mawson noticed there was no carpet. The police later told her Ridgway had probably used the carpet to wrap up a body.

Mawson said Ridgway would leave for work early in the morning some days and, later, assumed that he must have committed some of the murders while supposedly working those early shifts. She claimed that she had not suspected Ridgway before he was first contacted by the authorities in 1987 and had not even heard of the Green River Killer because she did not watch the news.

CUTTING A DEAL

For the Green River Task Force, Gary Ridgway's name had been in the frame since the beginning. In 1980, he was interviewed after a prostitute accused him of trying to throttle her. He said that she had bitten him and choked her to make her stop. The police picked him up with prostitute Kelly Kay McGinniss in 1982. She disappeared a year later and her body was never found.

Following the disappearance of 18-year-old Marie Malvar on 30 April 1983, Ridgway was a leading suspect. The police questioned him and he denied all knowledge of her, even though a friend of hers

The Green River is a beautiful if fairly insignificant stretch of water appreciated for its fishing and whitewater rafting. In the summer of 1982, it became the dumping ground for the bodies of Gary Ridgway's victims.

The Green River Task Force comb the landscape looking to retrieve the bodies of Ridgway's victims.

Ridgway was arrested and charged with the murders of Marcia Chapman, Opal Mills, Cynthia Hinds and 21-year-old Carol Ann Christensen, who went missing on 4 May 1983 and was found four days later by a family picking mushrooms. Her body had been displayed in a particularly gruesome way. Her head was covered by a paper bag, with a fish placed on top of her neck. There was another fish on her left breast and a bottle between her legs. Her hands were crossed over her stomach with freshly ground beef placed on top of them. Her body showed signs of having been in water, even though the river was miles away. Ridgway pleaded not guilty to all charges when arraigned.

In March 2003, three more counts of murder were added, those of Debra Bonner, Wendy Coffield and 15-year-old Debra Estes, who went missing on 20 September 1982 and was not found until 30 May 1988 – after a forensic scientist identified microscopic spheres of paint of the type used at the Kenworth truck factory where Ridgway worked as a spray painter. Again, he pleaded not guilty.

However, just before his trial in November 2003 Ridgway entered into a plea bargain to avoid the death penalty. He confessed to 48 killings – although he said the total might be more than 60. As it was, the number he confessed to was more than the 41 on the Green River Task Force's list, but less that the 71 he was actually suspected of.

On 5 November 2003, Ridgway pleaded guilty to 48 counts of aggravated first-degree murder, saying that he had been motivated by a deep hatred for prostitutes.

> **'I WANTED TO KILL AS MANY WOMEN I THOUGHT WERE PROSTITUTES AS I POSSIBLY COULD. I THOUGHT I COULD KILL AS MANY OF THEM AS I WANTED WITHOUT GETTING CAUGHT.'**

However, not all of his victims had been prostitutes. Some were teenage runaways and drug addicts. Others seem to have been selected at random. He picked up women sometimes by showing them a picture of his son from his second marriage to engender trust.

After having sex with his victim, Ridgway strangled the woman from behind. Initially he did this manually. But when victims, trying to defend themselves, inflicted possibly incriminating wounds and

had seen Marie get into a truck that was thought to be Ridgway's. Her body was not found until September 2003, after Ridgway had finally confessed to her murder.

In May 1984 he took a lie detector test, but the polygraph cleared him. Nevertheless, Ridgway remained 'a person of interest'. In 1988, the police obtained a warrant to search his house, but found nothing incriminating. They also got permission to take a saliva sample to determine his blood group. Although DNA fingerprinting had been introduced in 1985, it was not then a reliable procedure if the amount of DNA was small. However, scientists later developed methods of amplification. In November 2001, samples saved from the earlier blood tests were subjected to DNA analysis and it was found that Ridgway's DNA matched that of semen recovered from the bodies of four victims of the Green River Killer.

Police Lieutenant Dan Nolan stands beside a display of the Green River Killer's victims, many of whom were left in the forest and picked clean by scavengers. Ridgway may have killed many more women than he was arraigned for.

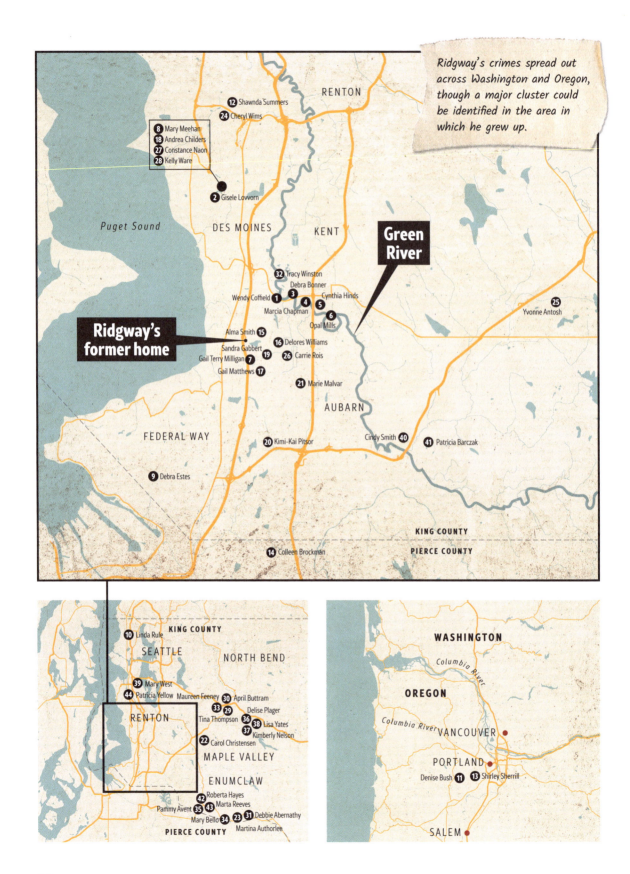

Gary Ridgway was found to have an IQ of just 82. As a boy he was a bed-wetter and his mother used to belittle him in front of his family.

bruises on his arm, he began to use ligatures to strangle his victims.

Most victims were killed in his home, in his truck, or in a secluded area. The bodies were often posed naked. They were left in clusters around certain areas, which gave Ridgway a thrill when he drove by. Sometimes he would return to a body and have sex with it. Later, he began burying his victims to remove that temptation.

A TROUBLED AND CONFUSED MAN

Ridgway was found to have a low IQ of just 82. As a boy he was a bed-wetter. His mother would use this to belittle him in front of his family. He admitted, from a young age, to having conflicted feelings of anger and sexual attraction towards her. At 16, he stabbed a six-year-old boy, saying he wondered what it would feel like to kill someone.

At 18, he joined the navy. Away from home a lot, Ridgway began to use prostitutes and his first wife also began to stray. His second wife accused him of trying to choke her. He became a religious zealot, while still using prostitutes. He also had an insatiable appetite for sex, forcing his wife to make love with him in public places, including areas where his victims' bodies were later discovered.

Before his sentencing, the families of Ridgway's victims were allowed to address the court.

'Gary Ridgway is an evil creature who I would condemn to many, many long years of anguish and despair,' said Nancy Gabbert, whose

Green River Killer Gary Ridgway cries in court as he listens to testimony from relatives of his victims. He avoided the death penalty by agreeing to help police find the bodies of those who were still missing.

17-year-old daughter, Sandra, was killed in 1983.

'I was only five when my mother died,' Sara King, daughter of Carol Ann Christensen, whose body was found in 1983, told him. 'The one thing I want you to know is that there was a daughter at home. I was that daughter… waiting for my mother to come home.'

The grieving relatives called Ridgway a coward, a monster, an animal, a devil, a vile killer and a paedophile. A handful angrily wished that he would burn in hell. More than a few said they hoped he would meet a violent end in prison.

'I can only hope that someday, someone gets the opportunity to choke you unconscious 48 times so you can live through the horror that you put our mothers and daughters through,' said Tim Meehan, brother of Mary Meehan, whose body was also found in 1983. 'To me you are already dead.'

Ridgway turned slightly from the defence table to face the speakers, but he appeared largely unaffected by their words until Robert Rule approached the microphone. Ridgway had murdered his 16-year-old daughter, Linda, in 1982.

'Mr Ridgway, there are people here that hate you,' Robert Rule said. 'I'm not one of them. I forgive you for what you have done.'

As Rule spoke, Ridgway wiped away tears.

A statement from Ridgway's family was also read in court: 'Be assured that we were shocked to hear that Gary could do the things he has admitted to doing. However, we love Gary, and believe that the Gary Ridgway America now knows is different from the person known by our family. Clearly, there were two Gary Ridgways.'

Ridgway himself read an apology from a yellow legal pad.

'I know how horrible my acts were,' he said. 'I have tried for a long time to get these things out of my mind. I have tried for a long time to keep from killing any more ladies.'

He read in a halting tone, stopping to remove his glasses and wipe his eyes once more.

'I have tried hard to remember as much as I could to help the detectives find and recover the ladies,' he said, adding, 'I'm sorry for killing these ladies. They had their whole lives ahead of them… I'm very sorry for the ladies that were not found. May they rest in peace. They need a better place than what I gave them.'

However, the judge dismissed Ridgway's emotions as 'Teflon-coated'.

'There is nothing in your life that was significant other than your own demented, calculating and lustful passion of being the emissary of death,' he said.

Ridgway was given 48 life sentences without the possibility of parole, plus another ten years for each victim for tampering with the evidence – giving him another 480 years to serve.

'You violated the sanctity of every relationship in your life,' the judge said. 'As you spend the balance of your life in your tiny cell surrounded only by your thoughts, please know that the women you killed were not throwaways or pieces of candy in a dish placed upon this planet for the sole purpose of satisfying your murderous desires.'

He asked Ridgway to turn around and look at the faces of the victims' relatives and friends who packed the courtroom.

'Mr Ridgway,' Judge Richard Jones said. 'Those are the families and friends of the people you killed. I truly hope that the last thoughts you have of the free world are of the faces of the people in this courtroom.'

Referring to Ridgway's method of strangling his victims from behind, the judge said: 'While you could not face them as you took their lives, if you have a drop of emotion anywhere in your existence, you will face those young women in your dreams.'

THE FINAL TALLY

In 2011, Ridgway pleaded guilty to a 49th murder – that of Rebecca 'Becky' Marrero, a 20-year-old mother last seen on 3 December 1982. Her skull was found in December 2010, not far from where Marie Malvar had been unearthed. Ridgway had already confessed to murdering her, but there was no evidence to charge him. Once the body part was identified by dental records, he submitted a guilty plea under the plea bargain he had entered into in 2003.

Ted Bundy had offered his help in the hunt for the person he called 'Riverman', fearing that the Green River Killer would eclipse his reputation as a serial killer. During one interview session, Bundy suggested that the killer was most likely revisiting his dump sites to engage in sexual intercourse with the bodies. He advised the investigators in case they find a fresh grave to stake it out and wait for the killer to return. Bundy went to the electric chair before Ridgway was caught.

The prosecutor shows a photo of the murder victim Rebecca Marrero at a press conference after her body was found in 2011, nearly 30 years after she disappeared.

ANATOLY ONOPRIENKO

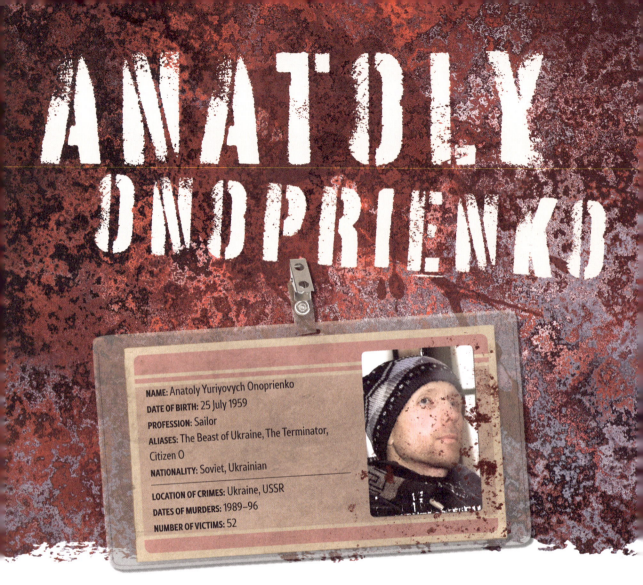

NAME: Anatoly Yuriyovych Onoprienko
DATE OF BIRTH: 25 July 1959
PROFESSION: Sailor
ALIASES: The Beast of Ukraine, The Terminator, Citizen O
NATIONALITY: Soviet, Ukrainian
LOCATION OF CRIMES: Ukraine, USSR
DATES OF MURDERS: 1989–96
NUMBER OF VICTIMS: 52

Anatoly Onoprienko was the second major serial killer to emerge in the former USSR after the collapse of communism, following the Rostov Ripper, Andrei Chikatilo. Onoprienko was a brutal killer with a particularly unusual pathology. Quite simply, Onoprienko liked to kill families – children and all – acting with a ruthlessness that led the newspapers to dub him 'the Terminator'.

Onoprienko was born in the town of Laski in Ukraine. His mother died when he was just four years old and his father placed him in an orphanage, though he kept his older son at home. This appears to have been the foundation of Onoprienko's rage at humanity and families in particular. He never forgave his father for discarding him, and he took a terrible revenge.

JACK OF ALL TRADES

After he left the orphanage, Onoprienko worked as a forester and as a sailor, and was known to the mental health authorities in the Ukrainian capital of Kiev. The first spate of killings with which he is associated happened in 1989. With an accomplice, Sergei Rogozin, Onoprienko carried out a series of burglaries. During one of these robberies the pair were interrupted by the house owners. Onoprienko promptly killed them. He followed this up by killing the occupants of a parked car.

Afterwards, Onoprienko split with Rogozin. His movements over the next six years, as communism collapsed and Ukraine became an independent state, remain mysterious. He is known to have roamed around central Europe for a while and was expelled from both Germany and Austria, but whether he was responsible for any further murders during that time remains unclear.

18 UNFORGIVING VIOLENCE

The town of Bratkovichi in Ukraine, the scene of many of Onoprienko's crimes.

BLOODIEST SPREE IN HISTORY

What is certain is that he was back in Ukraine at the end of 1995, for it was then that he began one of the bloodiest murder sprees in history, killing 43 victims in little more than three months. As before, Onoprienko targeted houses on the edge of small towns and villages across Ukraine; this time, however, he was not interested in burglary, only in killing.

He began on Christmas Eve 1995 by breaking into the home of the Zaichenko family. He murdered the couple and their two children with a double-barrelled shotgun, took a few souvenirs, then set the house on fire. Six days later in the town of Bratkovichi, a place that was to become a regular hunting ground, he broke into another house and killed the couple who lived there and the wife's twin sisters. Before his next family killing, almost as a side show, he spent 6 January killing motorists, four in all, along the Berdyansk-Dnieprovskaya highway.

'TO ME IT WAS LIKE HUNTING. HUNTING PEOPLE DOWN.'

Next, on 17 January, he headed back to Bratkovichi. There he broke into the house of the Pilat family, killing the five people who lived there and then setting the house on fire. As he left, two people saw him, so he shot both of them as well.

Later that same month he headed east to the town of Fastova, where he killed four more people, a nurse and her family. He then went west to Olevsk, where, on 19 February, he broke into the home of the Dubchak family. He shot the father and son, and battered the mother and daughter to death with a hammer. He later told investigators that the daughter had seen him murder her parents and was praying when he came up to her.

'SECONDS BEFORE I SMASHED HER HEAD, I ORDERED HER TO SHOW ME WHERE THEY KEPT THEIR MONEY. SHE LOOKED AT ME WITH AN ANGRY, DEFIANT STARE AND SAID, "NO, I WON'T." THAT STRENGTH WAS INCREDIBLE. BUT I FELT NOTHING.'

Just over a week later, Onoprienko drove to Malina, where he murdered all four of the Bodnarchuk family, shooting the husband and wife and using an axe to despatch their two daughters, aged seven and eight.

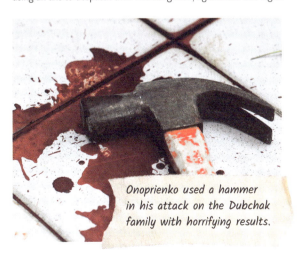

Onoprienko used a hammer in his attack on the Dubchak family with horrifying results.

Onoprienko in prison, minded by a guard.

ONOPRIENKO'S MURDERS

14 June 1989 – Oleg and Ludmila Melnik
16 July 1989 – Victor and Anna Vasylyuk
16 August 1989 – The Podolyak family
5 October 1995 – Galina Gryshchenko and Alexander Svetlovsky
28 October 1995 – Maria Parashchuk
24 December 1995 – The Zaichenko family
2 January 1996 – The Kryuchkov family, Mikhail Malinowski
5–6 January 1996 – Sergei Odintsov, Tamara Dolinin, Alexander Rybalko, Sergei Garmash, Victor Kasayev, Anatoly Savitsky, Nadezhda Kochergina
17 January 1996 – The Pilat family, Galina Kondzela, Stepan Zakharko
30 January 1996 – The Marusina family, Sergei Zaghranichny
19 February 1996 – The Dubchak family
26 February 1996 – Victor Gudz
27 February 1996 – The Bodnarchuk family, Boris Tsalk
22 March 1996 – The Novosad Family

Once again a passer-by who was unfortunate enough to witness the killer leaving the house was added to the death list.

Just over three weeks passed before Onoprienko struck again on 22 March 1996. He travelled to the small village of Busk, just outside the beleaguered town of Bratkovichi, to slaughter all four members of the Novosad family, shooting them and then burning their house. At this stage, the terrified villagers demanded help from the government, who responded by sending a full National Guard Unit, complete with rocket launchers, to ward off this unknown menace. Meanwhile, 2,000 officers became part of a gigantic manhunt.

CACHE OF WEAPONS

In the end, however, it was a relative of Onoprienko who brought about his capture. Onoprienko was staying with a cousin who, on finding a cache of weapons in his room, told him to leave the house and phoned the police. The police tracked Onoprienko to his girlfriend's house, where he was arrested on Easter Sunday, 16 April 1996. They found him listening to music on a tape deck stolen from the Novosad family. Further investigation revealed weapons used in the murders, plus a collection of souvenirs taken from his victims.

Once in custody Onoprienko demanded to speak to 'a general', and as soon as one was provided he confessed to 52 murders. He claimed to have been hearing voices that told him to commit the crimes. He also said that he had been treated for schizophrenia in a Kiev mental hospital. Disturbingly, Kiev's Interior Ministry initially disclosed that Onoprienko was an outpatient whose therapists knew him to be a killer, but they then refused to say any more about the matter.

In 1999, Onoprienko was convicted on 52 counts of murder and sentenced to life imprisonment. He died of heart failure in prison in 2013.

A TOZ-34ER hunting gun, Onoprienko's favourite weapon, though despite his extensive arsenal, he was happy to use whatever came to hand.

CARL PANZRAM

NAME: Charles Panzram
DATE OF BIRTH: 28 June 1891
PROFESSION: Farmer and soldier
ALIASES: Carl Panzram, Jefferson Davis, Jack Allen, The River Pirate, Copper John
NATIONALITY: American
LOCATION OF CRIMES: USA
DATES OF MURDERS: 1905–29
NUMBER OF VICTIMS: 5–21

Carl Panzram was a true misanthrope – a man who positively loathed his fellow human beings. His 39 years on Earth saw him drift from an abusive childhood to a nomadic adulthood spent in and out of a hellish prison system. In between, he took his revenge by killing as many as 21 victims, and robbing and raping many more. When he was put to death in 1930, his last action was to spit in the hangman's face and say: 'Hurry it up, you Hoosier bastard, I could hang a dozen men while you're fooling around.'

Panzram was born on a farm in Warren, Minnesota, on 28 June 1891, one of seven children in a dirt-poor German immigrant family. Theirs was a desperately hard life that became even harder when Carl was seven years old: his father walked out one day and never came back. His mother and brothers struggled to keep the farm going, working from dawn till dusk in the fields. During this time, his brothers used to beat him unmercifully for no reason at all. At the age of 11 he gave them a good reason: he broke into a neighbour's house and stole whatever he could find, including a handgun. His brothers beat him unconscious when they found out.

22 UNFORGIVING VIOLENCE

Panzram stole a military issue Colt M1911 and it became one of his most treasured possessions. He used the stolen weapon to kill most of his victims.

BRUTAL CORRECTIONAL INSTITUTION

Panzram was arrested for the crime and sent to the Minnesota State Training School in 1903, aged 12. This was a brutal institution in which he was regularly beaten and raped by the staff. Here he acquired a taste for forced gay sex and an abiding hatred of authority. In 1905 he expressed this hatred by burning part of the school down. He was not identified as the culprit, however, and was able to persuade a parole panel that year that he was a reformed character. The opposite was closer to the truth: the Carl Panzram who emerged from the school was in reality a deformed character.

Panzram returned home for a while, went to school briefly, then left after an altercation with a teacher. He worked on his mother's farm until, at 14, he jumped on a freight train and headed westwards. For the next few years he lived the life of a teenage hobo. He committed crimes and was the victim of them; he was sent to reform schools and broke out of them. When he was 16, in 1907, he joined the army but refused to accept the discipline and was then caught trying to desert with a bundle of stolen clothing. He was dishonourably discharged and sent to the fearsome Leavenworth Prison, where he spent two hard years, breaking rocks and becoming a very strong, dangerous man. On his release, he returned to his roaming. He was arrested at various times and under various names for vagrancy, burglary, arson and robbery. The one crime he was not arrested for, but took particular pleasure in carrying out, was homosexual rape. Once he even raped a policeman who was trying to arrest him. His crimes escalated in savagery and so did his prison sentences; he served time in both Montana and Oregon.

In 1918, Panzram escaped from Oregon State Prison, where he had been serving a sentence under the name Jefferson Baldwin. He decided to leave the north-east, where he had become very well known to the police. He changed his name to John O'Leary and headed for the east coast, where he would make the transition from robber and rapist to cold-blooded killer.

BAIT

He began by carrying out a string of burglaries that made him enough money to buy a yacht. He would lure sailors on to the yacht, get them drunk, rape them, kill them and then dump their bodies in the sea. This went on until his boat crashed and sank, by which time he reckoned he had killed ten men. Broke once more, Panzram stowed away on a ship and ended up in Angola, Africa. He signed on

Panzram's sadism knew no bounds. In Angola, he hired six locals to act as guides and assist in a crocodile hunting expedition. Once downriver, with the crocodiles in sight, he shot all six and fed the men to the beasts.

UNFORGIVING VIOLENCE

During one of his frequent stints in jail, Panzram was sent to Sing Sing but proved so unruly he was moved – only to go on to murder a fellow inmate.

with an oil company who were drilling off the coast of the Congo. While he was there, he raped and killed a 12-year-old boy. Then he went on a crocodile hunting expedition that ended when he killed the six local guides he had hired, raped their corpses and fed them to the crocodiles.

CAPTURED

Panzram returned to the States soon after, as witnesses had seen him engage the guides. He went on to rape and murder an 11-year-old boy, George McMahon, in the town of Salem, Massachusetts. Over the next months, he carried out two more murders and numerous robberies. Finally, he was captured while in the act of burgling a railway station. This was to be his toughest sentence yet: he began it in Sing Sing, but proved so unruly that he was sent on to Dannemora, an infamous establishment where he was beaten and tortured by the guards. His legs were broken and left untreated, leaving him semi-crippled and in constant pain for the rest of his life.

'I WAS SO FULL OF HATE THAT THERE WAS NO ROOM IN ME FOR SUCH FEELINGS AS LOVE, PITY, KINDNESS OR HONOUR OR DECENCY. MY ONLY REGRET IS THAT I WASN'T BORN DEAD OR NOT AT ALL.'

Prisoners at Fort Leavenworth Penitentiary march towards the mess hall for dinner. Panzram did three years' hard labour here, during which time he was chained to a 50 lb (23 kg) metal ball and frequently beaten.

On release in July 1928, Panzram immediately carried out a string of burglaries and at least one murder before being rearrested. By now he was evidently tired of life. On arrest he gave his real name for the first time and, while in prison in Washington DC, confessed to several murders of young boys. Encouraged by a prison guard with whom he struck up an unlikely friendship, he went on to write a 20,000-word account of his terrible life and crimes. This remains a remarkable document, a horrifying but unusually even-handed account of a serial killer's inner life. Following the confessions, and amid a flurry of media interest, Panzram was tried for the most recent of his murders: the strangling of Alexander Uszacke. He was found guilty and sentenced to serve 25 years at the federal prison in Leavenworth, Kansas. Following the sentence, Panzram warned the world that he would kill the first man who crossed him when he was inside. He was as good as his word. He was given work in the laundry and one day murdered his supervisor, Robert Warnke, by staving in his head with an iron bar.

This time, Panzram was sentenced to hang. He positively welcomed the court's verdict and claimed that now his only ambition was to die. When anti-death penalty campaigners tried to have his sentence commuted, he ungraciously wrote to them to say: 'I wish you all had one neck and I had my hands on it.' Shortly afterwards, on 3 September 1930, his wish to die was granted, and he was duly hanged.

Panzram seemed to positively welcome his sentence of death by hanging, going so far as to curse campaigners who tried to get the decision overturned.

DANIEL CAMARGO BARBOSA

NAME: Daniel Camargo Barbosa
DATE OF BIRTH: 22 January 1930
PROFESSION: Door-to-door salesman
ALIASES: The Sadist of El Charquito, The Mangrove Monster
NATIONALITY: Colombian
LOCATION OF CRIMES: Colombia, Ecuador
DATES OF MURDERS: 1974–86
NUMBER OF VICTIMS: 72–180

PARENTAL ABUSE

It is thought that **Daniel Camargo Barbosa** killed as many as 180 people – and probably raped many more. Like many serial killers it was the peculiar circumstances of his childhood that perhaps set him on his course.

Born to a relatively prosperous family in the small town of Anolaima in the Colombian Andes in 1930, he was the son of a local businessman named Daniel Camargo Briceño. His mother, Teresa Barbosa, was his father's second wife and he had an older half-sister from his father's first marriage. When Camargo was two years old his mother died and his father remarried shortly afterwards.

Camargo was very intelligent and did well in school, but his father remained distant and would dismiss the boy as useless and a lost cause. His upbringing was left to his stepmother, Dioselina Fernández, who was a mere adolescent at the time of her marriage and wanted to have a daughter of her own. When she found she was

28 UNFORGIVING VIOLENCE

In the 1940s, Camargo's father sent him to a prestigious, all-male Catholic school in the Colombian capital, Bogotá. When young, Barbosa had been abused by his stepmother. She punished him for getting into a fight by taking away his trousers and forcing him to wear girls' clothes.

unable to have children she doted on her stepdaughter but abused her stepson. Her cruelty for minor infractions extended to forcefully undressing him from his waist down and beating his bare buttocks with a bullwhip.

Understandably, Camargo developed violent tendencies. After he got into a fight at school, his stepmother punished him by taking away his trousers and forcing him to wear girls' clothes. Schoolmates were invited to witness this humiliation and he became the victim of bullying. From then on, Camargo came to despise women and everything feminine.

In the early 1940s, his father sent him to a prestigious, all-male Catholic boarding school in the Colombian capital, Bogotá. Camargo excelled academically, but any plans for him to continue his studies were curtailed when his family was hit by the economic downturn caused by La Violencia, Colombia's civil war that started in 1948. He was then forced to work as a door-to-door salesman to support them. Despite the hardship the country was suffering, he was charming, convincing and relatively successful.

LOVER LURES YOUNG GIRLS

In 1957, he began a relationship with a young client named Alcira Castillo. After a few dates, he rented a house and they moved in together. Soon they had a growing family and to make ends meet he took to crime. On 24 May 1958, he was arrested for robbing a shop owned by another client. Convicted of petty theft, he was sent to a minimum-security prison, but he was not there long. Taking advantage of the confusion caused by the widespread mass arrests, Camargo simply walked out with the staff, clutching a clipboard. He then returned home and seemingly there were no repercussions.

In 1962, Camargo fell in love with another woman named Esperanza and decided to leave Alcira, even though they had two children. He intended to marry Esperanza, but when they got engaged he discovered that she wasn't a virgin. Then he found her in their bed with another man. Angry at first, Camargo soon realized that he could manipulate the situation to his own advantage. He insisted on Esperanza bringing him young girls, so he could take from them the virginity she had denied him.

Esperanza reluctantly complied and lured five young girls to their apartment. She then drugged them with sleeping pills, so Camargo could rape them while they were unconscious. However, the fifth child realized what had happened to her and reported the couple. Esperanza and Camargo were arrested and on 10 April 1964 Camargo was convicted of sexual assault. Initially he was sentenced to three years but a second judge increased this to eight years. He served the full term but remained angry at what he saw to be an injustice.

LUST FOR VIRGINS

When he was released he moved to Brazil, but in 1973 he was arrested for being an undocumented immigrant and was deported back to Colombia. He used this as an opportunity to adopt a false identity. It is thought that he then resumed raping young girls, possibly as many as 80, and murdering them so that they could not go to the police.

In the northern town of Barranquilla, Camargo went to work as a street vendor selling televisions. On 2 May 1974, he was walking past a school there when he saw a nine-year-old girl who took his fancy. He lured her to a secluded area, then raped and strangled her. The following day, Camargo returned to dispose of the body and retrieve the TV set he had left there and was arrested. He was then convicted of the girl's rape and murder. Sentenced to 30 years in prison, he was sent to the island of Gorgona, Colombia's 'Devil's Island', situated some 30 km (20 miles) off the country's Pacific coast.

Ten years into his sentence, Camargo found a rowing boat that had been washed up on a beach. For years he had been studying the currents in the hope of escape, so he jumped in and after a few hours' paddling made landfall in Ecuador. Even though he was reported as a fugitive, the currents were particularly treacherous there and it was assumed he had died at sea. The Colombian press even reported that Camargo had been eaten by sharks. In fact, he was the first man to escape from the Colombian Alcatraz.

Ten years on Gorgona had not quenched his lust for virgins. On 18 December 1984, he abducted another nine-year-old girl in Quevedo, then raped and killed her. He went on to commit at least

Barbosa spent ten years imprisoned on the island of Gorgona, Colombia before managing to escape.

50 rapes and murders of girls and young women between 1984 and 1986.

His modus operandi was to target peasants, maids and students transitioning from primary school to college, though younger schoolgirls were also easy prey. He would approach them pretending he was a foreigner who was trying to find a Protestant pastor in a church on the outskirts of town, where he was to deliver a large sum of money. This was all the more convincing because he was fluent in English and Portuguese and was adept at adopting an accent. There would be a reward, of course, to any girl who would show him the way – a small part of the money or something as trivial as a pen. Younger girls would be given sweets while older victims were lured with the possibility of a job at the church. The journey often involved a bus trip. He insisted they alighted in a wooded area and then made off into the forest, claiming that he was now familiar with the area and remembered a shortcut. If the victim got suspicious and refused to follow him, Camargo would let her go and find someone new.

MEMORIZED VICTIMS' DETAILS

If the girl followed, Camargo would lead her to a secluded spot then rape her at knifepoint. Afterwards he would strangle her, stab her or cut her up with a machete. One adult woman hit him on the head with a rock while he was raping her, which enraged him so much that he decapitated her and threw her head away. Another victim was found dissected with all her internal organs removed. The bodies would be left to be stripped by scavengers, while he made off with their clothes and any valuables. He would urinate on his hands to wash off the blood and he always carried a clean shirt to change into. Before he left, he liked to memorize as many details about the victims as possible, such as scars, tattoos and moles, so he could relive the experience later. In some cases he even obtained the phone number of their families, so that he could call and taunt them about their missing daughters.

EXECUTED BY FELLOW PRISONER

Most of the murders happened in the Guayas province, but Camargo roamed all over Ecuador, following in the footsteps of Pedro López – 'The Monster of the Andes' – another Colombian serial killer active in Ecuador. In 1983, he was convicted of the murders of 110 girls in Ecuador and confessed to another 240 murders in Colombia and Peru.

As with López, Camargo's killings were so numerous that the police did not believe that the abductions were the work of one

Camargo used a machete to mutilate his victims.

man. Organized crime must be involved, they thought, or perhaps white slavers or a Satanic ring.

Camargo was arrested on 26 February 1986 by two Quito policemen, minutes after he had murdered another nine-year-old girl named Elizabeth Telpes. He was found in possession of a bag containing bloody clothes belonging to his final victim, along with a copy of Fyodor Dostoyevsky's *Crime and Punishment*.

After a local woman named María Alexandra Vélez survived an attack by a man matching his description, he was then taken to Guayaquil, where she identified him. Camargo admitted killing 71 victims in Ecuador following his escape from prison. He told investigators that he picked virgins 'because they cried'.

In 1989, he was convicted and sentenced to 16 years in jail, the maximum sentence in Ecuador. He was imprisoned at Quito's García Moreno Prison, the same penitentiary that was home to Pedro López. On 13 November 1994 Camargo was sitting in his cell when a new inmate, 29-year-old Giovanny Arcesio Noguera Jaramillo, came in and forced him to his knees. After saying 'it is the hour of vengeance', he stabbed Camargo eight times, killing him, and then he cut off one of his ears as a trophy. Noguera showed the ear to the guards, maintaining that his aunt was one of Camargo's victims and he had avenged her. Because nobody claimed Camargo's body, he was buried in a mass grave located in Quito's El Batán cemetery. He was 64 years old when he died.

López was released in 1994 but was deported back to Colombia, where he faced further murder charges. Found insane, he was committed to a mental hospital in Bogotá. Discharged in 1998, he was arrested again in 2002, but absconded.

HENRY LEE LUCAS

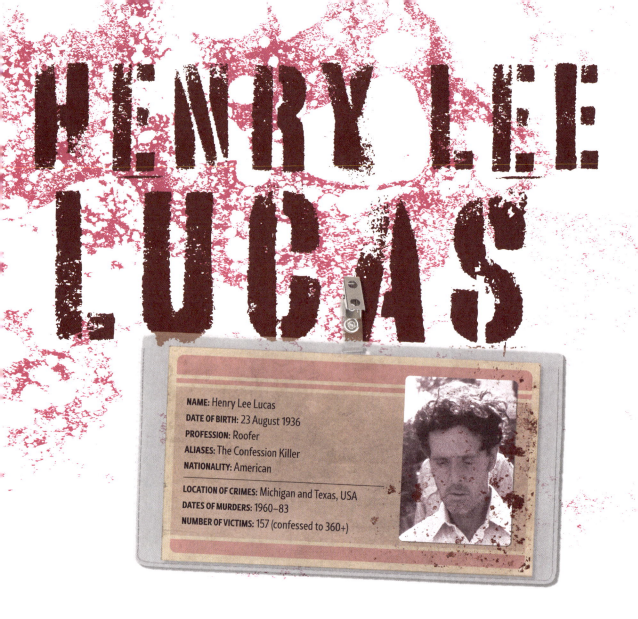

NAME: Henry Lee Lucas
DATE OF BIRTH: 23 August 1936
PROFESSION: Roofer
ALIASES: The Confession Killer
NATIONALITY: American
LOCATION OF CRIMES: Michigan and Texas, USA
DATES OF MURDERS: 1960–83
NUMBER OF VICTIMS: 157 (confessed to 360+)

Thought to be America's most prolific serial killer, Henry Lee Lucas had a partner in crime. With his accomplice, Ottis Toole, he confessed to over 360 murders – 157 of these confessions have been checked out by the authorities and proved to be genuine.

Lucas's mother was half-Chippawa. She was drunk most of the time on corn liquor which she bought with the proceeds of prostitution, conducted on the floor of her shack in front of her husband and children. She was known to be 'as mean as a rattlesnake' and packed the seven children from her first marriage off to a foster home. Lucas's father worked on the railways and lost both legs in an accident.

Lucas's mother and her pimp beat her children constantly. After one beating, Henry was unconscious for three days and suffered damage to his brain. Another accident left him with a glass eye.

Henry was made to grow his hair long and wear a dress, so that he could be pimped out to both men and women. The county court put an end to this forced cross-dressing when his school complained.

At the age of ten, Henry Lucas was introduced to sex by Bernard Dowdy, yet another of his mother's lovers. Dowdy was mentally retarded. He would slit the throat of a calf and have sex with the carcass; he encouraged the boy to do the same. Lucas enjoyed this activity and, from childhood onwards, he associated sex with death.

Throughout his childhood Lucas continued to have sex with

Henry Lee Lucas in court. He served just ten years of his initial sentence for murder and once he got out he went back to his violent ways.

animals, sometimes skinning them alive for sexual pleasure. At 14, he turned his perverted attention to women. He beat a 17-year-old girl unconscious at a bus stop and raped her. When she came to and started screaming, he choked the life out of her, or so he claimed.

> 'I HATED ALL MY LIFE. I HATED EVERYBODY. WHEN I FIRST GREW UP AND CAN REMEMBER, I WAS DRESSED AS A GIRL BY MY MOTHER. AND I STAYED THAT WAY FOR TWO OR THREE YEARS. AND AFTER THAT I WAS TREATED LIKE WHAT I CALL THE DOG OF THE FAMILY. I WAS BEATEN. I WAS MADE TO DO THINGS THAT NO HUMAN BEING WOULD WANT TO DO.'

At 15, he was sent to a reformatory for burglary. Two years of hard labour on a prison farm did nothing to reform him. When he was released, he returned to housebreaking. He was caught again and sent back to jail.

He escaped, then met and fell in love with a girl called Stella. They stayed together for four years and she agreed to marry him. Then his mother turned up demanding that her son take care of her. After a violent row, Lucas killed her. This time he got 40 years, but served just ten.

By 1970, the authorities considered Lucas a reformed character and released him. He killed a woman within hours of getting out. In 1971, he was arrested for attempting to rape two teenage girls at gunpoint. His only excuse was that he craved women all the time.

FEEDING THE FLAME

Released in 1975, he married a woman called Betty Crawford. The marriage broke up when Betty discovered that he was having sex with her nine-year-old daughter and trying to force himself on her seven-year-old. Lucas then moved in with his sister but was thrown out when he started having sex with her daughter too.

In 1978, he met another sex-murder freak called Ottis Toole in a soup kitchen in Jacksonville, Florida. He was a sadist with homosexual tendencies. He often dressed as a woman to pick up men in bars. He even started a course of female hormones as part of his ambition to have a sex change. Toole was also a pyromaniac and would achieve orgasm at the sight of a burning building.

Lucas and Toole became lovers and together they embarked on a series of violent robberies, which frequently involved murder – often for the sheer pleasure of it. In Toole's confession, he admitted that, around that time, they saw a teenage couple walking along a

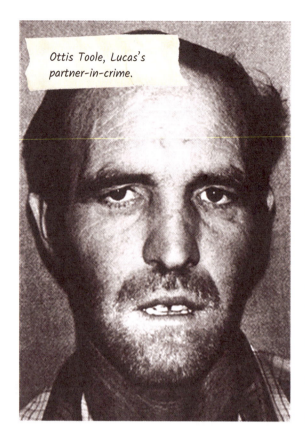

Ottis Toole, Lucas's partner-in-crime.

road after their car had run out of petrol. Toole shot the boy, while Lucas forced the girl into the back of the car. After he had finished raping her, he shot her six times and they dumped her body by the roadside. This was one of the cases the police could confirm.

Another killing occurred outside Oklahoma City. There, they had picked up a girl called Tina Williams when her car broke down. Lucas shot her twice and had sex with her dead body.

In 1978, Lucas and Toole were in Maryland when a man asked them whether they would help him transport stolen cars. This was too tame a sport for hardened criminals such as them, they explained. He then asked them whether they were interested in becoming professional killers. They said that they were. The one proviso was that they had to join a Satanist cult.

Lucas and Toole claimed to have been inducted into the Hand of Death sect in Florida by a man named Don Meteric. As part of the initiation, Lucas had to kill a man. He lured the victim to a beach and gave him a bottle of whisky. When the man threw his head back to take a swig, Lucas cut his throat.

As part of the cult activity, Lucas and Toole kidnapped young prostitutes who were forced to perform in pornographic videos, which often turned out to be 'snuff movies'. They also abducted children and took them across the border into Mexico where they were sold or used as sacrifices in Satanic ceremonies. These children may have been delivered to Adolfo de Jesus Constanzo, the bisexual high priest, and his one-time lover, the beautiful, American-college-educated Sara Maria Aldrete, known as La Bruja – 'The Witch'. They murdered and mutilated children in Mexico during Satanic rites. Their victims' genitals were cut out and their brains boiled. The flesh of 'gringos' was especially in demand.

MURDEROUS RAMPAGE

Around that time, Toole introduced Lucas to his 11-year-old niece, Becky Powell, who was slightly mentally retarded. She lived in Toole's mother's house in Florida where they were staying. Toole had been seduced by his older sister Druscilla, and he enjoyed watching his pick-ups make love to Becky or her older sister Sarah.

When Druscilla committed suicide, Becky and her brother Frank were put in care. Lucas decided to rescue them. By January 1982, they were on the run together, living off the money they stole from small grocery stores. Becky called Lucas 'Daddy'. But one night, when he was tickling her innocently at bedtime, they began to kiss. Lucas undressed her, then stripped off himself. Becky was only 12, he said, but she looked 18.

During his time with Becky, Lucas continued his murderous rampage with Toole. Lucas outlined a typical fortnight in Georgia. In the space of two weeks, they kidnapped and murdered a 16-year-old girl, then raped her dead body, and abducted, raped and mutilated a blond woman. Another woman was abducted from a parking lot and stabbed to death in front of her children. In the course of one robbery, the store owner was shot. Another man died in a second robbery. In a third, the store owner was stabbed. And in a fourth, a woman was tied up before being stabbed to death. Toole also tried to force his sexual attentions on a young man. On being spurned, Toole shot him. Becky and her brother Frank were often in on the robberies and witnessed several of the murders.

Eventually, Lucas and Toole parted company. Toole took Frank back to Florida, while Lucas and Becky got a job with a couple named Smart who ran an antique shop in California. After five months, the Smarts sent Lucas and Becky to Texas to look after Mrs Smart's 80-year-old mother, Kate Rich.

A few weeks later, Mrs Smart's sister visited her mother to find the place filthy. Lucas had been taking her money to buy beer and cigarettes. She found him drunk in bed with Becky and the two of them were fired.

They were hitch-hiking out of town when they were picked up by the Reverend Reuben Moore, who had started a religious community nearby called the House of Prayer. Lucas and his 15-year-old common-law wife quickly became converts and lived in a converted chicken barn. While they were staying at the House of Prayer, Becky seems to have had a genuine change of heart. She was homesick and she wanted to go back to Florida. Reluctantly, Lucas agreed and they set off hitch-hiking.

At nightfall, they settled down with their blankets in a field. It was a warm June night. A row broke out about Becky's decision to return home. She struck him in the face. He grabbed a knife and stabbed her through the heart. Then he had sex with her corpse, cut her body up and scattered its dismembered pieces in the woods.

After killing Becky, who Lucas later described as the only woman he had ever loved, he returned to the House of Prayer. He, too, seems to have had some sort of change of heart. One Sunday,

Lucas is escorted to court in Texas in June 1983 by law enforcement officials.

Lucas stuffed the body of Kate Rich into a nearby drainage pipe.

he dropped around to Mrs Rich's house to offer her a lift to church. She accepted. But during the journey, she began to question him about the whereabouts of Becky. Lucas pulled a knife and stabbed it into her side. She died immediately. He drove her to a piece of waste ground where he undressed and raped her corpse. He stuffed her naked body into a drainage pipe that ran under the road. Later, he collected it in a garbage bag and burned it in the stove at the House of Prayer.

Sheriff Bill F. 'Hound Dog' Conway of Montague County, Texas, had begun to have his suspicions about Lucas when he reappeared without Becky. Now he was linked to the disappearance of two women. Lucas was hauled in for questioning.

UNDER PRESSURE

Lucas was a chain-smoker and heavy caffeine addict. Conway deprived him of both cigarettes and coffee, but still he refused to break. Lucas maintained that he knew nothing about the disappearance of Kate Rich, and that Becky had run off with a truck driver who promised to take her back to Florida. Finally, Sheriff Conway had to release him.

Soon afterwards, Lucas told the Reverend Moore that he was going off to look for Becky. He headed for Missouri, where he saw a young woman standing beside her car in a petrol station. He held a knife to her ribs and forced her back into the car. They drove south towards Texas. When she dozed off, Lucas pulled off the road with the intention of raping her. She awoke suddenly to find a knife at her neck. He stabbed her in the throat, pushed her to the ground and cut her clothes off. After he had raped her dead body, he dragged it into a copse and took the money from her handbag. He abandoned her car in Fredericksburg, Texas and returned to the House of Prayer.

While he was away, the Reverend Moore had told Sheriff Conway that Lucas had given Becky a gun for safekeeping. Lucas was a convicted felon and had, consequently, forfeited his right to

The young woman awoke to find a knife at her throat.

bear arms. It was enough to put him back in the slammer. Sheriff Conway again deprived him of coffee and cigarettes. This time, Lucas began to crack. He was found hanging in his cell with his wrists slashed.

After being patched up in the prison hospital, Lucas was put in a special observation cell in the women's wing. The next night, he cracked completely. In the early hours of the morning, he started yelling. When the jailer arrived, Lucas claimed that there was a light in his cell and it was talking to him. The man on night duty, Joe Dan Weaver, knew that Lucas had already smashed the bulb in his cell and told him to get some sleep. Later in the night, Lucas called the jailer again and confessed that he had done some pretty bad things. Weaver advised him to get down on his knees and pray. Instead, Lucas asked Weaver for a pencil and paper.

Lucas spent the next half hour writing a note to Sheriff Conway. It read:

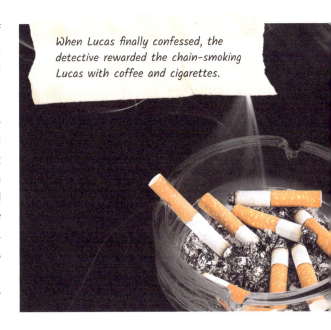

When Lucas finally confessed, the detective rewarded the chain-smoking Lucas with coffee and cigarettes.

'I HAVE TRIED TO GET HELP FOR SO LONG, AND NO ONE WILL BELIEVE ME. I HAVE KILLED FOR THE PAST TEN YEARS AND NO ONE WILL BELIEVE ME. I CANNOT GO ON DOING THIS. I HAVE KILLED THE ONLY GIRL I EVER LOVED.'

When the confession was finished, Lucas pushed it out of the cell door's peep hole. Weaver read it and called Sheriff Conway. He knew the sheriff would not mind being woken in the middle of the night under these circumstances.

When Sheriff Conway arrived, he plied Lucas with coffee and cigarettes – and asked about the murders. Lucas said that he had seen a light in his cell and it had told him to confess his sins. Then he told the sheriff that he had killed Kate Rich.

Later, Sheriff Conway and Texas Ranger Phil Ryan asked Lucas what had happened to Becky Powell. Tears flowed from his one good eye as Lucas told how he had stabbed, raped and dismembered her. The story left the two hardened law officers feeling sick and wretched.

'Is that all?' asked Ryan wearily, half-hoping it was.

'Not by a long way,' said Lucas. 'I reckon I killed more than 100.'

LITANY OF HORROR

The next day Montague County police began to check out Lucas's story. Near the drainage pipe where Lucas had temporarily hidden Mrs Rich's body, they found some of her underclothes and her glasses, broken. At the House of Prayer, they found some burnt fragments of human flesh and some charred bones.

Lucas took them to the field where he had killed Becky. They found her suitcase, full of women's clothing and make-up. Her skull, pelvis and other parts of her body were found in the woodland nearby, in an advanced stage of decomposition.

He began to confess to other murders too – often in breathtaking detail. These too checked out.

A week after he had begun to confess, Lucas appeared in court, charged with the murders of Kate Rich and Becky Powell. When asked whether he understood the seriousness of the charges against him, Lucas said he did and confessed to about 100 other murders.

The judge, shocked, could scarcely credit this and asked Lucas whether he had ever undergone psychiatric examination. Lucas said he had, but 'they didn't want to do anything about it … I know it ain't normal for a person to go out and kill girls just to have sex.'

Lucas's sensational testimony made huge headlines and the news wires quickly carried the story to every paper in the country. Police departments in every state and county began checking their records and Lucas's confessions were run through the computer at

Interstate 35 near Austin, Texas. Lucas and Toole cruised along this highway, murdering as they went.

the newly established National Center for the Analysis of Violent Crime.

Toole, it was discovered, was already in prison. He had been sentenced to 15 years for arson in Springfield. In jail, he had begun regaling a cellmate with the tale of how he had raped, murdered, beheaded, barbecued and eaten a child named Adam Walsh. Suddenly, in the light of Lucas's confession, the police began taking his stories seriously.

Both Lucas and Toole continued to confess freely. They admitted to a series of robberies of convenience stores. At one, they had tied up a young girl. She had wriggled free, so Lucas had shot her in the head and Toole had had sex with her dead body.

Lucas went on a thousand-mile tour of murder sites. In Duval County, Florida, Lucas confessed to eight unsolved murders. The victims had been women ranging in age from 17 to 80. Some had been beaten, some strangled, some stabbed and some shot. Lucas said that the Hand of Death said he should vary his MO.

Near Austin, Texas, Lucas pointed out a building and asked whether it had been a liquor store once. It had. Lucas confessed to murdering the former owners during a robbery in 1979. In the same county, Lucas led them to a field where he had murdered and mutilated a girl called Sandra Dubbs. He even pointed out where her car had been found.

Lucas and Toole had cruised Interstate 35, murdering tramps, hitch-hikers, men who were robbed of their money and old women who were abducted from their homes. They had killed more than 20 people up and down that highway alone, over a period of five years. One was a young woman who was found near Austin, naked except for a pair of orange socks. She had been hitch-hiking on the interstate when Lucas had picked her up. She refused to have sex with him, so Lucas strangled her and took what he wanted. She was never identified, but Lucas was sentenced to death for her murder.

Although he withdrew his confession to the Becky Powell murder and pleaded not guilty, he was found guilty anyway and sentenced to life. On top of that he received four more life sentences, two sentences of 75 years each and one of 67 years, all for murder.

During his confessions, Lucas told the police that Toole had poured petrol over a 65-year-old man and set him alight. They had hidden, so that they could watch the fire engines arrive. The police identified the man as George Sonenberg. He had died four days later. Until then, they had assumed that the fire was an accident. Toole freely admitted the murder and claimed to have started hundreds of other fires. But it was for this particularly horrific murder that Toole, as well, was sentenced to death.

Lucas and Toole enjoyed their brief celebrity and took a certain relish in revealing the ghoulish details of their shocking crimes. Both their death sentences were commuted. Toole died of cirrhosis at the Florida State Prison on 15 September 1996 at the age of 49. His body went unclaimed and he was buried in the prison cemetery. Lucas died of heart failure on 12 March 2001, aged 64, in the Texas State Penitentiary at Huntsville, Texas and was buried in Captain Joe Byrd Cemetery – aka Peckerwood Hill – in Huntsville, Texas. He lies in an unmarked grave after vandals repeatedly damaged or stole his tombstone.

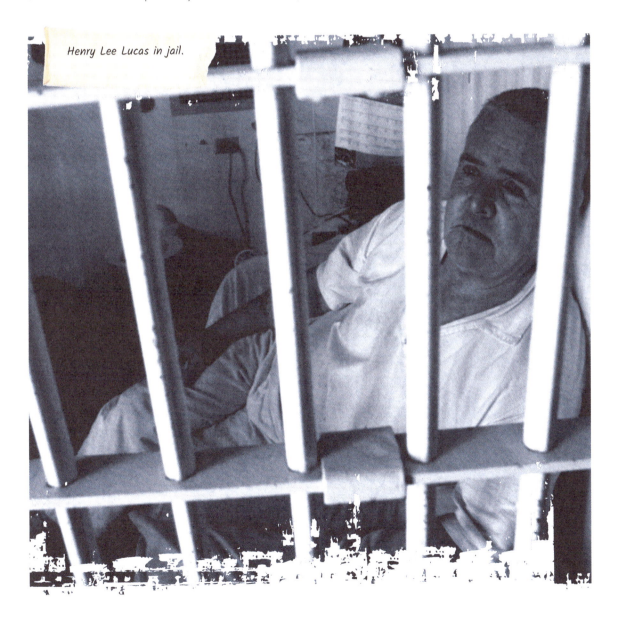

Henry Lee Lucas in jail.

DOUGLAS CLARK AND CAROL BUNDY

NAME: Henry Douglas Daniel Clark and Carol Mary Bundy (née Peters)
DATE OF BIRTH: 10 March 1948 (Clark) and 26 August 1942 (Bundy)
PROFESSION: Mechanic (Clark), Nurse (Bundy)
ALIASES: The Hollywood Slashers, The Sunset Strip Killers
NATIONALITY: American
LOCATION OF CRIMES: California, USA
DATES OF MURDERS: June–August 1980
NUMBER OF VICTIMS: 7

Doug Clark and Carol Bundy appeared to make an unlikely couple. Doug was a good-looking man from a well-to-do family, a 32-year-old charmer with a string of girlfriends pining after him. Carol was a divorcee with thick glasses and a weight problem. Five years older than Clark, she had recently split from an abusive husband and was working as a nurse. Underneath, however, the pair had a great deal in common: both were sexually driven, both lacked a moral compass and together they embarked on a rampage of sexually motivated murder.

'KING OF THE ONE NIGHT STAND'

Douglas Daniel Clark was born in 1948, the son of a Naval Intelligence officer, Franklin Clark. The family moved repeatedly during Doug's childhood, due to his father's work. He later claimed to have lived in 37 countries. In 1958, his father left the navy to take up a civilian position as an engineer with the Transport Company of Texas: some sources suggest that this was in fact merely a cover for continuing intelligence activities. Either way, it did not put a stop to the family's nomadic lifestyle. They lived

40 UNFORGIVING VIOLENCE

in the Marshall Islands for a time, moved back to San Francisco, and then moved again to India. For a while Doug was sent to an exclusive international school in Geneva. Later, he attended the prestigious Culver Military Academy while his father continued to move around the world. When he graduated in 1967, Doug naturally enough enlisted in the air force.

At this point, however, Clark's life began to unravel. He was discharged from the air force and for the next decade he drifted around, often working as a mechanic, but really concentrating on his vocation as a sexual athlete: 'the king of the one night stand' as he liked to call himself. The 70s was the decade when casual sex first became a widespread, socially acceptable phenomenon – at least in the big cities – and Doug Clark, a smooth-talking, well-educated young man, was well placed to take advantage of this change in the nation's morals.

Nowhere was this lifestyle more prevalent than Los Angeles, and eventually Doug Clark moved there, taking a job in a factory in Burbank. One of the bars he liked to frequent to pick up women was

Clark was always the picture of a charming and confident man in court.

DOUGLAS CLARK AND CAROL BUNDY **41**

a place in North Hollywood called Little Nashville, where, in 1980, he met Carol Bundy.

Bundy was 37 years old. She had had a troubled childhood: her mother had died when she was young, and her father had abused her. Then, when her father remarried, he had put her in various foster homes. At the age of 17, Bundy had married a 56-year-old man; by the time she met Clark she had recently escaped a third marriage to an abusive man, by whom she had had two young sons. Most recently, she had begun an affair with her apartment block manager, a part-time country singer called John Murray. She had even attempted to bribe Murray's wife to leave him. Murray's wife was not pleased at this and had told her husband to have Bundy evicted from the block. However, this had not ended the infatuation and Bundy continued to show up regularly at venues where Murray was singing. One of these was Little Nashville.

Clark, an experienced manipulator of women, quickly saw the potential in seducing the overweight and transparently needy Bundy. He turned on the charm and won her over immediately. Before long, he moved into her apartment and soon discovered that this was a woman with whom he could share his increasingly dark sexual fantasies.

PROSTITUTES

He started bringing prostitutes back to the flat to have sex with them both. Then he began to take an interest in an 11-year-old girl who was a neighbour. Carol helped lure the girl into sexual games and posing for sexual photographs. Even breaking the paedophile taboo was not enough for Clark, however. He started to talk about how much he would like to kill a girl during sex and persuaded Carol to go out and buy two automatic pistols for him to use.

The killing began in earnest during June 1980. Clark came home and told Bundy about the two teenagers he had picked up on Sunset Strip that day and subsequently murdered. He had ordered them to perform fellatio on him and then shot them both in the head before taking them to a garage and raping their dead bodies. He had then dumped the bodies beside the Ventura freeway, where they were found the next day. Carol was sufficiently shocked by this news to make a phone call to the police admitting to some knowledge of the murders but refusing to give any clues as to the identity of the murderer.

REFRIGERATED REMAINS

Twelve days later, when Clark killed again, Bundy had clearly got over her qualms. The victims were two prostitutes, Karen Jones and Exxie Wilson. Once again, Clark had picked them up, shot them and dumped the bodies in plain view, but this time he had decided to take a trophy: Exxie Wilson's head. He took the head back to Bundy's house and surprised her by producing it from her fridge. Almost unbelievably, she then put make-up on the head before Clark used it for another bout of necrophilia. Two days later, they put the freshly scrubbed head in a box and dumped it in an alleyway. Three days after this, another body was found in the woods in the San Fernando Valley. The victim was a runaway called Marnette Comer, who appeared to have been killed three weeks previously, making her Clark's first known victim.

Clark waited a month before killing again. Meanwhile Bundy was still infatuated with John Murray. She would go to see him singing in Little Nashville, and after a few drinks her conversation would turn to the kind of things she and Clark got up to. These hints alarmed Murray, who implied he might tell the police. To avert this, Bundy lured Murray into his van after a show to have sex. Once they were inside the van, she shot him dead and decapitated him. However, she had left a trail of clues behind her: Bundy and Murray had been seen in the bar together and she had left shell casings in the van. Bundy herself was unable to take the pressure. Two days later, she confessed to her horrified co-workers that she had killed Murray. They called the police and she began to give them a full and frank confession about her and Clark's crimes.

Clark was immediately arrested and the guns found hidden at his work. Bundy was charged with two murders: Murray and the unknown victim whose killing she confessed to having been present at. Clark was charged with six murders. At his trial he represented himself and tried to blame Bundy for everything, portraying himself as an innocent dupe. The jury did not believe him, and he was sentenced to the death penalty, while Bundy received life imprisonment. Ironically enough, it was Bundy who met her end first, dying in prison on 9 December 2003 at the age of 61. Clark died on death row aged 75 on 11 October 2023.

CHARLES SOBHRAJ

NAME: Hotchand Bhawnani Gurmukh Sobhraj
DATE OF BIRTH: 6 April 1944
PROFESSION: Con artist
ALIASES: Charles Sobhraj, The Serpent, The Bikini Killer
NATIONALITY: French and Vietnamese
LOCATION OF CRIMES: Thailand, Nepal, India, Malaysia, France, Afghanistan, Turkey and Greece
DATES OF MURDERS: 1963–76
NUMBER OF VICTIMS: 12–30

It is a fact that, while most crimes are committed for financial gain, serial murder very rarely has money as its primary object. Serial murderers often rob their victims, but this is usually a secondary motivation, the main purpose being sexual gratification of some kind. Charles Sobhraj, nicknamed 'the serpent', is a definite exception to the serial killer rule. He stands accused of around 20 murders. All his victims were backpackers travelling around South East Asia. In all cases, he murdered them for money. As he himself told a journalist at the time of his 1976 murder trial:

'IF I HAVE EVER KILLED, OR HAVE ORDERED KILLINGS, THEN IT WAS PURELY FOR REASONS OF BUSINESS – JUST A JOB, LIKE A GENERAL IN THE ARMY.'

Charles Sobhraj was born in 1944 to an Indian tailor and his Vietnamese girlfriend, Song. His father refused to marry his mother or to take much responsibility for his son. Song later married

44 UNFORGIVING VIOLENCE

a French soldier, Lieutenant Alphonse Darreau, and the family eventually moved to Marseilles, France. Charles was an unruly child, who did not feel part of his mother's new life; several times he stowed away on ships leaving Marseilles, in an effort to return to his natural father, but each time he was discovered. As he got older, he acquired a reputation for dishonesty. A slight, small boy, he became adept at manipulating people, especially his half-brother Andre, into carrying out his plans for him.

PRISON

In his late teens, Sobhraj left home and went to Paris, where he was arrested for burglary in 1963 and sentenced to three years in prison. This could have been a nightmare experience, but Sobhraj's talents for manipulating people – plus his martial arts skills – came into their own in the prison milieu. One of the people he charmed there was a rich young prison visitor called Felix d'Escogne.

On his release from prison, Charles went to live with Felix and was introduced into a world of glamour and money. Sobhraj felt in his element, and married an elegant young woman, Chantal. However, in order to keep up in this world he had to have money, and the only way he knew of getting money was to steal it. He began to burgle his wealthy friends' houses and write bad cheques. Finally, with his wife, he fled France. The couple spent the remainder of the 1960s scamming their way across eastern Europe and the Middle East before settling down in Bombay, India. Chantal gave birth to their son during this time.

MURDER

In 1971, the family had to flee India following a botched jewel robbery. They went to Kabul, Afghanistan, for a while. Here Charles specialized in robbing hippies who were passing through. However, by now Chantal had had enough and she returned to Paris with their son. Charles went back to his wanderings, accompanied for a while by his brother Andre. Their partnership ended in a Greek jail from which Charles managed to escape, leaving his brother behind. Soon Charles found a new partner, Marie-Andrée Leclerc, who fell madly in love with him. They moved to Thailand and set up home in the beach resort of Pattaya. Gradually Sobhraj built up an entourage around him, reminiscent of the 'Family' set up by Charles Manson.

It was at this time that Sobhraj started to add murder to

Charles Sobhraj and Marie-Andrée Leclerc wait outside court, New Delhi, 24 February 1977.

CHARLES SOBHRAJ **45**

Pattaya Beach, Thailand.

robbery. His first victim was an American called Jennie Bollivar. She was found dead in a tide pool in the warm waters of the Gulf of Thailand, wearing a bikini. At first it looked like an accident, but the autopsy revealed that she must have died by being held under the water. The next victim was a young Sephardic Jew, Vitali Hakim, who was robbed, beaten and set on fire.

A pair of Dutch students, Henk Bintanja and his fiancée, Cornelia 'Cocky' Hemker, were next to go, both strangled and their bodies burned. At that point, a friend of Hakim's, Charmaine Carrou, came looking for him. Like Bollivar, she was drowned in her bikini, causing the unknown murderer to be branded the 'bikini killer'.

DISCOVERY

After reports of the murders in the Thai press, Sobhraj decided to lie low for a while. He flew to Nepal, where he met and murdered another couple, Laddie Duparr and Annabella Tremont, then left the country using the dead man's passport.

Back in Bangkok, some of Sobhraj's erstwhile followers had found a stash of passports in his office and suspected him of murder. Sobhraj fled back to Nepal using Henk Bintanja's passport, then fled again to Calcutta (now Kolkata), India, where he carried out another murder, that of an Israeli called Avoni Jacob. A bewildering series of moves followed, until he eventually returned to Thailand. By now the fuss had died down, and Sobhraj was able to bribe his way out of trouble. He soon went back to robbing and killing tourists, until the heat built up again and he returned to India in 1976, where he was finally arrested for the murder of a Frenchman.

When he was brought to trial, two of his associates testified against him. However, he was sentenced to only 12 years in prison. Once there, he began to live a life of luxury: special food, drugs and books were brought in to him, and he was free to spend his time more or less as he pleased. In 1986 he contrived a daring escape, but soon afterwards gave himself up to police in Goa. He realized that he needed to go back to prison in order to avoid being extradited to Thailand, where he would have faced the death penalty.

Finally, after 21 years in captivity (by which time, under Thai law, he could no longer be charged for his crimes), he was released from prison and deported to France. There he sold the rights to his story and enjoyed living off his notoriety. For a while, it looked as though he had actually managed to get away with murder.

However, in 2003, for reasons that remain inexplicable, Sobhraj returned to Nepal, where he was arrested. He was charged with the murders of Duparr and Tremont, and sentenced to life imprisonment. In 2004 he was convicted of the murder of Connie Jo Bronzich, an American tourist, and in 2014, he was convicted of the murder of her Canadian friend Laurent Carrière in Kathmandu in 1975. He was released on 21 December 2022 from prison in Nepal on account of old age and deported to France.

During his trial, Sobhraj was always careful to cover his face.

PAUL KNOWLES

NAME: Paul John Knowles
DATE OF BIRTH: 25 April 1946
PROFESSION: Welder
ALIASES: The Casanova Killer
NATIONALITY: American

LOCATION OF CRIMES: USA
DATES OF MURDERS: July–November 1974
NUMBER OF VICTIMS: 18–35+

Journalists usually only meet serial killers once they are safely locked behind bars. British journalist Sandy Fawkes had a rather different experience when she met a good-looking young man named Paul Knowles in an Atlanta bar, and ended up spending several days with him. Ten days later, she was to see her lover's mugshot on the cover of the newspaper – arrested for the latest in a string of at least 18 murders.

A native of Florida, Paul Knowles was a serial killer who lacked the usual patterns of behaviour common to murderers of this type. He roamed from place to place, killing young and old, men and women. Sometimes he raped his victims, both men and women; sometimes he did not. Sometimes his crimes were financially motivated, sometimes sexually. The only common thread in his actions was an utter lack of moral scruple.

Born in 1946, from his teenage years Knowles was consistently in trouble with the law. He served his first prison sentence when he was 19 and from then on was constantly in and out of jail, mostly for burglary or car theft.

His first verified murder came shortly after being arrested following a bar fight in Jacksonville, Florida, on 26 July 1974. He escaped from prison using his lock-picking expertise and broke into the house of 65-year-old Alice Curtis. He stole her money and possessions, including her car, and left her bound and gagged. Later, she choked to death on the gag and, when news of her death hit the local media, Knowles decided to dump the car. As he did so, he saw two young girls, aged seven and 11, whom he thought

48 UNFORGIVING VIOLENCE

had recognized him. He abducted them both, strangled them and dumped their bodies in a swamp.

ON THE ROAD

Next, he headed south to Atlantic Beach, Florida, where he broke into another house and strangled the occupant. From there he went north, picking up a hitch-hiker and raping and strangling her along the way, before stopping off in Musella, Georgia, to break into yet another house where he strangled Kathie Pierce as her three-year-old son watched. He did, however, leave the boy unharmed.

Knowles spent the next two months driving aimlessly around the country, killing, raping and stealing as he went. On 3 September 1974, he robbed and killed a businessman named William Bates in Lima, Ohio. On 18 September, he murdered two campers in Ely, Nevada. On 21 September, in Texas, he saw a stranded motorist looking for help. He stopped to rape and kill her. Two days after that, heading back towards his home territory, he met a beautician named Ann Dawson in Birmingham, Alabama. They spent six days together as lovers, Dawson paying the bills, until, on 29 September, he killed her.

Three more weeks of drifting elapsed before Knowles found his next victim, Doris Hovey, whom he shot dead a little way north of Woodford, Virginia. Back south in Macon, Georgia, on 6 November, a man named Carswell Carr made the mistake of inviting Knowles back to his house for drinks. Knowles stabbed Carr to death and then strangled his 15-year-old daughter Mandy, attempting to have sex with her corpse.

Paul Knowles is escorted to jail on 20 November 1974.

ROAD BLOCK

Two days later, Knowles was in Atlanta, where he met Sandy Fawkes. She was immediately attracted to what she called his 'gaunt good looks'. Knowles was unable to perform sexually, however, and failed repeatedly over the next few days. When they parted, Fawkes had no idea how lucky she was to be alive; she found out when, on the following day, Knowles picked up one of her friends, Susan Mackenzie, and pulled a gun on her before demanding sex. Mackenzie managed to escape and alert the police, who were soon on Knowles' trail.

The chase lasted several days. Finally apprehended by a police officer, Knowles managed to draw his gun first and kidnap the officer, stealing his car. He then used the police car to stop another motorist, whose car he stole in turn. Now he had two hostages, the policeman and the motorist, James Meyer. He soon tired of them, and tied the two men to a tree in Pulaski County, Georgia, before shooting them both in the head.

Time was running out for Knowles, however. He ran into a police roadblock, and tried to escape on foot before finally

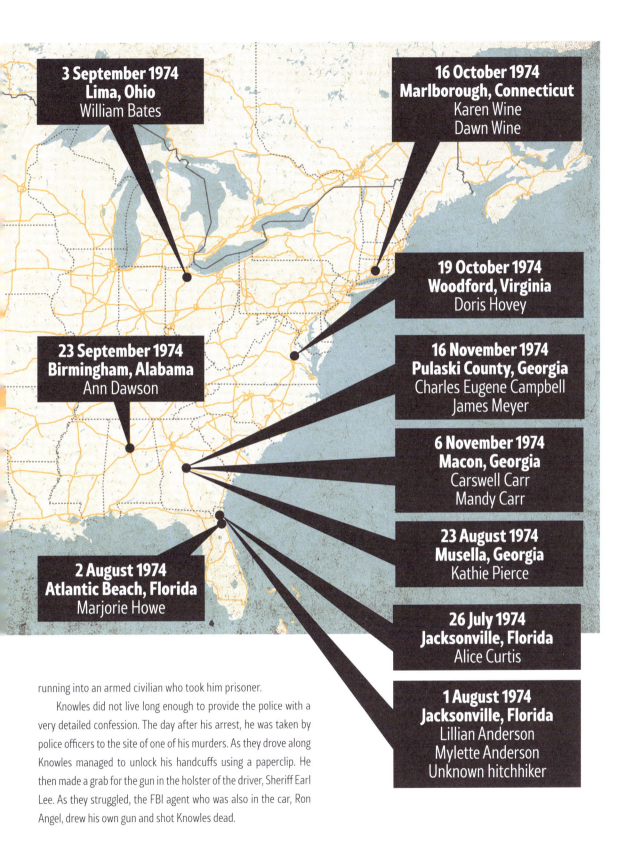

running into an armed civilian who took him prisoner.

Knowles did not live long enough to provide the police with a very detailed confession. The day after his arrest, he was taken by police officers to the site of one of his murders. As they drove along Knowles managed to unlock his handcuffs using a paperclip. He then made a grab for the gun in the holster of the driver, Sheriff Earl Lee. As they struggled, the FBI agent who was also in the car, Ron Angel, drew his own gun and shot Knowles dead.

PETER MANUEL

NAME: Peter Thomas Anthony Manuel
DATE OF BIRTH: 13 March 1927
PROFESSION: Gas engineer
ALIASES: The Beast of Birkenshaw
NATIONALITY: American
LOCATION OF CRIMES: Scotland, United Kingdom
DATES OF MURDERS: 1956–58
NUMBER OF VICTIMS: 7+

Born in New York to Scottish parents, Peter Manuel longed to be an American gangster even after the family returned to Scotland in 1932, when he was six. By the age of ten he had a well-deserved reputation as a juvenile delinquent and served his first term in custody at the age of 15 for sexual assault.

NOT YET A KILLER

In 1946 Manuel attacked a woman and was convicted of raping her. However, after reviewing the evidence for his book *Manuel: Scotland's First Serial Killer*, author and advocate Allan Nicol believes that he was wrongfully convicted. The victim had been dazed in the attack and only thought she had been raped. In addition, Nicol maintained that he was incapable of rape and only achieved sexual satisfaction from violence.

'Complete sperm [sic] were found on his trousers, shirt and singlet,' says Nicol. 'His dark secret meant he did not actually commit the full crime. He would have raped had he been capable.'

Manuel served nine years in Scotland's Peterhead prison in Aberdeenshire, where he pretended to be a safecracker – the glamour crime of the day. On his release in 1953 he moved to Glasgow, but he was jilted by his fiancée when she found out about his criminal record. That day Manuel took out his anger on 29-year-old Mary McLaughlan, dragging her into a field and threatening to cut her head off when she screamed for help. His eyes bulged as he groped her and forced kisses on her and he growled with rage as he described in detail what he would do.

Manuel followed 17-year-old Anne Kneilands to a golf course, where he assaulted her with an iron bar.

Throughout her ordeal, Mary sobbed and pleaded and then suddenly Manuel stopped and sat back. She was the last of his victims to escape with her life. He was charged with sexual assault and she testified against him in court. A small, dapper man, he defended himself and got a not proven verdict.

KILLING SPREE BEGINS

Manuel's killing spree began on the night of 2 January 1956 when he followed 17-year-old machinist Anne Kneilands on to a golf course in East Kilbride, not far from where he was laying pipes for the local gas board. There he smashed her head in with an iron bar and tore off her underwear, though there was no evidence of sexual interference. When Manuel turned up for work on 4 January there were scratch marks clearly visible on his face and as a known sex offender he was questioned, but he was released without charge after his father provided him with an alibi. Although he eventually confessed to Anne's murder, the case against him was dropped due to lack of evidence.

Then on 17 September 1956, Manuel broke into the home of 45-year-old invalid Marion Watt in the High Burnside district of Glasgow. Her husband William, a master baker who had several shops in Glasgow, was away on a fishing trip, but Marion's 41-year-old sister Margaret Brown and Marion's 16-year-old daughter Vivienne were in the house. They were shot dead in their beds and jewellery was taken.

The bodies were discovered by Mrs Helen Collison, the Watts' daily help, who turned up for work at 8.45 am. She was surprised to find the door still locked and the curtains drawn and then she noticed that a pane of glass in the kitchen door had been broken. When the postman, Peter Collier, arrived he put his hand through the broken pane and opened the door. Mrs Collison then went in to find the gruesome scene.

That same night a bungalow in nearby Fennsbank Avenue had been burgled and the police recognized the handiwork of local villain Peter Manuel. At the time, he was out on bail over a break-in at a local colliery. Although he was suspected of the murders he found himself off the hook when William Watt was arrested and charged with the killings. The police had interviewed a ferryman on the Clyde who thought that he had carried Mr Watt's car across the river on the night of the killings. It was a mistake, but Watt spent two months in jail before being released for lack of evidence. Nevertheless, the police continued to believe that he was the killer until Manuel was brought to book.

Manuel then served 18 months in prison for burglary. He was released in November 1957 and quickly resumed killing. His next victim was 36-year-old taxi driver Sydney Dunn, who was murdered on 8 December when Manuel was visiting Newcastle-upon-Tyne looking for work. Dunn was shot in the head and had his throat slit. His cab was found abandoned 30 km (20 miles) from Newcastle and his body was dumped on moorland, but Manuel had returned to Lanarkshire by the time it was found.

He then targeted 17-year-old Isabelle Cooke, who on 28 December 1957 was on her way to meet her boyfriend at a nearby

Peter Manuel's victims. Manuel was charged with the murder of eight people at his trial in 1958 and convicted for seven of them.

54 UNFORGIVING VIOLENCE

Manuel terrorized Glasgow and its surrounding areas in the 1950s.

bus stop. They were going to a dance at Uddingston Grammar School. Over the next few days, items of her clothing were found scattered in the area, but there was no sign of the girl herself. Manuel had strangled her and buried her body in a field. Initially, Isabelle's disappearance was not tied to Manuel and her body was only found when Manuel later pointed out the spot to the police.

BECOMES CARELESS

In the early hours of 1 January 1958, Manuel broke into the Uddingston home of the Smart family, where he shot Peter and Doris Smart, a couple in their early forties, and their ten-year-old son Michael. Manuel stayed in the house for nearly a week, eating the leftovers from their Hogmanay meal and feeding the family cat. There was some money in the house, as Peter had drawn some cash from the bank in preparation for a family holiday. The notes were new. Manuel took the money and the Smarts' car and even gave a lift to a policeman looking into Isabelle Cooke's disappearance. He told the constable that they were not looking in the right place.

Passers-by noticed that the curtains at the Smarts' house were opening and closing at strange times and they felt that they were being watched. Manuel seems to have used the house as a centre of operations. At about 5.45 am on 4 January, Mr and Mrs McMunn awoke to find a face peering around the bedroom door in their house in Sheepburn Road, Uddingston. Fortunately, Mr McMunn had the presence of mind to ask his wife: 'Where's the gun?' At that, the intruder fled.

Peter Smart did not return to work after the New Year break, which aroused suspicion, and then his car was found abandoned. Concerned, the police visited the Smarts' bungalow. Unable to get any response, they forced the back door and immediately noticed that the door to the main bedroom was covered with blood. The bodies of Mr and Mrs Smart were found inside the room and their son Michael's was found in his own bedroom.

NEW BANKNOTES LEAD

A barman in a pub became suspicious of Manuel, who was usually broke, when he paid for rounds of drinks using new banknotes. In the days before ATMs, new notes were not a common sight. He called the police, who took the notes to the bank. After checking the serial numbers, the bank confirmed that they had been given to Peter Smart when he had cashed a cheque.

On 13 January 1958, Manuel was arrested at his home in Birkenshaw, near Uddingston. He was put on an identification parade

Peter Manuel returns to jail after his appeal. He was hanged on 11 July 1958.

and the staff at the pub and some of its customers confirmed that he was the man who had handed over the new notes. The Smarts' murders were conspicuously similar to the murders at the Watts' house and the police also had the letters Manuel had written to William Watt, while Watt was on remand. These contained details that only the killer could have known.

Manuel then took the police to the field where he had buried Isabelle Cooke. Asked where her body was, he said: 'I'm standing on her now.'

While in custody, Manuel confessed to eight murders, but when the case came to trial at the Glasgow High Court before Mr Justice Cameron in May 1958, he changed his plea to not guilty and withdrew his confession, claiming it had been extracted under coercion. On the ninth day of the trial, he dismissed his lawyers and proceeded to conduct his own defence.

He then pleaded insanity but was unable to convince the judge. It took the jury just two and a half hours to convict him of seven murders. Lord Cameron had directed them to acquit Manuel on the charge of killing Anne Kneilands, but it made little difference as Manuel faced a death sentence anyway.

Northumbria police attended Manuel's trial and would have charged him with the murder of Sydney Dunn had he been acquitted of the Scottish killings. A button from his jacket had been found in Dunn's abandoned cab. There were still some doubts as to whether he had done it, but a coroner's jury found him responsible at a hearing after he was dead.

EXECUTION

The original execution date was set for 19 June but this had to be postponed, pending the hearing of Manuel's appeal on 24 and 25 June. However, the appeal was dismissed so a new execution date of Friday 11 July was set. Manuel then tried to feign insanity as he sat on his bed in Barlinnie prison's condemned suite. He refused to talk to the death-watch warders and just listened to the radio he had been allowed to have. As a Catholic he was also permitted the ministrations of Father Smith, who similarly got nothing out of him. His mother, Bridget, visited him in his final days. Enraged at his play-acting, she slapped his face, telling him: 'You can't fool me!'

At 8 am on Friday 11 July 1958, the hangman Harry Allen, assisted by Harold Smith, led Manuel the few paces from his cell to the gallows. Manuel's last words were: 'Turn up the radio and I'll go quietly.' His execution took just eight seconds to carry out and 24 seconds after the drop Manuel was certified dead by Dr David Anderson, the prison's medical officer. His body was taken down at 8.35 am and placed in an open coffin ready for a 9.30 am inquest before Sheriff Allan Walker. Father Smith conducted a burial service later that day, when Manuel was interred in an unmarked grave in the prison grounds near the wall of D Hall.

SHOULD HE HAVE DIED?

Little effort had been made to save Manuel from the hangman, even by those trying to abolish the death penalty. However, 50 years later, Dr Richard Goldberg of Aberdeen University's law school tried to get files on the case reopened. They had been sealed for 75 years. Dr Goldberg, whose father had witnessed a medical examination of Manuel while working as a consultant at the Western Infirmary in Glasgow, believed Manuel could have escaped the gallows if the court had been told the full extent of his mental health problems, which included a form of epilepsy many believe can cause criminal behaviour.

Journalist Russell Galbraith, who covered Manuel's trial, said: 'I don't remember any great enthusiasm from people trying to save Manuel, I must say, although there was obviously an abhorrence at the death penalty in many places.'

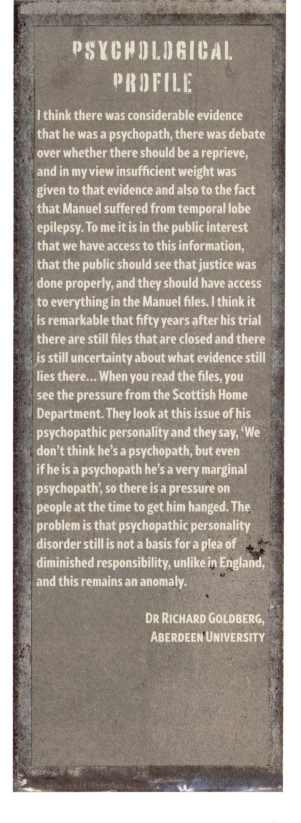

PSYCHOLOGICAL PROFILE

I think there was considerable evidence that he was a psychopath, there was debate over whether there should be a reprieve, and in my view insufficient weight was given to that evidence and also to the fact that Manuel suffered from temporal lobe epilepsy. To me it is in the public interest that we have access to this information, that the public should see that justice was done properly, and they should have access to everything in the Manuel files. I think it is remarkable that fifty years after his trial there are still files that are closed and there is still uncertainty about what evidence still lies there… When you read the files, you see the pressure from the Scottish Home Department. They look at this issue of his psychopathic personality and they say, 'We don't think he's a psychopath, but even if he is a psychopath he's a very marginal psychopath', so there is a pressure on people at the time to get him hanged. The problem is that psychopathic personality disorder still is not a basis for a plea of diminished responsibility, unlike in England, and this remains an anomaly.

DR RICHARD GOLDBERG, ABERDEEN UNIVERSITY

CHAPTER 2

DOUBLE LIVES

It is not always easy to detect a serial killer. Often, they seem to be normal, trustworthy members of society, well-liked in their community and holding respectable jobs. The ranks of serial killers include police officers and journalists who abuse their authority to indulge their most violent urges, while others take advantage of people's better nature to keep committing their crimes.

MIKHAIL POPKOV

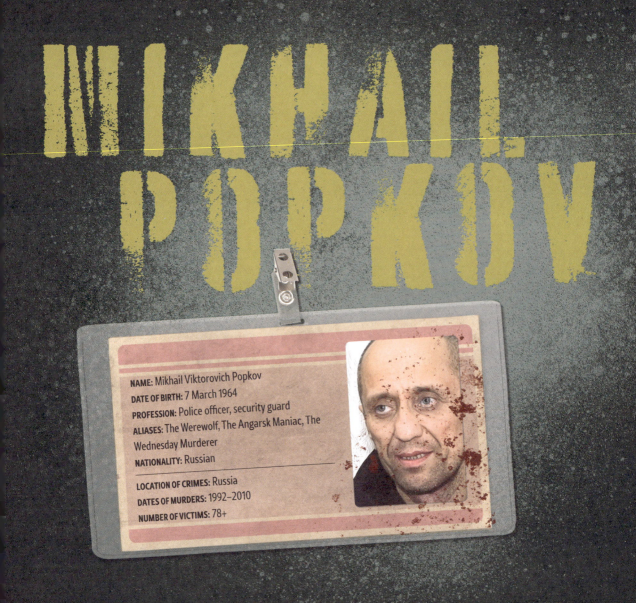

NAME: Mikhail Viktorovich Popkov
DATE OF BIRTH: 7 March 1964
PROFESSION: Police officer, security guard
ALIASES: The Werewolf, The Angarsk Maniac, The Wednesday Murderer
NATIONALITY: Russian
LOCATION OF CRIMES: Russia
DATES OF MURDERS: 1992–2010
NUMBER OF VICTIMS: 78+

Mikhail Popkov was known as 'The Werewolf' in the press because he struck at night, but the authorities more prosaically called him the 'Wednesday Murderer' because that was usually when the bodies were found. Nevertheless, he is much more scary than that name suggests, for as Russia's most prolific killer he admitted to the rape and murder of more than eighty women. The final total may have been even higher than that.

Having been sentenced to life imprisonment for twenty-two murders in 2015, Popkov claimed that he stopped killing in the year 2000 after one of his victims gave him syphilis, rendering him impotent. However, in 2017 he admitted that he continued for another ten years and confessed to killing another sixty people in the Irkutsk Oblast of central Siberia. And there may have been even more victims. After quitting his job as a police officer, he travelled regularly between his hometown of Angarsk and Vladivostok on Russia's Pacific coast, over two thousand miles away, and the detectives felt that he may have killed along the way. They believed that he was rationing his confessions to delay his transfer from the relative comfort of the regular prison, where he was then being held, to a tough penal colony where he would serve out the rest of his life sentence.

Popkov was dubbed 'The Werewolf Killer' by the press because of his tendency to kill at night.

KILLED THOSE OF 'NEGATIVE BEHAVIOUR'

Popkov began killing in 1992 when he found two used condoms in the rubbish at home and suspected that his wife Elena, who was also a police officer, was cheating on him. Though it seems that the condoms had been left by a house guest, one of Elena's work colleagues admitted that he had had a brief affair with her.

A few weeks after his discovery, Popkov killed 'spontaneously', he told investigators.

> 'I JUST FELT I WANTED TO KILL A WOMAN I WAS GIVING A LIFT TO IN MY CAR.'

In 2015, he claimed that his victims were prostitutes and that his aim was to 'cleanse' his hometown. He also thought that even if they were not involved in prostitution, women who went out by themselves at night, going to bars and drinking alcohol, needed to be punished. It has been speculated that Popkov was taking psychic revenge on an alcoholic mother who abused him as a child.

Women felt safe getting into Popkov's police car. He used his uniform and his job as a police officer to reassure victims.

> 'MY VICTIMS WERE WOMEN WHO WALKED THE STREETS AT NIGHT ALONE, WITHOUT MEN, AND NOT SOBER, WHO BEHAVED THOUGHTLESSLY, CARELESSLY, NOT AFRAID TO ENGAGE IN A CONVERSATION WITH ME, SIT IN THE CAR, AND THEN GO FOR A DRIVE IN SEARCH OF ADVENTURE, FOR THE SAKE OF ENTERTAINMENT, READY TO DRINK ALCOHOL AND HAVE SEXUAL INTERCOURSE WITH ME,' HE SAID. 'IN THIS WAY, NOT ALL WOMEN BECAME VICTIMS, BUT WOMEN OF CERTAIN NEGATIVE BEHAVIOUR, AND I HAD A DESIRE TO TEACH AND PUNISH THEM, SO THAT OTHERS WOULD NOT BEHAVE IN SUCH A WAY AND SO THAT THEY WOULD BE AFRAID.'

He used to have sex with them and then decide whether to murder them. The women were reassured by his police uniform and felt safe getting into a police car.

> 'I WAS IN UNIFORM. I DECIDED TO STOP AND GIVE A WOMAN A RIDE. I FREQUENTLY DID THAT BEFORE,' HE SAID. 'THE WOMAN BEGAN TALKING TO ME, I OFFERED TO GIVE HER A LIFT, SHE AGREED ... THAT SAME MORNING, I DROVE THE HEAD OF THE CRIMINAL INVESTIGATION TO THE MURDER SCENE.'

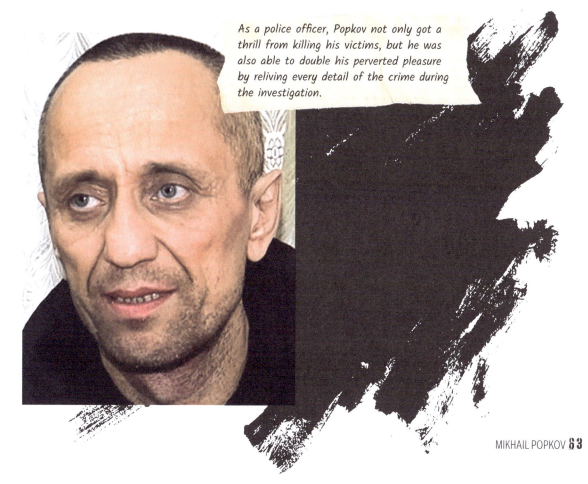

As a police officer, Popkov not only got a thrill from killing his victims, but he was also able to double his perverted pleasure by reliving every detail of the crime during the investigation.

THRILL FROM INVESTIGATIONS

Popkov not only got a thrill from killing his victims, but he was also able to double his perverted pleasure by reliving every detail of the crime during the investigation. He should have been caught much earlier, as one of his victims survived and identified him. On 26 January 1998, a 15-year-old known as Svetlana M said a police car had stopped to give her a lift. The officer took her into some woodland where he forced her to strip naked. He then smashed her head against a tree and she lost consciousness. The next day she was found alive near the village of Baykalsk, some 110 km (70 miles) from where Popkov had picked her up. Somehow she had survived the night naked in the sub-zero temperatures of a Siberian winter.

When she awoke in hospital she was able to identify the officer who had tried to kill her. It was Popkov. However, his wife provided him with a false alibi. Neither she nor their daughter Ekaterina, a teacher, could believe that he was a killer. They said he was a perfect husband and father.

Popkov's colleagues in the police force also found it hard to believe that he was a killer. Nor do there appear to have been any signs of mental instability.

'I was in the service, in the police, having positive feedback on my work,' he said. 'I never thought of myself as mentally unhealthy. During my police service, I regularly passed medical commissions and was recognized as fit.'

An axe was one of many weapons Popkov used to commit his crimes.

'I HAD A DOUBLE LIFE. IN ONE LIFE, I WAS AN ORDINARY PERSON ... IN MY OTHER LIFE I COMMITTED MURDERS, WHICH I CAREFULLY CONCEALED FROM EVERYONE, REALIZING THAT WHAT I WAS DOING WAS A CRIMINAL OFFENCE.'

'FASTIDIOUS'

A major clue that was overlooked was that the murder weapons were removed from the police storeroom. After wiping them to remove his fingerprints, he would throw them away near the scene of the crime.

'The choice of weapons for killing was always casual,' he said. 'I never prepared beforehand to commit a murder. I could use any object that was in the car – a knife, an axe, a bat.'

And he claimed to be fastidious.

'I never used rope for strangulation,' he said, 'and I did not have a firearm either. I did not cut out the hearts of the victims.'

Two bodies turned up in Angarsk after two women decided to accept a lift from a police officer.

However, one of his victims had had her heart gouged from her body. Others were mutilated or dismembered. One, a medical student, had been beheaded. Her body was found in a rubbish container in Angarsk, her head in another skip elsewhere.

On one occasion, the killing came close to home when he discovered that he had murdered a teacher at his own daughter's music school.

'Her corpse was found in the forest along with the body of another woman,' he said. 'My daughter asked me to give her money because the school was collecting to organize funerals. I gave it to her.'

DOUBLE MURDERS

He had another close call in 2000 when he returned to the scene of a crime. After he had left 35-year-old Maria Lyzhina and 37-year-old Liliya Pashkovskaya for dead, he found that a commemorative chain he wore around his neck was missing and he went to retrieve it before investigators found it.

'I realized that I lost it in a forest glade when I killed the two women,' he said. 'I realized that I would absolutely be identified by the lost chain, and experienced the greatest stress. I realized that I should return to the scene of the crime, if the police or the prosecutor's office had not been there yet.'

But when he returned to the scene he found more than he had bargained for.

'I found the chain right away, but saw that one of the women was still breathing,' he said. 'I was shocked by the fact that she was still alive, so I finished her off with a shovel.'

The two women had worked together in a shop. On 2 June they went to see Maria's sister and at midnight they decided they had better go home. At first they thought of taking a taxi but then they changed their minds.

It was a warm summer night and they decided to walk. On 5 June, their bodies were found in the forest near Veresovka village. Maria had a 14-year-old daughter and Liliya had a 12-year-old daughter and a three-year-old son, who would now have to grow up without their mothers.

The custom in Russia is for coffins to be left open at the graveside so mourners can bid the deceased a final farewell, but the two women were buried in closed coffins because they were so badly disfigured.

Another double murder occurred in 1998 when the bodies of 20-year-old Tatiana 'Tanya' Martynova and 19-year-old Yulia Kuprikova were found in a suburb of Angarsk. Tanya's sister Viktoria Chagaeva had given her a ticket for a concert, but Tanya was married with a small child and her 24-year-old husband Igor begged her not to go. Ignoring his pleas, she made the mistake of stopping for a quick drink with a few friends after the show. Then the two girls accepted a lift from a policeman.

'On the morning of 29 October, Igor called me saying Tanya had not come back home,' said Viktoria. 'I got truly scared. It was the first time she had ever done this. There were no mobile phones at that time; we could only call Yulia's parents, thinking Tanya must have stayed overnight there for some reason. But Yulia's parents said she had not come home either.'

They went to the police and were told that they must wait three days before the two young women could be listed as missing. There would be no need to wait. That night a shepherd found their naked bodies near Meget, a village close to Angarsk.

'It was 1 am when Tanya's husband Igor and I came to the police,' said Viktoria. 'We did not tell our mother yet. Igor was absolutely devastated and kept saying: "She was killed, she was killed." I was shocked too, but I simply could not believe it and replied: "What are you talking about?"'

Later they were told that their bodies were found next to each other. Both girls had been raped after they were killed and then mutilated.

'My elder brother Oleg went to the morgue to identify Tanya,' said Viktoria. 'He had just flown from Moscow. He felt sick when he saw the body, she was so mutilated. He was almost green when he came out of there. He just could not say a word. I did not dare to go in and look.'

The mutilation was confined to Tanya's body and the back of her head, so the coffin could be left open with her face showing. However, Yulia's coffin had to be kept closed as her face was so badly cut up.

'Many people attended Tanya's funeral,' said Viktoria. 'It felt as if the whole town was there. Our poor mother lost consciousness several times; she needed a lot of medicine to cope. Igor was in almost the same condition.'

Indeed, their mother Lubov never recovered from the loss of her daughter. 'She felt as if she had died with Tanya. Life became useless for her,' said Viktoria. 'She lived only because she was visiting various mediums one by one, looking for the killer and wasting her money. Nobody gave her any serious information but she kept doing it. She died in 2007, aged 66, from a heart attack. I think her heart could not cope with the pain any longer.'

VICTIM'S SISTER KNEW THE KILLER

When Popkov was arrested in 2012, Viktoria realized that she knew him. They had both competed in a biathlon at a local sports ground.

'I was struck with horror when I saw the picture of this maniac in the paper and online,' she said. 'My sister's killer was looking into my eyes. I immediately felt as if I'd met him. Looking at him, I could hardly breathe. Some minutes later I looked at him another time and thought – oh my God, I know him! I was so shocked, I even took a knife and cut his face in the newspaper, I needed to let this horror out of me.

'I remember him as a tall slim man, he was always alone, with a slippery and shifty glance. I think such people just must not live. This beast took the life of my sister, who had so many happy years in front of her. I cried a lot that day, but it is time to be quiet and just wait. He will be punished by law and criminals in jail will punish him too. I am sure he will pay for all the murders one day.'

That a fellow officer committed these terrible crimes under their noses perturbed the police. A former police colleague said: 'When I read about him in the press, I literally choked because I used to work with him and thought I knew him. He was an absolutely normal man. He liked biathlon; once on duty he shot a rapist during an arrest. There was an investigation and he was not punished as the chiefs considered he had taken fair action.'

Another ex-colleague said: 'I used to work closely with him for five years. He knew lots of jokes and stories, and could be the life and soul of the party.'

Popkov was caught when 3,500 policemen and former policemen were asked to give a DNA sample. His DNA matched that in sperm found on some of the victims.

'I couldn't predict DNA tests,' he told a reporter from *Komsomolskaya Pravda* in a jailhouse interview. 'I was born in the wrong century.'

When Popkov pleaded guilty to the two dozen murder charges, the judge asked him how many murders he had committed in total. In reply, the killer just shrugged.

'I can't say exactly,' he said. 'I didn't write them down.'

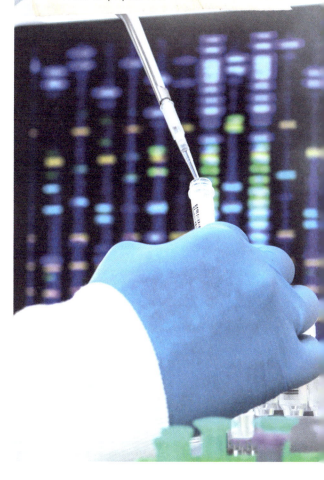

It took DNA testing to finally catch Popkov – the one eventuality he had failed to prepare for.

VLADO TANESKI

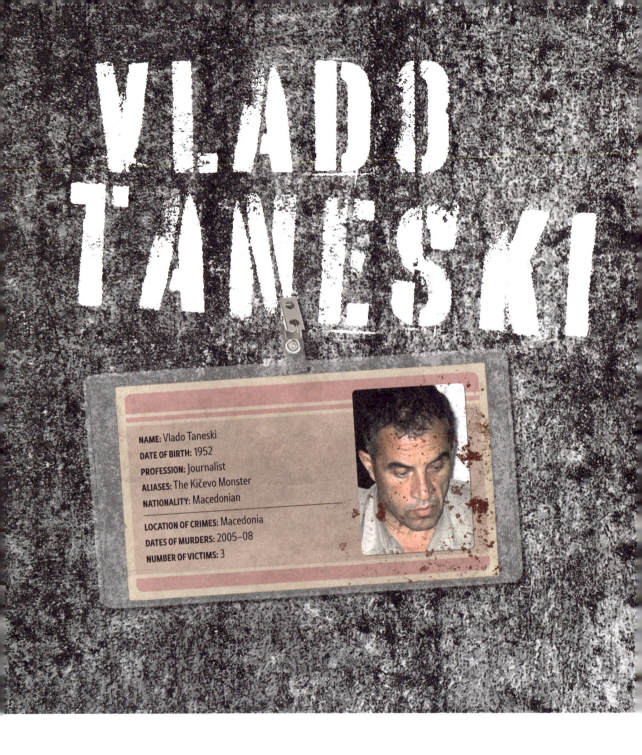

NAME: Vlado Taneski
DATE OF BIRTH: 1952
PROFESSION: Journalist
ALIASES: The Kičevo Monster
NATIONALITY: Macedonian
LOCATION OF CRIMES: Macedonia
DATES OF MURDERS: 2005–08
NUMBER OF VICTIMS: 3

On **19 May 2008**, Macedonia's biggest daily newspaper *Nova Makedonija* (New Macedonia) printed a story under the headline 'Serial Killer Stalks Kičevo Too'. Three women's bodies – naked, wrapped in telephone cable and stuffed into nylon bags – had been found around Kičevo, a poor mountainous town with a population of 27,000, about 120 km (75 miles) south-west of Macedonia's capital Skopje. The previous year a serial killer had stalked Ohrid, just 50 km (30 miles) away, though the MO was clearly different.

NOVA MAKEDONIJA

The people of **Kičevo** live in fear and panic after another butchered body of a woman from the town was found over the weekend. The local police, as well as the town populace, see the mysterious disappearances and terrible deaths of Živana Temelkoska and Lubica Ličoska as the work of a single person – a serial killer.

Both women were tortured and murdered in the same fashion, which rules out the possibility that this could have been done by two different people. The Ohrid serial killer murdered three people but his victims were all street-based money exchangers and his motive was to rob them.

The motives of the Kičevo monster remain unclear. Both women were friends and living in the same part of town. Police have a few suspects who they are interrogating.

The latest body was found in a rubbish dump. It had been tied up with a piece of phone cable with which the woman had clearly been previously strangled.

- Vlado Taneski

Nova Makedonija's story was bylined 'Vlado Taneski', a veteran reporter of 20 years who still used a typewriter and phoned in his copy, rather than send it by fax or even by laptop and email. There was usually little to report from Kičevo apart from local government incompetence or corruption, rising unemployment and petty crime, and then in November 2004 came a story Taneski could get his teeth into. Sixty-one-year-old Mitra Simjanoska, who some said was a woman 'of loose morals', went missing.

SUSPECTS JAILED

On 12 January 2005, her body was found dumped in a shallow hole in an abandoned construction site on the edge of town. She had been bound, brutally raped, strangled and then stuffed into a bag. The police quickly arrested two men in their twenties, Ante Risteski and Igor Mirčeski, who were charged with the murder of Simjanoska as well as that of Radoslav Bozhinoski, an old man who had been robbed and killed and horribly abused in the nearby village of Malkoetz. His penis and testicles had been squeezed with hot fire tongs and objects had been forced up his anus. It was reported that Risteski and Mirčeski had confessed to both murders, but in court they only admitted to killing Bozhinoski and said they had nothing to do with Simjanoska.

They were sentenced to life imprisonment for the two murders. However, semen had been found on Simjanoska's body and the DNA matched neither that of Risteski nor Mirčeski.

INTERVIEWS VICTIM'S SON

Then in November 2007 56-year-old Lubica Ličoska went missing from the same part of town as Simjanoska. Taneski interviewed Ličoska's son Duko, who said:

'Lubica was a quiet and gentle woman. She fought poverty and worked as a janitor of apartment buildings to feed her family. Two days after the disappearance of my mother, I informed the police. I talked to the residents of the buildings where my mother used to work and searched around a bit for

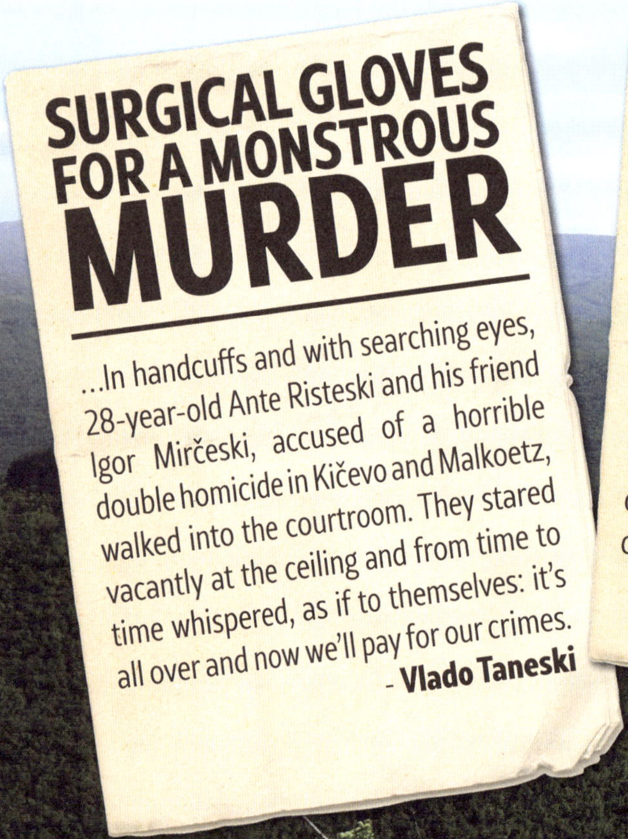

SURGICAL GLOVES FOR A MONSTROUS MURDER

...In handcuffs and with searching eyes, 28-year-old Ante Risteski and his friend Igor Mirčeski, accused of a horrible double homicide in Kičevo and Malkoetz, walked into the courtroom. They stared vacantly at the ceiling and from time to time whispered, as if to themselves: it's all over and now we'll pay for our crimes.

- Vlado Taneski

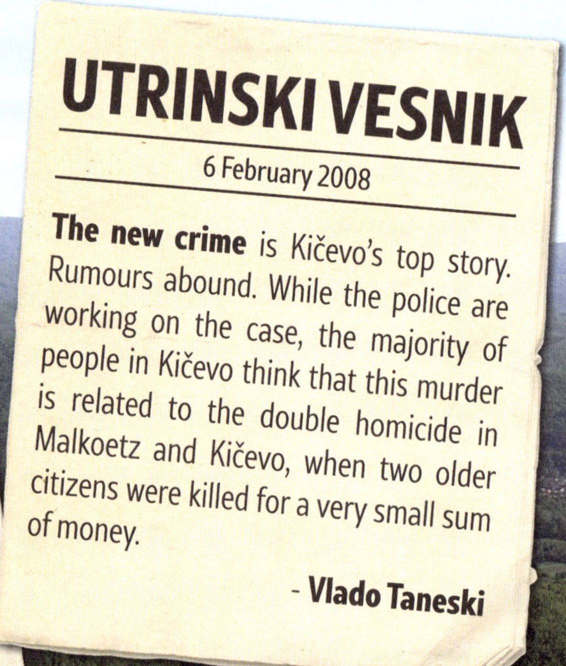

UTRINSKI VESNIK

6 February 2008

The new crime is Kičevo's top story. Rumours abound. While the police are working on the case, the majority of people in Kičevo think that this murder is related to the double homicide in Malkoetz and Kičevo, when two older citizens were killed for a very small sum of money.

- Vlado Taneski

clues, but I couldn't find any traces of her. The police told me they are on the case.'

Then locals remembered that in May 2003 another elderly woman, 73-year-old Gorica Pavelski, had also gone missing from the neighbourhood. No trace of her was ever found. However, Ličoska's body was found dumped near the road from Kičevo to Gostivar. Like Simjanoska, she had been bound, raped, strangled and stuffed into a bag. But it appeared that she had been killed only days before, while she had been missing for three months. In the meantime she had been kept prisoner, while being tortured and raped. Taneski's article appeared in *Utrinski vesnik* (Morning Herald) on 6 February 2008.

How could that be when the convicted killers of Simjanoska were already behind bars?

Taneski speculated that Ličoska had been hit by a car and instead of taking her to hospital someone took hideous advantage of her defenceless state. The police, he said, were on their way to solving the case.

REPORTER ARRESTED

Then the body of 65-year-old Živana Temelkoska was found on a rubbish tip outside town. Temelkoska had been bound, raped, strangled and stuffed into a bag in the same way as the others and during her torture she had been abused with a glass object and aftershave. She had numerous internal and external injuries, including five broken ribs and 13 lacerations to the head, and again there was semen on the body. Temelkoska had gone missing from the same part of town as the others, just a week before she was

Mitra Simjanoska's body was found in a shallow hole on an abandoned construction site in Kičevo (pictured below). She had been bound, brutally raped, strangled and then stuffed in a bag.

Taneski left the bodies in rubbish dumps outside town.

her son was injured. Taneski had also chided the police for pinning the murder of Simjanoska on Risteski and Mirčeski, as they were in jail when the other murders were carried out. But their innocence of that crime was only established when the DNA analysis was finalized. Eventually, he said Temelkoska had been strangled with the same cable with which she was bound, but detectives had not released that detail to the media. It was something only the killer or someone close to the case could have known.

Lab tests showed that Taneski's DNA exactly matched samples taken from the bodies of Mitra Simjanoska and Živana Temelkoska. Only later was it shown that seven hairs found near Ličoska's body came from Taneski.

The source of the women's clothing found in his house and his summer cottage some miles away is disputed, but it is thought that Taneski dressed his victims up in his mother's clothes before he raped and strangled them.

Taneski had continued living in the family home, even after he was married, and his wife confirmed that his parents were the only people he ever got angry with. But his life fell apart when his father apparently hanged himself and his mother died of an overdose of sleeping tablets. Around the same time, Taneski was made redundant from his staff job on *Nova Makedonija*, though he continued writing for them as a freelancer while his wife left to take a job in Skopje.

DIED WITHOUT TRIAL

He did not drink or smoke and had few friends. Colleagues were shocked, always finding him mild-mannered. The worst they could say of him was that he occasionally plagiarized – a sin most journalists are guilty of.

Stoutly maintaining his innocence to the police and his estranged wife, Taneski was transferred to the jail in the nearby town of Tetovo. At 2 am, three days after he had been arrested, a cellmate found him on his knees in the lavatory with his head in a bucket of water. He had drowned himself. A signed note in his pocket referred the finder to a second note under the pillow on his bed. This read: 'I have not killed the women. I'm proud of my family.'

Taneski's boss at *Utrinski vesnik*, Daniela Trpchevska, said: 'Police said it was suicide; others – like me – don't think so. And I'm not a hundred per cent convinced that Vlado was the killer, either. After all, he never stood trial.'

However, the veteran reporter, a dedicated journalist, did go out on the best story of his life.

Taneski was found drowned in a bucket of water by his cellmate.

JACK UNTERWEGER

NAME: Johann 'Jack' Unterweger
DATE OF BIRTH: 16 August 1950
PROFESSION: Journalist, playwright
ALIASES: Jack the Strangler, The Courier
NATIONALITY: Austrian

LOCATION OF CRIMES: Austria, West Germany, Czechoslovakia, USA
DATES OF MURDERS: 1974, 1990–92
NUMBER OF VICTIMS: 12–15

Jack Unterweger entered prison as an uneducated murderer and emerged a celebrated author. The toast of Vienna, he was feted and invited to openings and soirées – but his real interest was in murdering prostitutes.

He was born Johann Unterweger on 16 August 1950 to a prostitute in Judenburg, Austria. He never knew his father, nor did he know the man's identity. However, it was generally assumed then, as now, that Unterweger's father was an American soldier. Abandoned at birth, for his first seven years he was raised in extreme poverty by an alcoholic grandfather in a one-room cabin.

From an early age Unterweger displayed a wild and unpredictable temper. At 16, he was arrested for the first time after having assaulted a woman. Tellingly, Unterweger's victim was a prostitute. Other crimes followed in quick succession; he was charged with stealing cars, burglary and receiving stolen property. He was also accused of having forced a woman into prostitution and taking all the proceeds.

On 11 December 1974, he and a prostitute named Barbara Scholz robbed the home of an 18-year-old German prostitute named Margaret Schäfer. Afterwards, Schäfer was taken by car into the woods, where Unterweger tied and beat her. Then he removed her clothes and demanded sex. When she refused, he hit her with a steel pipe and she was strangled with her own bra. He was quickly caught. In his subsequent confession, Unterweger tried to defend his actions by saying that it was his mother whom he'd envisaged beating, and not Margaret Schäfer.

Unterweger was sentenced to life in prison for the murder. Having received little in the way of schooling as a child – he entered incarceration as an illiterate – he found prison could provide him with an education. His progress was dramatic. He soon learned to read and write, and developed an interest in the literary arts. In a short time, he was writing poetry, plays and short stories, as well as editing the prison's literary magazine.

In 1984, his first book, an autobiography entitled *Fegefeuer – eine Reise ins Zuchthaus* ('Purgatory: A Journey to the Penitentiary'), was published to great acclaim and went on to become a bestseller. Unterweger was soon giving interviews and publishing essays and more books – very much the public person, despite being incarcerated. In 1988, his life story – or part of it, at least – was played out on the silver screen when *Fegefeuer* was made into a feature film. Unterweger became a cause célèbre among those promoting the ideals holding prison as a place in which criminals can be reformed.

On 23 May 1990, having served 15 years of his life sentence,

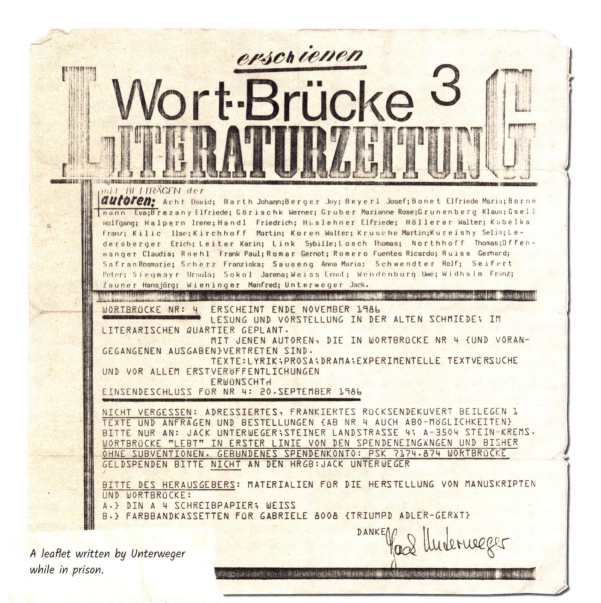

A leaflet written by Unterweger while in prison.

Special knowledge: Unterweger occupied a strange position where as a 'resocialized' ex-con and best-selling author he was in a position to duplicitously comment in the media on crimes he had actually committed.

76 DOUBLE LIVES

UNTERWEGER KEY EVENTS

11 December 1974 – Unterweger murders Margaret Schäfer.

1976 – Unterweger is sentenced to life in prison for Schäfer's murder.

1984 – Unterweger's autobiography *Fegefeuer – eine Reise ins Zuchthaus* (Purgatory: A Journey to the Penitentiary) is published.

23 May 1990 – Unterweger is released from prison.

15 September 1990 – The body of Blanka Bockova is discovered in Prague.

5 January 1991 – Brunhilde Masser's body is discovered near Ganz.

5 October 1991 – Elfriede Schempf's body is found outside Graz.

27 February 1992 – US marshals arrest Unterweger in California.

28 May 1992 – Unterweger is deported to Austria.

29 June 1994 – Unterweger is found guilty and commits suicide that evening.

Unterweger was granted parole. Thus, he began a new life involving opening nights, book launches and exclusive receptions. Articulate, handsome and stylish, Unterweger was in demand on talk shows and as a dinner guest. His career as a writer seemed to go from one height to another; he was sought after as a journalist and his plays were being performed throughout Austria.

Before long, as a journalist, he was covering a beat he knew well: murder. Much of his writing concerned a number of prostitutes who had recently been murdered. He put both his past and celebrity to good use, moving freely through the streets. In his writing and in television pieces he berated the authorities for not having solved the crimes, asserting that there was a serial killer in Austria who was preying on prostitutes.

The first of these prostitutes, Brunhilde Masser, had last been seen alive on 26 October 1990 on the streets of Graz. Less than six weeks later, another prostitute, Heidemarie Hannerer, disappeared from Bregenz, near the border with Germany and Switzerland. Her body was discovered on New Year's Eve by two hikers. Upon inspection, it was apparent that she had been strangled with a pair of tights. Though she was fully clothed, it was after her death that she had been dressed. On 5 January 1991, Masser's body was found outside Ganz. Though badly decomposed, the corpse revealed that she too had been strangled with tights. On 7 March, another Austrian prostitute, Elfriede Schrempf, disappeared.

By this point the authorities were becoming extremely concerned. Since it is a legal occupation in Austria, prostitution has fewer dangers than in many other Western nations. In an average year, the country would suffer no more than one murdered prostitute. And yet, in little more than four months two prostitutes had been murdered and another had gone missing. Worries increased when Schrempf's family received two phone calls in which they were threatened by an anonymous man. Though unlisted, their number was one that Schrempf carried on her person.

On 5 October, hikers discovered Schrempf's remains in the woods outside Graz. Within a month, another four prostitutes would disappear from the streets of Vienna. Looking at all the evidence, a team of investigators from Ganz, Bregenze and Vienna concluded that the murders and disappearances were not the work of a serial killer, a finding with which Unterweger took issue.

Another person who disagreed with the team's findings was August Schenner. A 70-year-old former investigator, Schenner had been involved in solving the 1974 murder of Margaret Schäfer, for which Unterweger had served his prison time. He noted that Schäfer had been strangled, as had another prostitute whom he had always suspected Unterweger of killing. And, of course, all the recent murders of prostitutes had been committed by means of strangulation. When the bodies of two of the missing prostitutes surfaced, both strangled, the authorities became convinced that

JACK UNTERWEGER **77**

Prostitutes began disappearing from the streets of Graz in the early 1990s.

they did indeed have a serial killer on their hands – and that he was most likely Jack Unterweger.

The celebrity author was placed under surveillance for three days. On the fourth day, Unterweger flew off to Los Angeles, where he was to write an article on crime in the city for an Austrian magazine. In his absence, the Austrian federal police tracked their suspect's movements since his release from prison. They discovered that he had been in Graz on the dates when Brunhilde Masser and Elfriede Schrempf had disappeared; in Bregenze when Heidemarie Hannerer had been murdered, and in Vienna when all four prostitutes had gone missing. They also learned that Unterweger had visited Prague in September 1990. A call to Czech authorities revealed that they had an unsolved murder of a young woman, Blanka Bockova, dating from that time. When found by the bank of the Vitava River, her body had a pair of grey stockings knotted around the neck.

After he returned from Los Angeles, Unterweger was questioned by officers of the criminal investigation bureau. One of the officers already knew the suspect as he'd been interviewed by the celebrity author for one of the articles he'd written on the murders. Unterweger denied knowing any of the prostitutes, saying that his knowledge of their respective fates was limited to what he'd found through his work as a journalist. He was let go due to lack of evidence. Soon thereafter, he resumed his attacks in print for what he described as the mishandling of the case.

In their hunt for evidence, the police discovered that Unterweger had sold the car he'd first bought after his release from prison. With the permission of the new owner, they went through

78 DOUBLE LIVES

the vehicle and discovered a hair fragment which, through DNA testing, was shown to be that of Blanka Bockova. With the hair sample, investigators now had enough to obtain a search warrant for Unterweger's apartment.

A call to the Los Angeles Police Department brought news that three prostitutes had been strangled during Unterweger's time in the city.

When Austrian police moved in to arrest Unterweger, they discovered that he had left the city, ostensibly to holiday with Bianca Mrak, his 18-year-old girlfriend. In reality, he was fleeing to avoid arrest. Unterweger managed to enter the United States by lying about his previous murder conviction. He settled with Mrak in Miami, from where he launched a campaign against the Austrian authorities. At the centre of his fight was the accusation that the police were fabricating evidence in an attempt to frame him. Connections in the media were called upon in an effort to have his version of events published.

On 27 February 1992, Unterweger was arrested by United States marshals after he picked up money that had been wired to him. They arrested him on the grounds that, in lying about his 1974 murder conviction, he had entered the country illegally. He fought deportation until he learned that California, the state in which he was suspected of murdering three prostitutes, had the death penalty.

On 28 May, he was returned to Austria. There Unterweger was subject to a law which permitted him to be charged for the murders he was accused of committing both inside and outside of the country's borders – 11 in total. Awaiting trial, Unterweger gave interviews and wrote letters to the media in which he professed his innocence. He was convinced that the public was on his side. However, the tide had long since begun to turn; even his former friends in the media doubted his innocence. Unterweger went on trial in June 1994 with the conviction that his popularity and charm would win over the jury.

On 29 June 1994, Unterweger was found guilty of all but two charges of murder. He was sentenced to life in prison without parole. That evening Unterweger used the string of his prison jumpsuit to hang himself. The knot he tied was the very same one he'd used on his victims.

Jack Unterweger on the first day of his trial.

SERHIY TKACH

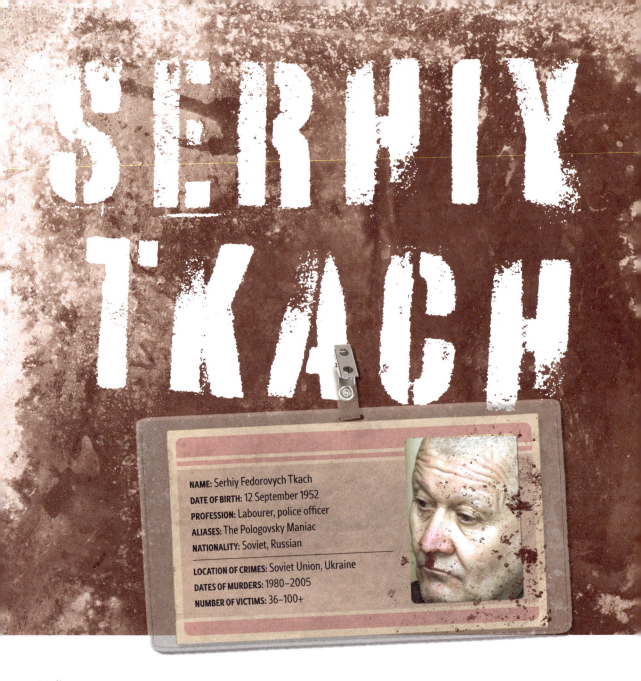

NAME: Serhiy Fedorovych Tkach
DATE OF BIRTH: 12 September 1952
PROFESSION: Labourer, police officer
ALIASES: The Pologovsky Maniac
NATIONALITY: Soviet, Russian

LOCATION OF CRIMES: Soviet Union, Ukraine
DATES OF MURDERS: 1980–2005
NUMBER OF VICTIMS: 36–100+

Short in stature, a quiet man who shied away from eye contact, Serhiy Tkach didn't much look like a murderer, yet for a quarter of a century he took one life after another. It's possible that he was the most prolific serial killer in Ukrainian history. After he was caught, Tkach would happily tell anyone who would listen that his victims numbered over 100. This was no confession, but a boast. Tkach was, and remains, proud of the murders he committed.

Serhiy Tkach was born on 12 September 1952 in Kiselyovsk, a Russian city that was then a part of the Soviet Union. By all accounts he did well academically, though he wasn't much interested in higher learning. After fulfilling his compulsory military service, Tkach continued his studies briefly in order to become a police officer. Upon graduation, he became a criminal investigator in Kemerovo, an industrial city in the central Soviet Union. However, what looked to be a long, successful career in law enforcement ended abruptly when Tkach was caught committing fraud. He was only able to avoid prison by writing a letter of resignation.

The city of Kemerovo, where Tkach worked as a criminal investigator before embarking on his insane spree of killings.

According to Tkach, he killed for the first time in 1980, not long after his exit in disgrace from the police department. A pleasant, pastoral afternoon, fuelled by numerous bottles of wine, turned horrific when the then 27-year-old grabbed a young woman, dragged her into some bushes and strangled her. Rape, he told one reporter, was his intent; the murder had taken place only because he was fearful that his victim might somehow escape before he'd completed the assault.

INTO THE COLD

Tkach never identified the woman by name, saying only that she was a former schoolmate whom he had dated on and off for nine years. He added that, in all that time, the two had not had sexual relations. Tkach claimed that on the day of her death, the unnamed woman had slapped his face at the mere suggestion.

'Do you want to know why I killed?' he asked one journalist. 'My main motive was revenge!'

After he returned home, Tkach called the police to report his

Ex-policeman Tkach used his specialized knowledge to escape along railway lines treated with tar to throw police dogs off the scent.

crime, but was irritated when the officer on the other end of the line refused to identify himself.

'I was going to tell him where to find the corpse,' Tkach told investigators pursuing the case. 'I was going to help my former colleagues, but changed my mind.'

With the loss of his respected position in law enforcement, Tkach became a man adrift. The former criminal investigator worked in mines, on farms and as a low-paid factory worker. He moved from one city to another, leaving a trail of cold bodies in his wake.

Tkach was as meticulous as he was calculating. He was always careful to strip his victims of their jewellery and clothing, some of which he would keep as trophies. Tkach used his police training in making certain that no fingerprints or traces of semen would be left behind. So as to lend the impression that his murders had occurred far away, he left the bodies close to roads and railways.

It's likely that most of the murders took place in Ukraine. He killed in the cities of Zaporizhia, Kharkov and, finally, in Dnipropetrovsk, where he lived his final years as a free man.

The vast majority of Tkach's known victims were between nine and 17 years of age, a fact that has led to doubts about the story of his first killing. His final victim, a nine-year-old identified in the media only as 'Kate', was the daughter of one of Tkach's friends. The girl had been playing with four other children one August 2005 day when she was grabbed. Tkach drowned the girl and, as he had with so very many others, left the body to be found.

Zeroing in on a child whom he had known and carrying out the abduction in front of her friends was uncharacteristically sloppy. Tkach pushed his luck even further by attending the little girl's funeral. He was recognized immediately by her playmates. The former criminal investigator would later express regret that he hadn't bothered to kill them as well.

Tkach was soon dubbed 'The Pologovsky Maniac' after the area of Dnipropetrovsk he had called home. News of his crimes came as a shock to neighbours. Known as a former criminal investigator, the killer had a certain stature within the immediate community. While he was a bit of a loner, and a man of few words, these qualities only added to Tkach's reputation as someone who was highly intelligent. True, Tkach had two failed marriages in his past, but he appeared for all the world to be a devoted husband to wife number three. Unlike so many men in his neighbourhood, he never said a negative word about women. As far as anyone knew, he'd never so much as raised a hand against his wife and four children.

NO REMORSE

More than two years passed before Tkach was put on trial. Much of the delay had to do with the significant challenges that faced investigators.

It wasn't that they had no experience of investigating serial killers – the previous decade, Anatoly Onoprienko, 'The Beast of Ukraine', had been convicted of 52 murders – but with Tkach, the number of victims looked to be much higher. What's more, the

Pologovsky Maniac's killing spree had lasted five times longer and stretched to hundreds of kilometres.

There were also legal issues that needed attention. Over the decades, nine innocent men were tried and sentenced for murders that Tkach committed. One of the convicted had committed suicide in prison.

Finally, there were the questions about Tkach's sanity. It beggared belief that anyone in his right mind could commit such horrible acts. Psychiatrists, however, were unanimous in their opinion that Tkach was a sane man. Though he routinely consumed a litre of vodka before each rape and murder, all were convinced that he'd been fully aware of the crimes he had been committing.

Even before the lengthy investigation truly got under way, Tkach began taunting the police. At his arrest, he told officers that he had been expecting them for years, adding that they should have figured things out much sooner.

In interviews with the press Tkach painted those investigating his case as lazy. 'The police couldn't be bothered exhuming bodies,' he said, 'they'd rather I write a letter of confession. I've long laughed at them!'

When it finally began, the trial lasted almost all of 2008.

Speaking from a cage within the courtroom, Tkach demonstrated that the memories of his victims remained fresh in his mind. Twenty-eight years after his first murders, he was able to recall in detail each victim, and the manner in which he'd hunted them down.

Tkach expressed no remorse – not for his victims, not for the wrongly accused. He defended his actions with the claim that the killings had been committed for no other reason than to expose the police as a group of bumbling incompetents. Yet, he would also describe himself frequently as a beast, a creature who not only deserved, but desired the death penalty.

Ultimately, Tkach would be disappointed in his wish for a quick end to his life. Ukraine having abolished capital punishment, Tkach was sentenced to life in prison for the murders of 36 of the more than 100 girls and women that he claimed to have deprived of life. 'No one has been able to determine the motives for his actions,' declared Judge Serhiy Voloshko after delivering his verdict.

Christmas Day 2008 marked the first full day of his sentence, but to Tkach the date meant nothing. 'I do not believe in God or the Devil,' he'd declared. Perhaps not, but to many his actions were clear evidence of the existence of the latter.

Dnipropetrovsk, home to Serhiy Tkach. He was named 'The Pologovsky Maniac' by the media after the region of the city he lived in.

ALEXANDER PICHUSHKIN

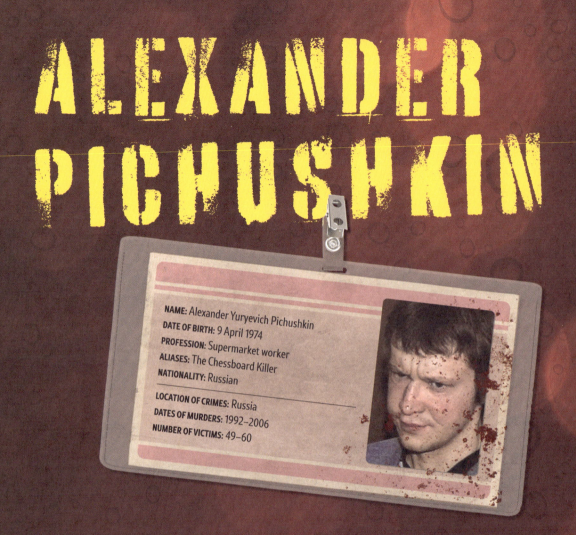

NAME: Alexander Yuryevich Pichushkin
DATE OF BIRTH: 9 April 1974
PROFESSION: Supermarket worker
ALIASES: The Chessboard Killer
NATIONALITY: Russian

LOCATION OF CRIMES: Russia
DATES OF MURDERS: 1992–2006
NUMBER OF VICTIMS: 49–60

In June 2006, Moscow police found a chessboard with dates written on 61 of its 64 squares. Alexander Pichushkin was only too willing to explain its significance. He was trying to break the record set by the prolific Russian serial killer and cannibal, Andrei Chikatilo, who had murdered a minimum of 52 women and children and eaten their body parts. Each covered square on the board represented a victim. He was caught with just three to go before completing his horrific game. In 2007, he was convicted of 48 murders although he claimed to have been responsible for over 60. His crimes were so terrible they led to a serious consideration of reinstating the death penalty.

A CHILDHOOD ACCIDENT

Alexander Pichushkin was born in 1974 in Mytishchi, a small city on the outskirts of Moscow. A year after his birth his father left. He said himself that he had a 'difficult life' because he had never known his father. He spent much of his childhood in Bitsevsky Park (or Bitsa Park), a sprawling and densely wooded area where locals would hang out, smoke and drink alcohol.

As a young child he was known to be friendly and sociable, but early on in his young life an accident would change this. When he was four years old he fell off a swing and was struck in the forehead by the seat. The injury damaged the frontal cortex in his brain – an area that is used to regulate impulses and limit aggression. Soon after the accident he became hostile and aggressive and he was transferred to a school for those with learning disabilities. He was soon beset by bullying from children from his old school who referred to him as 'that retard'.

Encouragement from his grandfather led him to the game of chess. Pichushkin was fascinated by chess and soon became an outstanding player. He began to participate in regular exhibition games, usually against older men in Bitsa Park, with great success.

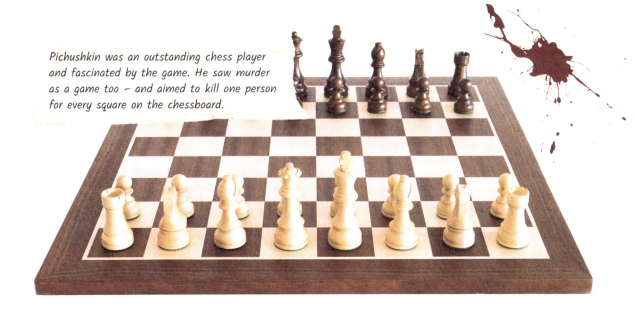

Pichushkin was an outstanding chess player and fascinated by the game. He saw murder as a game too – and aimed to kill one person for every square on the chessboard.

He was also an animal lover – his neighbour, Svetlana Mortyakova, once found him in tears over the death of his cat. Towards the end of his school days, Pichushkin's grandfather died which came as a great blow to him and he began to drink heavily to dull the pain. Psychologists would later suggest that Pichushkin's murders were prompted by anger at his grandfather for 'abandoning' him.

Around this time, he also developed a disturbing passion for filming young children and watching the footage, which allegedly gave him a feeling of superiority. Pichushkin began to take a camera with him if he knew he would come into contact with children. On one occasion, he held a child upside down by one leg and spoke into the camera: 'You are in my power now … I am going to drop you from the window … and you will fall 15 metres to your death.'

Pichushkin was obsessed by Andrei Chikatilo. He committed his first murder while he was still a teenager during the serial killer's trial in 1992. Pichushkin pushed a boy out of a window and remembered the experience fondly. When questioned by the police, he said, 'This first murder, it's like love, it's unforgettable.'

He treated murder as a game: the 64 squares on his chessboard functioned as his motivation to achieve a set target. His life, otherwise, was very dull. He worked as a supermarket shelf-stacker and lived in an apartment with his mother near Bitsa Park. The setting was important to Pichushkin because the size of the park, spanning some 10 km (6 miles) and covered in forests, provided the ideal location for a determined serial killer to practise his art.

For Pichushkin, murder was the only change to his dull routine. He targeted elderly homeless men – similar to those he had spent his teenage years playing chess against – and lured them to his house with the offer of free vodka. He often talked to his victims about his dog as a way to befriend them. Usually they were elderly men, but when the opportunity arose, he had no qualms killing women and children. Not all of his victims were killed in this cold, calculating manner. He was motived to kill his neighbour, Valery Kulyazhov, because the man had told him 'to take away his enormous, mongrel mutt'. Pichushkin could not tolerate an insult to the one thing he loved most in the world – his dog.

> **'IN ALL CASES I KILLED FOR ONLY ONE REASON. I KILLED IN ORDER TO LIVE … FOR ME, LIFE WITHOUT MURDER IS LIKE LIFE WITHOUT FOOD FOR YOU.'**

He always attacked his victims from behind. He did not like to get blood on his clothes. Psychoanalyst Tatyana Drusinova said he was 'detached from human beings … Human beings were no more than wooden dolls, like chess pieces, to him.'

In 2001 people began vanishing from Bitsa Park. Maria Viricheva was a shop clerk from Tatarstan. In 2001, she entered a secluded part of the forest with Pichushkin, lured by the promise of black market goods. Pichushkin grabbed her by the hair and threw her down a well 9 m (30 ft) deepl. Unbeknown to Pichushkin she survived the ordeal, but, unbelievably, police refused to investigate.

Pichushkin was allowed to roam free and became more brazen in his attacks. Only years later did Viricheva finally came forward to identify her attacker, after he had already been arrested for his other crimes.

In October 2005, one of Pichushkin's victims was found along one of the park's footpaths. The skull had been smashed and a vodka bottle driven into the brain. By June 2006, police had found 13 more bodies, all killed in the same way. They dubbed the killer the 'Bitsa Park Maniac'.

Pichushkin's last victim was Marina Moskalyova. Moskalyova had told her son of her plans to go on a date with a co-worker, and even left the man's phone number – this man's name was Alexander Pichushkin. This was the police's first major lead. Next, when they discovered the dead body of Moskalyova they also discovered her metro ticket in the pocket of her jacket. They were able to identify Pichushkin from the security cameras at the metro station walking alongside Moskalyova. Pichushkin was arrested on 15 June 2006 for Moskalyova's murder. He told police: 'I kept thinking whether to kill her or take caution. But finally I decided to take a risk. I was in that mood already.'

Soon Pichushkin was confessing to a bewildering array of crimes. Detectives checked his confessions against missing persons

Moscow's Bitsa Park, where Pichushkin preyed on his victims.

reports. They quizzed him on the locations of the murders and he recalled them with astounding accuracy. His victims included old men, young women and even a nine-year-old boy. Forty-three of the bodies he had disposed of by throwing them in the sewer pits of the park. He showed no hint of remorse.

His trial lasted six weeks. Like his old hero, Chikatilo, he was kept inside a glass cage for his own protection during the trial. Moscow prosecutor Yury Syomin stated, 'This is the first such case in Moscow. We are charging him with 52 murders. He insists that he killed 63, but there are no bodies, no murder weapons, no testimony, and not even records of people gone missing.'

The jury only needed three hours to make their decision. Pichushkin was found guilty of 48 counts of murder and of three counts of attempted murder. He was sentenced to life imprisonment and during his first 15 years he was to be kept in solitary confinement.

Tamara Klimova, the wife of one of Pichushkin's alleged victims, told Russian media, 'He should be handed over to the public for punishment rather than allowed to live in prison at our expense.'

Pichushkin had one last thing to say. If he had reached his goal of 64 murders, it would not have been enough.

'I never would have stopped, never. They saved a lot of lives by catching me.'

CHAPTER 3

BLOODY BUTCHERS

For some depraved individuals, it is not enough to merely kill their victims. They must dismember and butcher the bodies too. They seek not just to kill, but to inflict pain on their victims too in their search for absolute power and control. In some cases, anger and passion explain the lengths they will go to inflict pain – but even more disturbingly, some of these criminals see their victims simply as objects to be used for their own pleasure, with no thought for the humanity of the people who suffer so terribly at their hands.

ROBERT PICKTON

NAME: Robert William Pickton
DATE OF BIRTH: 24 October 1949
PROFESSION: Farmer
ALIASES: The Pig Farmer Killer, The Butcher
NATIONALITY: Canadian

LOCATION OF CRIMES: British Columbia, Canada
DATES OF MURDERS: 1978–2001
NUMBER OF VICTIMS: 6–49

When Robert Service first cast his eyes on British Columbia, the poet described what he saw as being 'something greater than my imagination had ever conceived'. Canada's westernmost province is known for its natural beauty. Robert Pickton saw these wonders on a daily basis, but his immediate surroundings were much less attractive.

Pickton lived on a pig farm, a muddy, run-down 17-acre parcel of land in Port Coquitlam that he and his siblings had inherited from their parents. On the occasions that he left his home, Pickton could often be found 30 km (20 miles) away hunting down the drugged and desperate in Vancouver.

For runaways, the homeless and those who were simply down on their luck, British Columbia's biggest city holds an understandable allure.

Nestled by the warm Pacific Ocean, it enjoys a much milder winter than any other major Canadian city. For the drug addict, there's a steady supply of illegal narcotics flowing through its port. For those who still dream of sudden fame, there is fantasy to be found in the city's healthy film industry; 'Hollywood North' is just one of Vancouver's many nicknames.

Sadly, Vancouver is also by far the most expensive city in Canada; in North America it is surpassed only by Manhattan proper.

Port Coquitlam stands near beautiful countryside. PoCo, as it is known, is Canada's 88th-largest city by population.

Real estate is at a premium, and rental units are expensive and hard to come by. This city, with the highest concentration of millionaires in North America, is also home to the poorest neighbourhood in the country. Haunted by glorious buildings, reminders of long-gone days as a premier shopping district, Vancouver's Downtown Eastside is a blight on the utopian landscape. The banks disappeared years ago, as did the well-stocked department stores. The few shops that aren't boarded up house lowly pawnbrokers. Outside their doors, and in the blocks that surround them, prostitutes – some as young as 11 years old – ply their trade.

MONSTROUS APPETITES

Pickton did not prey on children. It's thought that his first victim was a 23-year-old woman named Rebecca Guno, who was last seen on 22 June 1983. She was reported missing three days later – a very short time period compared to the many that followed. The next victim, Sheryl Rail, was not reported missing for three full years. The lives of Guno and Rail were just two of the six Pickton is known to have taken in his first decade of killing. With as much as 28 months separating one murder from the next, the pig farmer had no clear pattern. These early erratic and seemingly spontaneous killings enabled Pickton to pass under the radar. It wasn't until the closing years of the millennium that speculation began to surface that a serial killer just might be at work on the seedier streets of Vancouver. By then Pickton had picked up the pace; it's believed that he killed nine women in the latter half of 1997 alone.

The next year, the Vancouver Police Department began reviewing cases of missing women stretching back nearly three decades. By this time, talk of a serial killer was a subject of conversation in even the most genteel parts of the city, and still authorities dismissed speculation.

When one of their own, Inspector Kim Rossmo, raised the issue, he was quickly shot down. 'We're in no way saying there is a serial murderer out there,' said fellow inspector Gary Greer. 'We're in no

The death of Dawn Crey, 43, was only confirmed when police found her DNA on the farm.

way saying that all these people missing are dead. We're not saying any of that.'

The police posited that the missing women had simply moved on. After all, prostitutes were known to abruptly change locations and even names. Calgary, 970 km (600 miles) to the east and flush with oil money, was often singled out as a likely destination.

Years later, veteran journalist Stevie Cameron would add this observation: 'There were never any bodies. Police don't like to investigate any case where there isn't a body.'

Even as the authorities dismissed the notion of a serial killer, Pickton continued his bloody work. Among those he butchered was Marcella Creison. Released from prison on 27 December 1998, she never showed at a belated Christmas dinner prepared by her mother and boyfriend. Sadly, 14 days passed before her disappearence was reported.

The waters were muddied by the fact that some of the women who had been reported missing were actually found alive. Patricia Gay Perkins, who had disappeared leaving a one-year-old son behind, contacted Vancouver Police after reading her name on a list of the missing. One woman was found living in Toronto, while another was discovered to have died of a heroin overdose. However, the list of missing women continued to grow, even as other cases were solved.

Accepting, for a moment, that there was a serial killer on the loose, where were the police to look? There was, it seemed, an embarrassment of suspects – dozens of violent johns who had been rounded up on assault charges during the previous two decades.

However, Robert Pickton was not among them. Should he have been?

In 1997, Pickton got into a knife fight with a prostitute on his farm that resulted in both being treated in the same hospital.

Nurses removed a handcuff from around the woman's wrist using a key that was on Pickton's person. He was charged with attempted murder, though this was later dismissed.

In 1998, Bill Hiscox, one of Pickton's employees, approached police to report on a supposed charity, the Piggy Palace Good Times Society, that was run by Robert and his brother Daniel. Housed in a converted building on the pig farm, Hiscox claimed that it was nothing but a party place populated by a rotating cast of prostitutes.

It wasn't the first police had heard of the Piggy Palace Good Times Society. Established in 1996 to 'co-ordinate, manage and operate special events, functions, dances, shows and exhibitions on behalf of service organizations, sports organizations and other worthy groups', it had continually violated Port Coquitlam city bylaws. There were parties – so many parties – drawing well over 1,000 people to a property that was zoned as agricultural.

The strange goings-on at the Piggy Palace Good Times Society might have been a concern, but Hiscox's real focus had to do with the missing women. The Pickton employee told police that purses and other items that could identify the prostitutes would be found on the pig farm.

Police visited the Port Coquitlam property on at least four occasions, once with Hiscox in tow, but found nothing. Robert Pickton would become nothing more than one of many described as 'a person of interest'.

MISSION TO MURDER

The years passed, women kept disappearing, and still the notion of a serial killer at work in the Downtown Eastside was dismissed.

By 2001, the number of women who had gone missing from

The last remaining barn on the Pickton property, the home of the Piggy Palace Good Times Society.

the neighbourhood had grown to 65 – a number that police could no longer ignore. That April, a team called 'The Missing Women Task Force' was established. The arrest of Gary Ridgway seven months later by American authorities brought fleeting interest. Better known as the 'Green River Killer', Ridgway killed scores of prostitutes in the Seattle area, roughly 240 km (150 miles) south of Vancouver. The many murders coincided with the disappearances of the missing women, but it quickly became clear that Ridgway had had nothing to do with events north of the border. The Missing Women Task Force looked into other American serial killers, as well, including foot fetishist Dayton Rogers, 'The Malolla Forest Killer', who had murdered several prostitutes in Oregon.

Despite the newly established task force, prostitutes continued to disappear. No one foresaw the events of February 2002.

Early in the month, Pickton was arrested, imprisoned and charged with a variety of firearms offences, including storing a firearm contrary to regulations, possession of a firearm without a licence and possession of a loaded restricted firearm without a licence. In carrying out the search warrant that led to the charges, police uncovered personal possessions belonging to one of the missing women.

Pickton was released on bail, but was kept under surveillance. On 22 February, he was again taken into custody – this time to be charged with two counts of first-degree murder in the deaths of prostitutes Serena Abotsway and Mona Wilson. The pig farmer would never again experience a day of freedom.

The Pickton farm soon came to look like something out of a science fiction film. Investigators and forensics specialists in

Police went through Pickton's property with a fine-tooth comb – their diligence produced over 10,000 pieces of evidence.

contamination suits searched for signs of the missing women. Severed heads were found in a freezer, a wood chipper contained further fragments, and still more were found in a pigpen and in pig feed. These were easy finds; a team of 52 anthropologists were brought in to do the rest, sifting through 14 acres of soil in search of bones, teeth and hair. Their diligence brought over 10,000 pieces of evidence – and, for Pickton, a further 24 counts of murder.

But to the citizens of Vancouver, particularly the friends and families of the missing women, the breakthrough had come far too late. In place of praise came criticism. How was it that the police had found nothing at all suspicious when they'd visited the farm just a few years earlier? Serena Abotsway, Mona Wilson and several other women whose body parts were found on the farm had disappeared after those initial searches. Might their lives have been saved?

We might add to these questions: What do we now make of Robert Pickton? A decade after he made headlines as Canada's most prolific serial killer, his picture is still coming into focus.

Pickton promised prostitutes not only cash, but drugs and alcohol, if they would only come to Piggy Palace. It's thought that he would almost invariably accuse each of his victims of stealing. He bound each woman, before strangling them with a wire or a belt. Pickton would then drag his victim to the farm's slaughterhouse, where he would use his skills as a butcher.

Some remains he buried on the farm, while others were fed to his pigs. Still more was disposed of at West Coast Reduction Ltd, an 'animal rendering and recycling plant' located well within walking distance of Main and Hastings, the worst corner in the country. In fact, dozens of prostitutes strolled the streets in the shadow of the plant. Eventually, the remains would find their way into cosmetics and animal feed.

Testing found the DNA of some victims in the pork found on the farm. The meat processed on the farm was never sold commercially, though Pickton did distribute it amongst friends and neighbours.

'NAILED TO THE CROSS'

It took nearly five years and $100 million to prepare the case against Pickton. The pig farmer denied his guilt to all but one person: a police officer who had been posing as a cellmate. The pig farmer's words were caught by a hidden camera: 'I was gonna do one more, make it an even 50. That's why I was sloppy. I wanted one more. Make… make the big five O.'

Pickton seemed to acknowledge that he was stuck, that there was no way he would be found not guilty. 'I think I'm nailed to the cross,' he told the bogus cellmate. 'But if that happens there will be about 15 other people are gonna go down.'

The statement only added to suspicions that the remains found on the pig farm weren't solely Pickton's work. Yet, on 22 January 2007, when the pig farmer finally had his day in court, he went alone.

The trial proceeded on a group of six counts that had been drawn from the 26 that Pickton faced. As explained by Justice James Williams, the severing had taken place in the belief that a trial dealing with all 26 might take as long as two years to complete, and would place too high a burden on the jury.

As it turned out, Pickton's trial on the six charges lasted nearly 11 months, and was the longest in Canadian history. Pickton, who had pleaded not guilty on all counts, sat barely paying attention as 128 witnesses took the stand.

That he was found guilty came as a surprise to no one, though the details of the verdict were unexpected. On 9 December 2007, after nine long days of deliberation, jurors found Pickton guilty only of six counts of second-degree murder. The men and women were not convinced that Pickton had acted alone.

Robert Pickton was sentenced to life in prison. He died on 31 May 2024 after being assaulted by another inmate.

An artist's sketch of Robert Pickton in court.

KATHERINE KNIGHT

NAME: Katherine Mary Knight
DATE OF BIRTH: 24 October 1955
PROFESSION: Slaughterhouse employee
NATIONALITY: Australian

LOCATION OF CRIME: New South Wales, Australia
DATES OF MURDER: February 2000
NUMBER OF VICTIMS: 1

Katherine Knight once worked in Australian slaughterhouses where she discovered a talent for decapitating pigs. She used the very same knives from her work to murder her common-law husband. John Price was skinned and beheaded; portions of his buttocks were cut from what remained of his body. All this was in preparation for a stew intended for his children. But it was not the work of a madwoman; courts determined that Katherine was quite sane. She had planned the murder, knew that it was wrong and was well aware of the consequences of her grizzly actions.

Katherine Mary Knight was born on 24 October 1955 at Tenterfeld, New South Wales, one of many communities in which her father, Ken, had found employment as a slaughterhouse worker.

Kath lived a semi-transient life until 1969, when her family settled in Aberdeen, 170 miles (270 km) north of Sydney. The town may have been small – with just over 1,500 inhabitants – but the Knight family was fairly large. A twin, Kath was one of eight children.

VIOLENT BULLY

Barely literate, she wasn't much of a student; Kath still made a mark at the schools she attended by being a violent bully. At the age of 16, following in the footsteps of her father, brother and twin sister, Kath became a slaughterhouse worker herself. The following year, she

96 BLOODY BUTCHERS

It was her partner's misfortune that Katherine Knight was destined to take the skills she had learnt in the slaughterhouse back home with her.

met and moved in with David Kellett, a 22-year-old truck driver. The couple married in 1974, a happy occasion that was marred when the bride, disappointed by his sexual performance on their wedding night, tried to strangle her groom.

As the relationship progressed, so too did the abuse. In what, by comparison, seems a trivial incident, Kath burned all David's clothing. Early in the marriage, he arrived at work with the imprint of an iron burned on to the side of his face. The truck driver once awoke to find his wife astride his chest holding a knife to his throat.

And yet, he stayed with Kath long enough to father, and witness the birth of, a daughter, Melissa, born in 1976. It was a joyous occasion in an otherwise unpleasant and disturbing period.

'I never raised a finger against her,' David said, 'not even in self-defence. I just walked away.' Within two months he had done just that, leaving his wife for another woman.

In retaliation, Kath placed Melissa on railway tracks just minutes before a train was scheduled to pass. The baby was discovered and saved by a local drifter, and, incredibly, the mother suffered no repercussions.

Kath was not so lucky when, a few days later, she disfigured a 16-year-old girl's face with a butcher's knife. A stand-off ensued, during which Kath held a young boy hostage. She was placed in a psychiatric hospital, only to be released a few weeks later. There was a reunion with David, who worked to save what was left of the marriage.

DOOMED

The attempt was doomed from the start. Despite the medication and therapy she'd received, Kath was, if anything, more violent. And yet, in 1980 the couple had a second daughter, Natasha.

It would have been understandable had David again walked away, yet it was Kath who ended the relationship. He returned home one day to discover his house stripped of its contents and Kath, Melissa and Natasha gone.

In 1986, she began seeing a man named Dave Saunders, with whom she had a daughter, Sarah, the following year. Kath soon left her slaughterhouse job, citing a back injury. With Dave's help, and the aid of a significant compensation package, she bought a rundown house in an undesirable area of town, and, setting health concerns aside, began renovating and decorating. Kath's tastes were fairly unconventional: cow hides, steer horns, a stuffed baby deer, rusted animal traps and a scythe hung on a rope above her couch. And the pattern of her life was unchanged. Kath cut up her boyfriend's clothes, vandalized his car, hit him with an iron, stabbed him with scissors and beat him with a frying pan until he was unconscious. Even more disturbingly, Kath took one of Dave's dogs, an eight-week-old puppy, and, making certain he was watching, killed the creature by cutting its throat.

As their relationship drew to an end, Kath took an overdose of sleeping pills and wound up in another psychiatric hospital. And yet, somehow, she managed to obtain an Apprehended Violence Order that kept Dave away from her and his child.

By May of 1990, Kath had moved on to another man. John Chillington, a cab driver, became another victim of her abuse. She smashed glasses grabbed from his face and destroyed his false teeth. Despite the drama, in 1991 the pair had a child, Eric, together.

In 1994, Kath dumped John for her final partner, John Charles Price, known as 'Pricey'. He was a well-liked man; even his former wife, with whom he'd had four children, spoke of him only in glowing terms.

Knight had unusual tastes. She filled her home with stuffed animals, hides, horns and even a scythe.

John Price (second from the left) and his original family in much happier times.

After a little more than a year together, Kath abandoned her shoddy, bizarrely decorated home for Pricey's more tasteful, well-built bungalow. Even before moving in, the relationship had taken several bad turns. The pair had been seen fighting – typical behaviour for Kath, but very much out of character for Pricey.

Frustrated by Pricey's refusal to marry her, Kath presented a videotape to her boyfriend's employers depicting items allegedly stolen from his work. Though the goods featured, all well past their expiry dates, were probably scavenged from the trash, Pricey was fired – an abrupt end to 17 years of dedicated service. Kath and Pricey split up. But within a few months they were back together.

Unable to read or write, Pricey's employment options were extremely limited. Pricey sank into drink for a time, until, by chance, he happened upon a job at Bowditch and Partners Earth Moving. It was just the sort of break he needed. A year after being hired, Pricey was made supervisor.

He'd begun to share elements of his unhealthy relationship with the boys from work, telling them that Kath had a history of violence and that he wanted her out of the house. Pricey also claimed his wife could throw a punch as good as any man alive and that she'd once chased him with a knife. Pricey's stories were at odds with the woman known to his friends at work. The Kath they'd seen might have been a bit of an odd bird, but to an outsider she seemed pleasant enough. By the early months of 2000, Pricey had begun making an effort to share his concerns.

On 21 February, he was forced to flee the house after Kath had grabbed a knife in an argument. Though some of Pricey's friends encouraged him to leave, he felt the need to stay in order to protect the children. Eight days later, during his noon-hour break, Pricey went to a local magistrate. He feared for his life and showed a wound he'd received when Kath had stabbed him. After returning to work, his boss offered him a place to stay, but Pricey declined.

KATHERINE KNIGHT 99

John Price, seen here with his son Johnathon, was a typical product of smalltown Australia – a conscientious worker with a love of beer and 'cigs'.

EERIE PREMONITION

A family video, shot just a few hours later, captures Katherine singing nursery rhymes to her children. Her sole grandchild, a girl, sits on her lap. It was an out-of-character performance, complete with the peculiar message: 'I love all my children and I hope to see them again.' After the camera was switched off, she and the children enjoyed a dinner at a local Chinese restaurant. Again, it was something out of the ordinary. Kath told the children, 'I want it to be special.'

Aged 20, Natasha had a vague feeling of unease about the meaning of her mother's unusual behaviour. As Kath left to see Pricey, she said, 'I hope you are not going to kill Pricey and yourself.'

Later, Kath claimed that she had no recollection of the evening after having watched *Star Trek* at Pricey's house.

Much of what we now know is drawn from forensic evidence gathered at the scene. We know that at some point Kath donned a black negligee bought at a local charity shop. It's highly probable that she was wearing the flimsy garment when they had sex – it is certain that Kath had on the negligee when she began stabbing Pricey. The wounded man managed to make it outside his front door before being dragged back into the house, where the stabbing continued. The coroner determined that Pricey received at least 37 stab wounds, destroying nearly all of his major organs.

When Kath began skinning, beheading and otherwise carving up her lover is unknown, though cameras did manage to record her movements at 2.30 am, when she made a withdrawal from an ATM.

It was at Bowditch and Partners that the first concerns for Pricey were raised. Such was Pricey's dedication and reliability that at 7.45 am his boss phoned local police to report that he had not yet arrived at work.

The authorities visited Pricey's bungalow, forced the door and found his skin hanging in a doorway. The decapitated corpse was lying in the living room. Pricey's head was in a large pot, simmering away on the kitchen stove.

The dining room table held two servings of food, consisting of baked potato, pumpkin, courgette, cabbage, squash and generous portions of the cooked corpse.

Placement cards indicated that the two settings were intended for Pricey's children. Barely literate notes containing baseless allegations were addressed to the children. Having taken a mild overdose, the author, Kath, lay semi-comatose on the bed she and Pricey had once shared.

In October 2001, Kath admitted her guilt in Pricey's death. The following month she became the first woman in Australia to receive a life sentence without the possibility of parole. Speculation remains as to whether she ate any of the meal prepared from Pricey's body.

The authorities found Pricey's head simmering in a large pot when they visited his bungalow after receiving a report he hadn't turned up to work.

DENNIS RADER

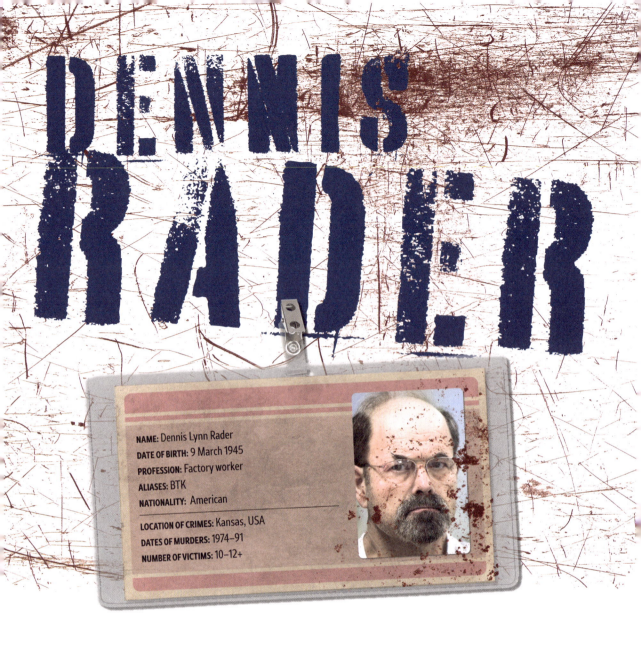

NAME: Dennis Lynn Rader
DATE OF BIRTH: 9 March 1945
PROFESSION: Factory worker
ALIASES: BTK
NATIONALITY: American
LOCATION OF CRIMES: Kansas, USA
DATES OF MURDERS: 1974–91
NUMBER OF VICTIMS: 10–12+

Although he appeared to be a normal, God-fearing American from a normal, God-fearing American family, Dennis Rader called himself BTK – standing for 'Bind them, Torture them, Kill them' – in letters he sent to the newspapers taunting the police for their inability to catch him. Despite this, he got away with killing ten people between 1974 and 1979. Then he stopped. It was only when he resumed writing letters in 2004 that he got caught.

Rader was born in Pittsburg, Kansas in 1945, after his father returned from serving in the Marine Corps during World War II. He was the first of four boys. When he was still a child, the family moved to Park City, a town just outside Wichita.

From the age of eight, Rader grew obsessed with the true crime and detective magazines of the era, with names such as *True Detective, Revealing Detective, Master Detective, Front Page, Climax, Vintage Sensation*, etc., that his father hid in his car. The stories were accompanied by photographs and artworks intended to titillate the male readership. In them, women were often hunted, tied up, tortured and killed. A solitary boy, Rader practised these techniques on animals and continued doing so until he enlisted in the US Air Force, aged 21.

His mother was a strict disciplinarian. She would beat her children, giving Rader the first inklings of sexual stimulation. This

102 BLOODY BUTCHERS

Dennis Rader's home in Park City with a police cordon around it, shortly after his arrest.

led him to masturbate while torturing small animals.

At school, he supplemented this with drawing women being subjugated and murdered. He would cut pictures of women out of magazines and underwear catalogues, adding gags, chains and ligatures around their necks. He earned a badge for knot-tying in the Boy Scouts.

From the age of 14, he became a peeping Tom and stalker, and would also break into homes in the neighbourhood to steal women's underwear. In his parents' basement, he would rig up ropes, pulleys and other bondage paraphernalia. Then he would photograph himself naked or in stolen women's clothes while restrained.

He enjoyed the military discipline of the air force, studied electronics and was posted to the Far East. In Japan, he visited brothels where he studied the finer points of bondage, domination, submission and autoeroticism. After four years in the service, he was honourably discharged and returned to Park City as well as to the old practices of photographing himself wearing women's clothes and make-up, or a mask, in bondage.

ON THE PROWL

Meanwhile, he married, became the father of two children and took a job in the meat department of a supermarket where his mother worked. In the evenings and weekends, he studied criminal justice, with an emphasis on law enforcement, graduating with a bachelor's degree. He tried to join the police, but failed on psychological evaluation. However, he did work as a reserve police officer in a number of jurisdictions around the Wichita area. And he took a job in a security company, installing burglar alarms. This gave him a good knowledge of the districts and the homes where he would commit his murders.

He began picking people he would target for bondage, torture and killing. He would also build a number of 'hit kits', containing guns, knives, cords from Venetian blinds, black electrical tape, screwdrivers, wire-cutters, plastic bags, handcuffs and gloves. These would be carried in a small bag, attaché case or just stuffed in his pockets.

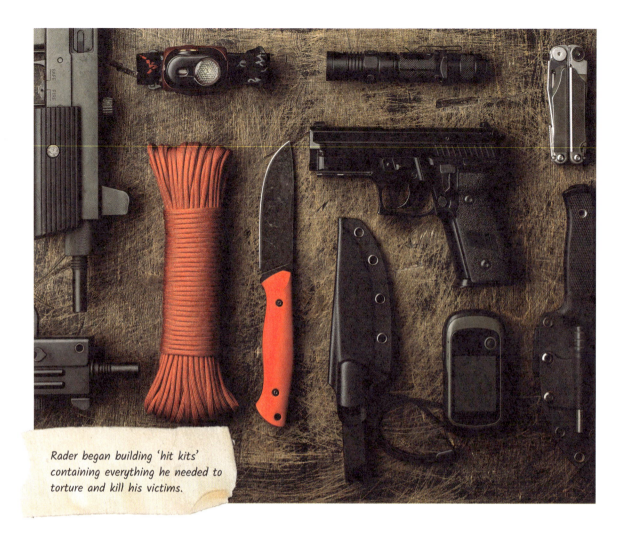

Rader began building 'hit kits' containing everything he needed to torture and kill his victims.

He came up with detailed plans for future crimes. These were known as projects. The murder of Vicki Wegerle was known as Project Piano since she played the piano, while Project Fox Hunt referred to the murder of Nancy Fox. These would join his ever-growing collection of autoerotic photographs and pictures showing men, women and children in bonds. As his murderous career got under way, he would also add press cuttings of his crimes, copies of letters and poems he sent about the offences, and, eventually, books about the BTK killer, to his mother lode, all neatly filed in ten three-ring binders. As time went on, computer disks were added.

While these files swelled, he worked for the US Census Department as a city compliance officer, equipped with a badge, a gun, a citation book and authorization to prowl the streets at night. He was also elected to two city policy boards and the assembly of the Christ Lutheran Church in Wichita, where he rose to become vice-president.

His first murder took place in January 1974, when he killed four members of the Otero family in Wichita – 38-year-old Joseph Otero, his 33-year-old wife Julie, both from Puerto Rico, their 11-year-old daughter Josephine and nine-year-old son Joseph Jnr. Their bodies were found by their three older children, who had been at school.

'My dad's tongue was halfway bit off. He had a belt around his neck,' said Charlie Otero, who was 15 at the time. 'My mom was beaten, her nails were busted up. They were cold. We tried to get the ligatures undone, the belt undone and then I realized this was for nothing and that I had to get my brother and my sister out of the house.'

Rader had been lurking outside their home at 8.30 am. Ten minutes later, the door opened as Joseph Jnr stepped out. Rader grabbed him and pushed him back inside. He threatened the family with a knife and gun, reassuring them that it was only a robbery. In fact, little Josephine was his target. Rader made her and Joseph watch as he killed their parents in their bedroom.

He then dragged Joseph to his bedroom and wrapped two T-shirts around his head and covered it with a plastic bag. Pulling up a chair, he watched as the boy struggled as he suffocated to death. Then he put a noose around the neck of the barely conscious Josephine and led her down to the basement.

Rader asked her if she had a camera as he wanted to take a picture. She didn't. Tying the noose over the sewer pipe, he pulled her clothes off and toyed with her.

'What's going to happen to me?' she asked. He said she would soon be in heaven with the others. Then he placed a gag in her mouth and hoisted her off the floor. As she writhed, Rader masturbated.

Asked if he ever wore a mask to disguise his identity, Rader said: 'No, because they weren't going to be alive when I left.'

THE MONSTER IN THE DARK

Rader wrote a letter detailing the murders, which he left inside the book *Applied Engineering Mechanics* in Wichita Public Library in October 1974. On 22 October, he called Don Granger of the *Wichita Eagle* and *Beacon* newspapers telling them it was there. Granger retrieved the letter. Its authenticity was not in doubt as it contained details only the police and the killer could have known. It said that the three individuals being questioned for the Otero murders were not involved.

It was addressed to the 'Secret Witness Progam', where informants could pass on information to the police anonymously via the newspaper. The police asked the paper not to publish the contents of the letter to prevent them from having to deal with a spate of false confessions.

However, a reporter for a new rival newspaper called the *Wichita Sun* received a copy of the letter and printed part of it in an article on 11 December 1974. Although the letter was unsigned, it contained a postscript which gave him his famous tag, BTK.

A body of an Otero family member is taken out from their home in 1974.

'I write this letter to you for the sake of the tax payer as well as your time. Those three dude you have in custody are just talking to get publicity for the Otero murders. They know nothing at all. I did it by myself and with no ones help. There has been no talk either. Let's put this straight ...' [The killer provides details of the crimes and crime scene that were not published in the paper.]

'I'm sorry this happen to society. They are the ones who suffer the most. It hard to control myself. You probably call me "psychotic with sexual perversion hang-up." When this monster enter my brain I will never know. But, it here to stay. How does one cure himself? If you ask for help, that you have killed four people they will laugh or hit the panic button and call the cops.

'I can't stop it so the monster goes on, and hurt me as well as society. Society can be thankful that there are ways for people like me to relieve myself at time by day dreams of some victims being torture and being mine. It a big complicated game my friend of the monster play putting victims number down, follow them, checking up on them, waiting in the dark, waiting, waiting ... the pressure is great and sometimes he run the game to his liking. Maybe you can stop him. I can't. He has already chosen his next victim or victims. I don't know who they are yet. The next day after I read the paper, I will know, but it to late. Good luck hunting.

'YOURS, TRULY GUILTILY'

'P.S. Since sex criminals do not change their M.O. or by nature cannot do so, I will not change mine. The code word for me will be ... Bind them, torture them, kill them, B.T.K., you see me at it again. They will be on the next victim.'

Before the letter had been delivered, on 4 April 1974 he murdered 21-year-old Kathryn Bright in Operation Lights Out. He had decided that it would be easier to kill a woman who did not have any male family members – and a woman who did not have any children as they would be easier to subdue.

While she was out, he cut the phone lines and broke in through the back door. However, when she arrived home, she was accompanied by her brother William. Rader pretended to be an escaped felon and, threatening him with a .22, he ordered William to tie his sister up. He took William into another room and tied him up too.

Concerned that he might try and rescue his sister, he decided to strangle William first. When he fought back, Rader shot him. He intended to strangle or suffocate Kathryn when she was naked, or partially naked. But when she too struggled, he stabbed her.

William was not dead and, while Rader was slipping on Kathryn's blood, he made it out of the front door to call for help. Panicking, Rader fled. He tried to steal Kathryn's car, but it would not start. He could not get William's truck to start either, so he ran back to Wichita State University where he had left his car. Kathryn was still alive when the police arrived, but died from her wounds in hospital.

INSIDE JOB

On 12 November 1974, 23-year-old Sherry Baker was found dead less than 5 km (3 miles) from the Otero house and just 3 km (2 miles) from where Kathryn Bright had lived. She was found face down on the living room floor, in her negligee and panties, with her hands bound behind her back with telephone cable torn from the wall; she had been gagged with a torn piece of a towel. As usual, the telephone line had been cut. The post-mortem revealed she had been stabbed over 60 times. A pair of scissors were found in the back of her neck. The blow had been so vicious that a blade broke.

Rader had installed the burglar alarm at her home, saying he 'rigged a home once that I felt like I could maybe get back in ... she hired our company to protect her home ... I think it's the only one I did.' He also admitted acts of petty theft while he was at work, saying: 'Nylons or socks, something they wouldn't miss. Have you ever been – I don't know, have you ever been in a woman's dresser? They got pantyhoses and hoses. They don't know what they got in there. You know, all you got to do is reach way back there and pick something out, they won't miss it.'

On 17 March 1977, Shirley Vian was the next victim. Rader was pursuing a woman named Cheryl who he had met in the Blackout Tavern near Wichita State University. This was Project Green. She was

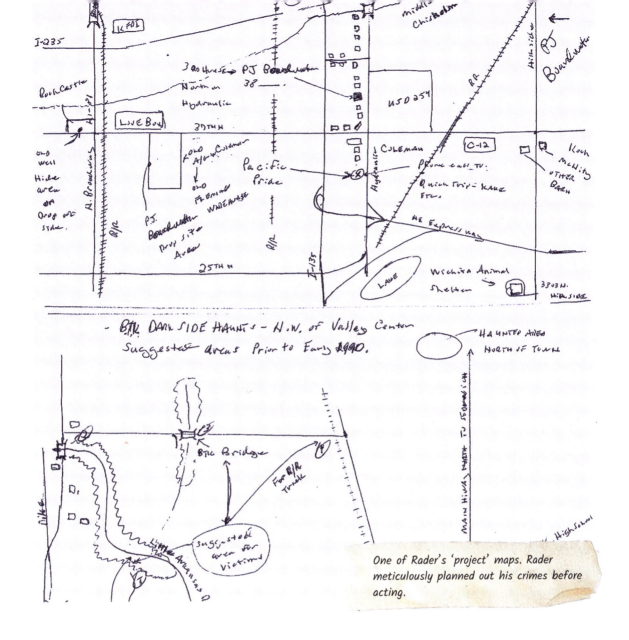

One of Rader's 'project' maps. Rader meticulously planned out his crimes before acting.

a single mother with a six-year-old son, but she was not at home. Then he saw a boy walking down the street. After he went into his home, Rader knocked on the door, posing as a detective. There were three children in the house. Rader switched off the TV and closed the blinds. Then their mother appeared from another room.

At gunpoint, he ordered the children to go into the bathroom and locked the door. He told Vian that he planned on having his way with her. To calm her down, he gave her a glass of water and smoked a cigarette with her. While the children were screaming in the bathroom, Rader tied her up, put a cord around her neck and strangled her. There was semen on her panties, which were found next to her body. In his confession, he said he would have killed the children too, if the phone had not rung.

Operation Fox Hunt was planned more carefully. Nancy Fox, he told investigators, appealed to him as a 'sexual female victim'. He recorded how he picked one target over another.

'The trolling stage was wide open. I might be looking and see someone else, say, well, this is even better yet ... and then I would drop this person, or I might leave them in the project box,' he wrote. 'Usually once – once I got narrowed down and started homing in, it became a stalking stage ... but there's only been a couple that went the way I wanted them.'

DENNIS RADER **107**

Detective Sam Houston shows a mask used in one of the crimes during Rader's sentencing hearing.

He had studied her daily routine, what time she went to her two part-time jobs and her other habits. On 8 December 1977, he struck. As with Kathryn Bright and Sherry Baker, he cut the phone lines and broke in through the back door. He then rifled though her closet and drawers, stealing various items of clothing. When she returned home, he threatened her with a gun and told her that he was going to rape her and photograph her, but first he let her smoke a cigarette and go to the bathroom. Meanwhile, he began to undress.

She was still wearing a sweater, bra and panties when he handcuffed her and wrapped his belt around her legs, pulling it up and around her neck. Then he told her that he was BTK and he was going to kill her.

'And then she really, really squirmed and then … and then I pulled, put the pressure down on it,' he said.

While being strangled, Nancy fought for her life and grabbed 'a hold of my nuts. Yeah, she did. And she was squeezing pretty hard. But it actually made me more excited.'

When she was dead, he took his belt, then tied her up with panty hose and scarves. He masturbated into her nightgown and threw it on the floor, next to her head. Then he left, taking with him some of her scarves, underwear and jewellery, which he later gave to his daughter when she was in high school. He stole her car to drive back to his own.

BTK messages leading to Rader's arrest

❶ 19 March 2004
Wichita Eagle receives BTK letter containing copy of Vicki Wegerle's driving licence

❷ May 2004
KAKE receives a letter containing chapter headings for 'The BTK Story' as well as fake IDs and a word puzzle

❸ June 2004
Police receive a letter from BTK

❹ 17 July 2004
Package found at Central Library

❺ 22 October 2004
Package found at Omni Center

❻ 14 December 2004
Package found in Murdock Park

❼ Unknown location and date
Postcard from 25 January suggests a package was sent on 8 January

❽ 25 January 2005
KAKE receives a postcard

❾ 16 February 2006
KSAS receives an envelope containing a computer disk and jewellery

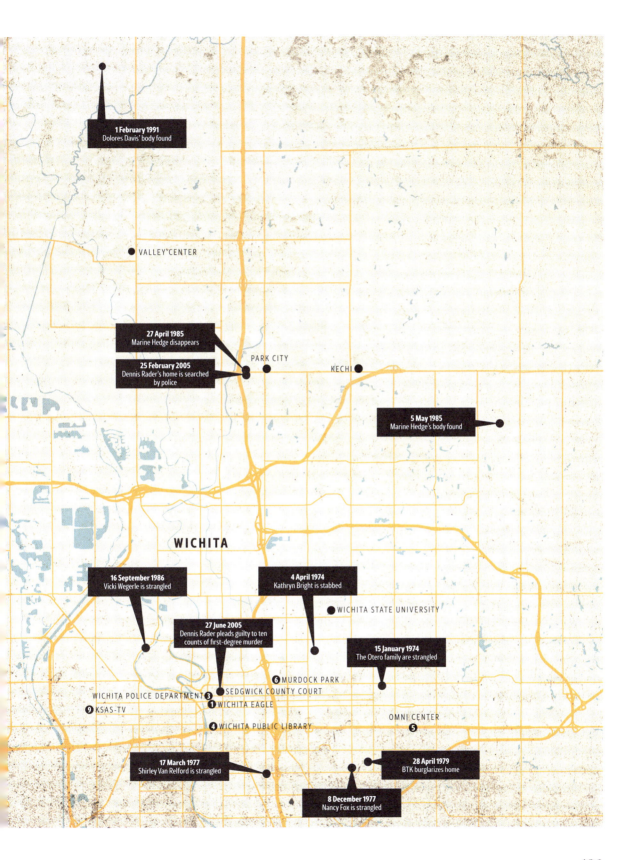

EVIL POETRY

On 10 February 1978, he wrote a four-page letter to the television station KAKE in Wichita describing the murders of the Oteros, Shirley Vian and Nancy Fox. In it, he enclosed a poem that parodied the lyrics of the American folk song 'Oh! Death'.

OH! DEATH TO NANCY
What is this taht [sic] I can see,
Cold icy hands taking hold of me,
For Death has come, you all can see. Hell has open it,s
    [sic] gate to trick me.
Oh! Death, Oh! Death, can't you spare me, over for
    another year!
I'll stuff your jaws till you can't talk
I'll blind [sic] your leg's [sic] till you can't walk
  I'll tie your hands till you can't make a stand.
And finally I'll close your eyes so you can't see
I'll bring sexual death unto you for me.
B.T.K.

There had been another poem after the death of Shirley Vian which appears to have been in the partially suppressed letter in 1964. In the 1978 letter, he wrote: 'I find the newspaper not writing about the poem on Vian unamusing. A little paragraph would have enough. I know it not the media fault. The Police Chief he keep things quiet, and doesn't let the public know there a psycho running around lose strangling mostly women, there 7 in the ground; who will be next?'

He was plainly miffed that he was not getting the attention from the media that he thought he deserved. The letter continued:

'How many do I have to Kill before I get a name in the paper or some national attention. Do the cop think that all those deaths are not related? Golly-gee, yes the M.O. is different in each, but look a pattern is developing. The victims are tie up-most have been women-phone cut- bring some bondage mater sadist tendencies-no struggle, outside the death spot-no wintness except the Vain's Kids. They were very lucky; a phone call save them. I was go-ng to tape the boys and put plastics bag over there head like I did Joseph, and

Shirley. And then hang the girl. God-oh God what a beautiful sexual relief that would been. Josephine, when I hung her really turn me on; her pleading for mercy then the rope took whole, she helpless; staring at me with wide terror fill eyes the rope getting tighter-tighter. You don't understand these things because your not under the influence of factor x). The same thing that made Son of Sam, Jack the Ripper, Havery Glatman, Boston Strangler, Dr. H.H. Holmes Panty Hose Strangler OF Florida, Hillside Strangler, Ted of the West Coast and many more infamous character kill. Which seem s senseless, but we cannot help it. There is no help, no cure, except death or being caught and put away. It a terrible nightmare but, you see I don't lose any sleep over it. After a thing like Fox I come home and go about life like anyone else. And I will be like that until the urge hit me again. It not continuous and I don't have a lot of time. It take time to set a kill, one mistake and it all over. Since I about blew it on the phone-handwriting is out-letter guide is to long and typewriter can be traced too. My short poem of death and maybe a drawing; later on real picture and maybe a tape of the sound will come your way. How will you know me. Before a murder or murders you will receive a copy of the initials B.T.K. , you keep that copy the original will show up some day on guess who?

'May you not be the unluck one! P.S. How about some name for me, its time: 7 down and many more to go. I like the following How about you?

'"THE B.T.K. STRANGLER", "WICHITA STRANGLER", "POETIC STRANGLER", "THE BOND AGE STRANGLER OR PSYCHO" "THE WICHITA HANGMAN THE WICHITA EXECUTIONER", "THE GAROTE PHATHOM", "THE ASPHIXIATER". B.T.K'

At the time it was suggested that his poor spelling and lack of literacy was a ruse, disguising a highly intelligent man – which serial killers often are. But after he was arrested, the same standard of illiteracy appeared in his college work.

In 1979, he sent two identical packages, one to 63-year-old Anna Williams – intended victim in Project Pine Cone – who was not at home when he broke into her house, and the other to KAKE. These contained drawings of what he intended to do to his victim, some small items he had pilfered from Anna's home and another poem:

> OH, ANNA WHY DIDN'T YOU APPEAR
> Oh, Anna Why Didn't You Appear
> T' was perfect plan of deviant pleasure so bold on that Spring nite
> My inner felling hot with propension of the new awakening season
> Warn, wet with inner fear and rapture, my pleasure of entanglement, like new vines at night
> Oh, Anna, Why Didn't You Appear
> Drop of fear fresh Spring rain would roll down from your nakedness to scent to lofty fever that burns within,
> In that small world of longing, fear, rapture, and desparation, the game we play, fall on devil ears
> Fantasy spring forth, mounts, to storm fury, then winter clam at the end.
> Oh, Anna Why Didn't You Appear
> Alone, now in another time span I lay with sweet enrapture garments across most private thought
> Bed of Spring moist grass, clean before the sun, enslaved with control, warm wind scenting the air, sun light sparkle tears in eyes so deep and clear.
> Alone again I trod in pass memory of mirrors, and ponder why for number eight was not.
> Oh, Anna Why Didn't You Appear
> BTK

Apparently, Rader had broken into her home, as usual cutting the phone lines and forcing entry through the back door. He collected scarves, nylons, jewellery and panties from Anna's bedroom and that of her daughter. Scattering these alongside clothes on the floor he made a comfortable nest for himself, where he could wait for her. He lingered for several hours inside the home, not realizing that she had gone to her sister's for the evening. He eventually got tired of waiting and went away, leaving a note saying: 'Glad you weren't here, because I was.' Then he stole her car to drive back to where he had parked his own vehicle.

MISSING FROM BOY SCOUT CAMP

Next time he would make no mistake. The victim, 53-year-old Marine Hedge, lived on the same street as Rader, just a few houses away, so he could keep an eye on her comings and goings. This appears to have taken years as she was killed eight years after the murder of Nancy Fox.

The local houses of women he was tracking looked to him like cookies, so Rader called the targeting, stalking and killing of Marine Hedge Operation Cookie. On the night of 26 April 1985, he cut the phone lines and broke into her house. When she returned home, she was with a male friend. He hid in the closet until 1 am, when her friend had left and she had gone to sleep.

'She didn't wake up until I got into bed with her,' Rader said.

When she did, she found that he had already put his 'belt around her neck ... and throttled her to get her under control'. Once she was dead, he handcuffed her and took her underwear, stockings, her car keys and driver's licence, and some jewellery. Then he stripped her, wrapped her in blankets and put her in the trunk of her car. Then he drove to Christ Lutheran Church and put her in a basement room there that he had already prepared.

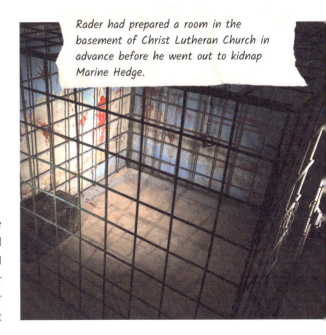

Rader had prepared a room in the basement of Christ Lutheran Church in advance before he went out to kidnap Marine Hedge.

For several hours, he said he 'photographed her in bondage ... different poses for her'. Then he masturbated over her body. After he had cleaned up, he dumped her corpse, returned her car, retrieved his own and drove back to the Boy Scout camp he had been supervising earlier, slipping back in, so that no one noticed he had been missing.

Marine's son-in-law informed the police that she was missing. They found her car in a shopping centre. There was bed linen in the trunk that had otherwise been wiped clean. Her decomposing body was found in a ditch where people dumped trash. Rader said that he had returned to it several times to retrieve the ligatures he had used, but it was thought he actually returned to take more pictures of her naked corpse.

Rader had stalked 28-year-old Vicki Wegerle for three weeks. He supplemented his hit kit with a fake telephone-company ID, a hard hat and a tool belt. On 16 September 1986, he approached the elderly couple who lived next door to her, pretending to check their line. Then he moved on to Vicki's house and pretended to check her line, before pulling a gun from his briefcase.

Leaving her 18-month-old son to his own devices, he ordered her into the bedroom, where he tied her up. He said she was crying, but somehow broke the bonds he had been tying and fought back. She scratched his hands and arms while he strangled her. Once she was dead, he pulled her clothes off and masturbated, then posed her and took some photographs.

After that, he stole her car and dumped his briefcase and hard hat. Asked what he would have done if he'd been stopped by a police officer, he said: 'I hope I would have been faster than him with a gun.'

Vicki's body and distraught son were found by her husband when he came home for lunch.

TAUNTING WORDS

In 1988, after the murders of three members of the Fager family in Wichita, a letter was received from someone claiming to be BTK. In it, he denied being the perpetrator in this case, but he credited the killer with doing admirable work. However, a week after Mrs Fager came home to find her husband and two daughters dead, Rader sent her a poem called 'Oh God He Put Kelli Sherri in the Tub'. Although the events related in the poem were accurate, the drawings of the bound and murdered girls were not. Mr Fager had been shot with a .357. Ten-year-old Sherri was found bound in the hot tub, where, it appears, she drowned. The naked body of her 16-year-old sister Kelli was put in the hot tub eight hours later. She had been strangled with a ligature and was dead when she was dumped in the water.

Dennis Rader is escorted to a correctional facility in El Dorado, Kansas, 19 August 2005.

Next came the killing of 62-year-old Dolores Davis. This was called Project Dog-Side as she had a dog kennel on her property, which was just two blocks from Rader's house.

He had tried to break into her home several times. Once he had been repulsed by her cat, which caused such a commotion that it alerted Dolores. On the night of 19 January 1991, he used the cover of a Boy Scout winter camp to go about his lethal business. His parents were away, so he went to their house to change. Then he drove to the church where he had stashed his hit kit, and walked to Dolores's home.

THE 'PROJECTS' OF BTK

OPERATION COOKIE
Date: 26 April 1985
Target: Marine Hedge, 53 years old
Location: Wichita, Kansas
Status: Victim murdered

PROJECT DOG-SIDE
Date: 19 January 1991
Target: Dolores Davis, 62 years old
Location: Park City, Kansas
Status: Victim murdered

PROJECT PIANO
Date: 16 September 1986
Target: Vicki Wegerle, 28 years old
Location: Wichita, Kansas
Status: Victim murdered

PROJECT FOX HUNT
Date: 8 December 1977
Target: Nancy Fox, 25 years old
Location: Wichita, Kansas
Status: Victim murdered

PROJECT LIGHTS OUT
Date: 4 April 1974
Target: Kathryn Bright, 21 years old
Location: Wichita, Kansas
Status: Victim murdered

PROJECT PRAIRIE
Target: Unknown
Date: 1983
Location: Hays, Kansas
Status: Victim missing

PROJECT GREEN
Date: 17 March 1977
Target: Shirley Vian, 25 years old
Location: Wichita, Kansas
Status: Victim murdered

PROJECT PINE CONE
Date: 1979
Target: Anna Williams, 63 years old
Location: Wichita, Kansas
Status: Victim survived, no one present at house

He got in by throwing a cinder block through a sliding glass door, waking her. When she confronted him, he pretended to be an escaped convict on the run. What he wanted was some money and her car, so he could drive to California. He warned her that he had a gun and a knife, saying: 'Take your choice how you want it.'

He said he really wanted to spend some time with her, but once he had handcuffed her and tied her up, he strangled her with panty hose. When he was done with her, he put her body in the trunk of her car along with her driver's licence, a camera, a box of jewellery and some clothing. After he dumped her body, he returned the vehicle and walked back to the church to retrieve his car. Then he went to recover Dolores's body, which he stowed under a bridge, returning several times to take photographs of her tied up and wearing a mask to make her 'look prettier'. The mask, he explained, was the one he had used in self-bondage – 'I would try to take pictures, so I looked like maybe I was a female or a person in distress.'

There were other 'projects' that did not come off. Project Prairie was planned in a town in north-east Kansas when he was a census-taker. Again, he broke into a woman's house, but she was saved when she did not come home that evening. Rader wrote to the Wichita police about Project Bell on 8 December 2004. When Rader was finally arrested and his records seized, it was found that he detailed the habits and routines of hundreds of possible targets. Children were picked out as potential victims.

'If I could get a younger person or could have got a younger person I would do it,' he wrote. 'Just not sure, what's the term – like adults where they are attracted to kids: Paedophile, yeah. Probably have some of that in me ... occasionally I draw a kid tied up or something.'

Although there had been no murders he had claimed credit for since 1991, clearly Rader had been missing the attention. On 19 March 2004, the *Wichita Eagle* received an envelope containing the driver's licence of Vicki Wegerle and three photographs of her bound lying on the floor. The return address was 'Bill Thomas Killman ... 1684 South Oldmanor'. The name was fictitious and the address a vacant lot, but clearly it came from BTK.

In April, Wichita's KSN-TV received a letter allegedly from BTK, containing a photograph of an unidentified baby. Then on 4 May 2004, KAKE-TV received a fake ID card, a word puzzle and a list of chapters from 'The BTK Story' published by Court TV's Crime Library in 1999. Some of the chapter titles were changed, indicating that there might be more murders. The return address this time used the name Thomas B. King – or TBK.

Another list of chapters from 'The BTK Story', along with sheets from the chapter 'Death on a Cold January Morning' and pictures of naked women, bound, gagged and hanging were found taped to a stop sign in June. It also contained a graphic description of the Oteros' murder and a drawing entitled 'The Sexual Thrill Is My Bill', along with a proposed chapter list for his own version of 'The BTK Story' – 'Chapter One: A Serial Killer is Born'.

More bizarre material was found in the return slot of the Wichita Public Library, the UPS box and Nancy Fox's driver's licence was in another package found in Wichita's Murdock Park.

Another letter was in a cereal box dropped in a pick-up truck at Wichita's Home Depot, but the driver threw it out. However, it was retrieved from the garbage after Rader asked whether they had got it. A check of the CCTV at the parking lot showed the driver of a Jeep Cherokee dropping the box into the pick-up. Another cereal box was found in the countryside with a bound doll in it, while KAKE-TV got a series of postcards.

In a letter to the police, Rader asked whether, if he put further communications on computer disks, he could be traced. Naturally, in their reply in the *Wichita Eagle*, they said he could not, so, on 16 February 2005, he sent a floppy disk to KSAS-TV in Wichita, along with a copy of the cover of *Rules of Prey* by John Sandford, a novel about a serial killer.

On the disk there were traces of a deleted file. In the metadata, they found 'Christ Lutheran Church' and a record that it had last been modified by 'Dennis'. This led the police directly to Dennis Rader. But they needed more. Obtaining a medical sample from Rader's daughter, they found a partial match for the DNA left at the crime scenes. And when they went to arrest Rader on 25 February 2005, they found a Jeep Cherokee parked outside his house.

He waived his right to silence and spoke for over 30 hours before a court-appointed public defender shut him up. At the arraignment he kept silent, so not guilty pleas were entered on his behalf. But at the trial, he pleaded guilty to all ten charges of murder and was given ten life sentences without the possibility of parole.

In jail, he was kept in solitary confinement for his own protection. His wife was granted an emergency divorce, waiving the usual waiting period. However, his daughter Kerri stayed in touch and continued to write to him, though she found it difficult to reconcile the psychopathic killer with the loving father she knew.

'We were living our normal life,' she said. 'We looked like a normal American family because we were a normal family. And then everything upended on us.'

114 BLOODY BUTCHERS

A letter sent by Dennis Rader to the *Wichita Eagle* from his jail cell after learning that Stephen King had based one of his novels on Rader's actions. Even after his conviction he remained obsessed with his own notoriety.

DAVID PARKER RAY AND CINDY HENDY

NAME: David Parker Ray and Cynthia 'Cindy' Lee Hendy

DATE OF BIRTH: 6 November 1939 (Ray) and 6 February 1960 (Hendy)

PROFESSION: Soldier, mechanic (Ray) and park official (Hendy)

ALIASES: The Toy-Box Killer (Ray)

NATIONALITY: American

LOCATION OF CRIMES: Arizona and New Mexico, USA

DATES OF MURDERS: 1950–99

NUMBER OF VICTIMS: 3–60+

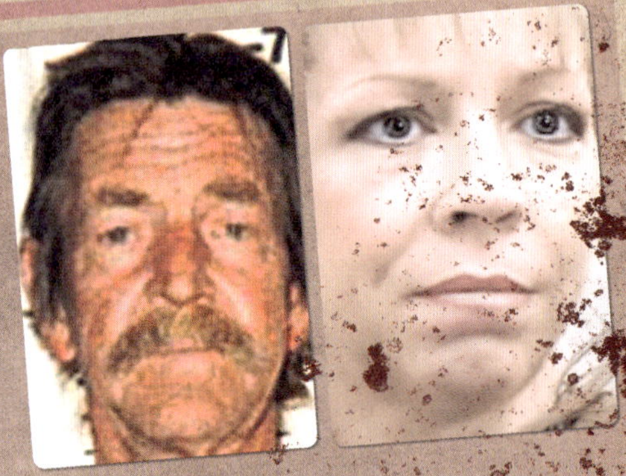

Truth or Consequences, New Mexico was once a place of relaxation. The first people to enjoy its hospitality arrived over one hundred years ago. They were there to soak in the Geronimo Springs at John Cross Ranch. It would be the first of several dozen spas to be built around the heated groundwater that continues to bubble up in this city of less than 8,000 souls. The entire community was built around this natural phenomenon. Anyone who wonders how important it once was to the local

economy need look no further than the city's original name: Hot Springs. The city became Truth or Consequences in 1950, when the popular radio quiz show of that name offered to broadcast from the first community to rename itself after the show. It was all good fun.

The first indication of David Parker Ray's crimes came on 26 July 1996, when the sheriff's office in Truth or Consequences received a call from a young Marine. On the previous day he had argued with his wife Kelly Van Cleave and he had not seen or heard

116 BLOODY BUTCHERS

Elephant Butte State Park: Kelly Cleave went missing and was found wandering in a dazed and incoherent state near here.

from her since. The anxious husband received only advice.

His wife had been gone such a short time that she could not be considered as a missing person. Based on past experience, the office had every reason to believe that Kelly would turn up.

Sure enough, the young man's wife returned home on the very next day. She had been brought back by an employee of nearby Elephant Butte State Park, where she had been found wandering in a dazed and incoherent state.

Kelly could account for only a few of the many hours she had been missing. After the fight with her husband, she remembered going to a friend's house. This was followed by trips to a number of bars, the last of which was the Blue Waters Saloon. It was there that Kelly ordered a beer, her first drink of the evening.

She soon began to feel dizzy. The sensation was not dissimilar to being drunk, but something was not quite right. Kelly could recall little else from this point onwards, though she was certain that an old friend, Jesse Ray, had offered to help. Those missing hours brought an end to Kelly's marriage. Her husband could never accept her disappearance, or her claim that she could not remember what had happened.

NIGHTMARES

Jesse Ray might have been able to help... but she could not be found. Kelly soon left Truth or Consequences, never to return. She would never see Jesse again.

Now separated, Kelly began to suffer from nightmares. The horrifying images were remarkably consistent – she saw herself being tied to a table, being gagged with duct tape and having a knife held to her throat. Nothing quite made sense so Kelly never did report her strange experience to the authorities. All the sheriff's office at Truth or Consequences had on file was a seemingly trivial phone call from a distrusting husband. They could not have known that the woman who walked through their door on 7 July 1997 was bringing information that was related to Kelly's disappearance.

The woman had come to report that she had not heard from her 22-year-old daughter, Marie Parker, for several days. This time, there would be an investigation. In such a small city, it was not difficult to track the young woman's movements. Marie had last been seen on 5 July at the Blue Waters Saloon. She had been drinking with Jesse Ray. Jesse told the authorities that Marie had been drinking heavily so she had driven her home, but she had not seen her since.

But Jesse was not the only person that Marie had been drinking with on the night of her disappearance. Roy Yancy, an old boyfriend, had also been raising a glass at the Blue Waters Saloon. A Truth or Consequences boy born and raised, there was nothing in Roy's past to make the community proud.

As a child he had been part of a gang that had roamed Truth or Consequences strangling cats, poisoning dogs and tipping over gravestones, acts that led the city to cancel that year's Hallowe'en festivities. He had also received a dishonourable discharge from the navy.

Marie might well have been in the company of an unsavoury character, but the Truth or Consequences sheriff's office saw nothing unusual about her disappearance. After all, the city was known for its transient population. They were all too ready to accept someone's hazy recollection of a girl accepting a ride out of the city. It was a typical story.

At around this time a new woman arrived in the small city. Cindy Hendy's history was anything but enviable. A victim of sexual abuse, she had been molested by her stepfather before being turned out on the street at the age of 11. Cindy had been a teenage mother, but only in the sense that she had given birth – other people had taken on the job of raising her daughter. When she arrived in Truth or Consequences, Cindy was on the run from a drugs charge. Several months earlier, she had supplied cocaine to an undercover agent. She was a violent woman with a short fuse, so it was not long before she found herself in the local jail. Days later she was sent out to Elephant Butte Lake on a work-release programme. It was there that she first met David Parker Ray, the father of her friend Jesse.

He was a quiet, though approachable and friendly man. Ray had been a neglected child. Unloved by his mother, his only real contact with his drifter father came in the form of periodic drunken visits. These invariably ended with the old man leaving behind a bag of pornographic magazines that portrayed sadomasochistic acts. His adult life was one of many marriages and many jobs. He had

Police say David Parker Ray may have killed as many as 60 people in the small city of Truth or Consequences.

Angie Montano left Truth or Consequences as soon as she could after her encounter with the Rays.

lived a transient life before 1984, when he settled down with his fourth wife in Elephant Butte. After acquiring a run-down bungalow on a little piece of property, Ray supported them by working as an aircraft engine repairman.

By 1995, his wife had left him. The fourth Mrs Ray would be the final Mrs Ray, but she was not his last companion. In January 1999, Cindy Hendy moved into Ray's bungalow. It mattered little that he was two decades older because the 38-year-old had met her soulmate – someone who, like herself, was obsessed with sadomasochistic sex.

LONELY NEWCOMER

Cindy had been living with Ray for just one month when, on 16 February, she invited Angie Montano over for a visit. Angie, a single mother, was new to Truth or Consequences, and was eager to make friends. She had come to the wrong place, because she was blindfolded, strapped to a bed and sexually assaulted. Ray and Cindy's sadistic tastes went beyond rape. Angie was stunned by cattle prods and various other devices that Ray had made himself. After five days, Angie managed to get Ray to agree to her release. He drove her to the nearest highway and let her out. As luck would have it, she was picked up by a passing off-duty police officer. Angie shared her story with him, but she would not agree to making an official report. Just as Kelly Van Cleave had done four years earlier, Angie left Truth or Consequences, never to return.

Even as the assaults on Angie Montano were taking place, Cindy's mind was sometimes elsewhere. Though her 39th birthday had only just passed, she was about to become a grandmother. She made plans to attend the birth in her old hometown of Monroe, Washington, but before she could go she needed to find a sex slave for Ray, someone who would meet his needs in her absence.

On 18 March, they drove through the streets of Albuquerque in Ray's motorhome, where they came upon Cynthia Vigil. She was a prostitute, so it was not difficult to get her into the vehicle, nor was it hard to overpower the 22-year-old. After being bound, Cynthia was taken back to the Elephant Butte bungalow, where she was collared, chained, blindfolded and gagged. A tape was then played to her. The voice was Ray's.

'HELLO, BITCH. WELL, THIS TAPE'S GETTIN' PLAYED AGAIN. MUST MEAN I PICKED UP ANOTHER HOOKER. AND I'LL BET YOU WONDER WHAT THE HELL'S GOIN' ON HERE. THE GAG IS NECESSARY BECAUSE AFTER A WHILE YOU'RE GOIN' TO BE DOIN' A LOT OF SCREAMING.'

A named wristband kept as a trophy by Ray, found during the FBI's investigation.

Those were just the first few sentences in a recording that lasted over five minutes. Ray went on to describe how he and his 'lady friend' were going to rape and torture the listener.

True to the words of the tape, Ray and Cindy tortured and raped the prostitute over the course of the next three days. The assaults had no effect on Ray's work habits. As the fourth day began, he donned his state park uniform and drove off. Cindy was charged with keeping their victim under control. But his lady friend wasn't quite up to the task. In fact, she was downright sloppy.

When Cindy left the room to prepare a lunch of tuna sandwiches, the young prostitute noticed that her abductor had left behind the keys to her chains. After releasing herself, she grabbed the phone and called the Sierra County Sheriff's Office. Before she could say a word, Cindy was back in the room, bottle in hand. She took a violent swing at the prostitute, cutting her with the breaking glass. Cynthia noticed an ice pick while she was lying on the floor. She quickly grabbed it and stabbed her captor in the back of the neck.

It was not a lethal blow, but it was enough to give Cynthia time to get out of the house. Naked except for a dog collar and chain, she ran out of the door and down the dusty, unpaved street. She was spotted by the drivers of two cars, but they just swerved to avoid the distressed, bleeding woman.

After about a mile, she came upon a trailer home. She burst through the door and fell at the feet of a woman watching television.

SCENE OF THE CRIME

Just minutes after the first interrupted call, the Sierra County Sheriff's Office received a second one. When the authorities arrived at the mobile home they heard a horrific tale of torture and assault. As Cynthia Vigil was being transported to the local hospital, the sheriff's department decided to call in the state police.

Over a dozen officers converged on Ray's bungalow, only to find that Cindy had fled.

The house was a mess, with garbage littering the floor. If there was any order, it was found in Ray's instruments of torture, which were arranged on hooks hanging from the walls of several rooms. His library included books on Satanism, torture and violent pornography. There were also a number of medical books, which presumably enabled him to carry out many of his fantasies.

The hunt was now on for Ray and Cindy. The chase was as short as it was easy. The couple had not fled – instead, they were driving along the nearby roads, looking for their captive. Ray and Cindy were spotted within 15 minutes, a mere two blocks from their home. They

Victim Cynthia Vigil escaped naked with a metal collar round her neck. Hendy received a 36-year sentence for her crimes against Vigil.

quickly admitted that they had been looking for Cynthia Vigil, but they also came up with an implausible explanation for their actions. The abduction of the prostitute had been a humanitarian act, claimed Ray and Cindy. Her confinement had been nothing more than an effort to help the young woman kick her addiction to heroin.

The story fooled no one. Ray and Cindy were arrested and taken into custody. As the investigation of Ray's property began, the state law enforcement officials realized that they did not have the resources to deal with their discoveries. Lieutenant Richard Libicer of the New Mexico State Police explained the situation:

> 'I THINK IT'S SAFE TO SAY THAT NOTHING THAT WAS INSIDE THAT HOUSE WAS ANYTHING ANY OF US HAD EXPERIENCED BEFORE – OR COME ACROSS BEFORE – EXCEPT MAYBE IN A MOVIE SOMEWHERE. IT WAS JUST COMPLETELY OUT OF THE REALM OF OUR EXPERIENCE.'

The assortment of shackles and pulleys and other instruments of torture inside the bungalow appeared almost mundane compared to what was discovered inside a padlocked semi-trailer that was parked outside.

What Ray described as the 'Toy Box' contained hundreds of torture devices. Many of them, such as a machine that was used to electrocute women's breasts, had been designed and built by the former mechanic. At the centre of this horror was a gynaecology table. Cameras were installed, so that the women could see what was happening to them. Ray had also videotaped his assaults,

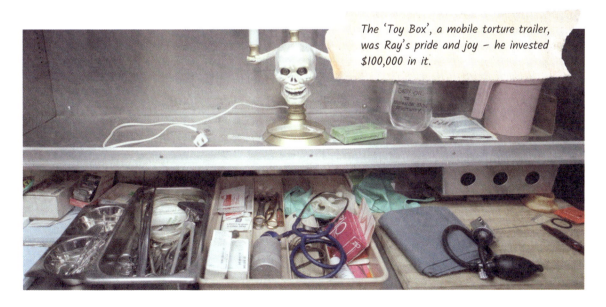

The 'Toy Box', a mobile torture trailer, was Ray's pride and joy – he invested $100,000 in it.

The New Mexico State Police display the gynaecology table that Ray built.

including the one involving Kelly Van Cleave. She had supposedly been found wandering by a state park official – but the state park official was David Parker Ray.

The videotapes were a revelation. For a start, they linked Jesse Ray to her father's crimes. Kelly's evidence also proved useful, but the most damning testimony came from Cindy Hendy.

Within days of her arrest, the 39-year-old turned on her boyfriend. She told the investigators that Ray had been abducting and torturing women for many years. What is more, Ray had told Cindy that his fantasies had often ended in murder.

Subsequent searches of Elephant Butte Lake and the surrounding countryside revealed nothing, but the police remained convinced that Ray had killed at least one person. Cindy also confirmed that Jesse had participated in at least some of the abductions. She added that she often worked in tandem with Roy Yancy.

SOFT CENTRE

Despite his tough demeanour, Roy caved in when he was arrested. He told the police that he and Jesse had drugged Marie Parker, the young woman who had gone missing three years earlier. They had taken her to Elephant Butte, where she was tortured. When Ray

Jesse Ray abducted women for her father.

RAY'S ACCOMPLICES

CINDY HENDY
Relationship: Ray's girlfriend
Priors: Forgery, theft, possession of drugs
Crimes: Kidnapping, criminal sexual penetration, torture

GLENDA JEAN 'JESSE' RAY
Relationship: Ray's daughter
Priors: N/A
Crimes: Kidnapping, criminal sexual penetration, accomplice to murder of Marie Parker, torture.

DENNIS ROY YANCY
Relationship: Marie Parker's boyfriend
Priors: Poisoning dogs, dishonourably discharged from the Navy.
Crimes: Murder of Marie Parker

tired of her, he instructed Roy to kill the woman who had once been his girlfriend.

The body was never found.

Roy Yancy pleaded guilty to second-degree murder and was sentenced to 20 years in prison.

After pleading guilty to kidnapping Kelly Van Cleave and Marie Parker, Jesse Ray received a nine-year sentence.

Facing the possibility of 197 years in prison, Cindy Hendy made a deal with the prosecutors. After pleading guilty to her crimes against Cynthia Vigil she received a 36-year sentence, with a further 18 years on probation.

Even Ray appeared to co-operate with the authorities, but only to the extent of describing his fantasies. He denied abducting or murdering anyone. Any sadomasochistic activities had been between consenting adults. 'I got pleasure out of the woman getting pleasure,' he told one investigator. 'I did what they wanted me to do.'

Ray faced three trials for his crimes against Kelly Van Cleave, Cynthia Vigil and Angie Montano. He was found guilty in the first trial, but part of the way through the second he too made a deal. Ray agreed to plead guilty in exchange for Jesse's release. The case concerning Angie Montano was never heard because she had died of cancer.

On 30 September 2001, David Parker Ray received a 224-year sentence for his crimes against Kelly Van Cleave and Cynthia Vigil. In the end, Ray did not serve so much as a year. On 28 May 2002 he slumped over in a holding cell, killed by a massive heart attack.

'Satan has a place for you. I hope you burn in hell forever,' Cynthia Vigil's grandmother had once yelled at him.

One wonders whether the words meant anything to Ray. The one sign he had put up in his 'Toy Box' read: 'SATAN'S DEN'.

CHAPTER 4

CHAMBERS OF HORROR

Many killers commit their crimes at home. These houses can be terrifying places. There are purpose-built dungeons and soundproofed walls to hide the crimes from prying neighbours. Corpses may be hidden around the property or victims may be locked up, tied down, and tortured for remarkable spells of time. What's amazing is how long many of these ordeals continue when there are so many clues to give the game away.

LEONARD LAKE AND CHARLES NG

NAME: Leonard Thomas Lake and Charles Chi-tat Ng
DATE OF BIRTH: 29 October 1945 (Lake) and 24 December 1960 (Lake)
PROFESSION: Soldier, technician
ALIASES: Leonard Hill, Alan Drey, Randy Jacobsen, Charles Gunnar
NATIONALITY: American (Lake) and British Hong Kong (Ng)
LOCATION OF CRIMES: California, USA
DATES OF CRIMES: 1950–99
NUMBER OF VICTIMS: 11–25

As individuals, Leonard Lake and Charles Ng were both unsavoury characters. Together, they were a deadly combination. In the space of little over a year, they killed, tortured and raped at least 11 and perhaps as many as 25 people, including men, women and two baby boys. The men were mostly killed for money; the women, for sexual thrills; and the babies simply for being in the way.

When it is compared to the horrific crimes that have been committed by Charles Ng, shoplifting seems such a trivial offence. Yet the simple theft of a bench vice was enough to seal Ng's fate and that of his partner in crime, Leonard Lake.

Ng was born in Hong Kong on Christmas Eve, 1960, to a wealthy, if unstable, family. His father, a highly-placed company executive, maintained discipline through constant beatings. The adolescent Ng was a poor student with no real friends, so he distinguished himself by attacking and beating younger children. At the age of 15 he was caught shoplifting for the first time. He was then sent to an English boarding school, but he was expelled after setting fire to a classroom.

At the age of 18 he moved to the United States, where he attended Notre Dame de Namur University, a small Catholic institution that is located in Belmont, California. He lasted just one semester.

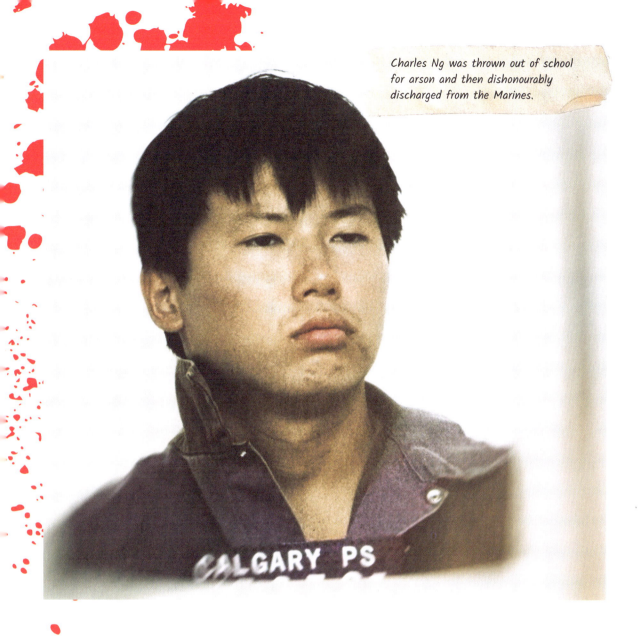

Charles Ng was thrown out of school for arson and then dishonourably discharged from the Marines.

Despite his dismal academic background, Ng was accepted into the United States Marine Corps in 1980. Less than a year later, he was caught stealing various kinds of weapons, including machine guns, from the Hawaiian base at which he was stationed. His attempt to escape added a charge of desertion to his record. After being dishonourably discharged, he was sentenced to 14 years in a military prison, but was released in late 1982.

Ng's bad experience with the Marines was something he shared with Leonard Lake. Born on 29 October 1945 in San Francisco, Lake had not enjoyed anything like Ng's privileged childhood. His parents had separated when he was six years old, which resulted in the Lake children being sent to live with their grandparents. Unlike Ng he had been a fairly good student as a child. He had also pursued some odd hobbies. He kept mice and, when they died, watched with interest as he dissolved their bodies in acid. He also enjoyed taking nude photographs of his sisters, an activity that was encouraged by his grandmother. His favourite book was *The Collector* by John Fowles, a novel about a seemingly mild young man who imprisons an attractive art school student, Miranda Grey, while he tries to make her love him.

LEONARD LAKE AND CHARLES NG

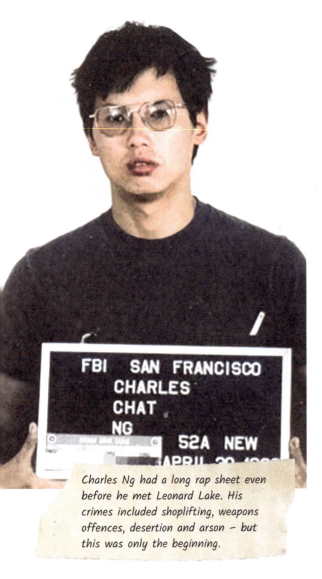

Charles Ng had a long rap sheet even before he met Leonard Lake. His crimes included shoplifting, weapons offences, desertion and arson – but this was only the beginning.

PERSONALITY DISORDER

Lake was 19 when he joined the Marines. He completed two tours of duty in Vietnam as a radar operator, but he was discharged in 1971 after having been diagnosed with schizoid personality disorder. Once more a civilian, he enrolled in San José State University, but he lasted only one semester. Lake's 1975 marriage was equally brief. It ended when his wife learned that he had been making amateur pornographic films. Even worse, he had been starring in them. He remarried in 1981, though his return to marital status was brief. His second wife did not want to act in his pornographic films, most of which featured bondage and sadomasochism. By the time he was arrested on a firearms violation in the following year, Lake had already gone through his second divorce.

It was Lake's second brush with the law. He had already served some time for car theft and he had no intention of returning to prison. Skipping bail, he hid out on an isolated property in Calaveras County, California, that belonged to his wife. It was not long before Lake met Charles Ng. They were both visiting San Francisco's red-light district at the time. The two men immediately recognized each other as kindred spirits. Among other things they shared a common interest in firearms and other weapons, as well as a belief in a coming nuclear holocaust.

Before long, Ng joined Lake in Calaveras County, where he assisted him in setting up 'Operation Miranda', a project that was named after the woman who had been held captive in *The Collector*. Leonard Lake explained the plan in a video he had made of himself in October 1983, shortly before his 38th birthday.

> 'WHAT I WANT IS AN OFF THE SHELF SEX PARTNER. I WANT TO BE ABLE TO USE A WOMAN WHENEVER AND HOWEVER I WANT. AND WHEN I'M TIRED OR BORED I SIMPLY WANT TO PUT HER AWAY.'

To this end, the pair built a bunker in the side of a hill. It was intended as the first of many that would house the pair's sex slaves. The women would be used to repopulate the planet after the expected nuclear war. Crudely constructed, it consisted of a main room that contained power saws and the other tools that were needed for disposing of bodies. There was also a smaller, sparsely-furnished room. Beneath it there was a cramped, windowless cell, which could be accessed through a trapdoor in the floor. On its walls were photographs of the young women that Lake and Ng had abducted, tortured, raped and killed.

The pair had also murdered a number of men and children – usually those who had been with the women when they were captured.

Most of the victims' bodies were burned in a home-made crematorium that had been built beside the bunker. Exactly how many people Ng and Lake killed is unknown, though the number is usually estimated at between 15 and 25. What can be said with more certainty is that Operation Miranda came to an end on 2 June 1985.

Leonard Lake loved animals, but when his pet mice died he dissolved their bodies in acid.

MURDERS AT THE OPERATION MIRANDA BUNKER

- **22 May 1983** – Charles Gunnar
- **July 1983** – Donald Lake
- **25 July 1984** – The Dubs family
- **October 1984** – Randy Johnson
- **12 April 1985** – Michael Carroll
- **After 12 April** – Kathleen Allen
- **19 April 1985** – The Bond family
- **April 1984** – Jeffrey Askren
- **12 July 1984** – Donald Giulietti
- **2 November 1984** – Paul Cosner
- **20 January 1985** – Clifford Parenteau
- **24 February 1985** – Jeff Gerald

On that day, customers at a San Francisco hardware store noticed Ng stealing a bench vice. Police officers caught sight of the former Marine as he was putting the stolen item in the back of a Honda, but he managed to flee on foot. Lake had been sitting at the wheel, so he was easily apprehended. He was taken to the local police station where a quick search uncovered a revolver, complete with silencer.

As the detectives prepared to question their suspect, the driving licence he provided was run through the system. The name on the document, Robin Scott Stapley, was that of a man who had been missing for nearly four months. It was then discovered that the Honda was registered to Paul Cosner, a man who had disappeared in the previous November while delivering the vehicle to a prospective purchaser.

While he was waiting in the interrogation room, Lake asked for a pencil, a sheet of paper and some water. Minutes later, he was found slumped in his chair, barely alive.

He was rushed to hospital, where it was discovered that he had swallowed cyanide pills. He died four days later. The pencil and paper had been used to write one last letter to his second wife, the owner of the Calaveras County property:

LEONARD LAKE AND CHARLES NG

> Dear Lyn,
> I love you. I figure your Freedom is better than all else. Tell Fern I'm sorry. Mom, Patty and all. I'm sorry for all the trouble.
>
> Love,
> Leonard

After Lake's death, investigators from the local sheriff's office visited his isolated mountain home. There was some suspicion that he and Ng had been trading in stolen goods. They had, after all, been advertising used items for sale. One look at the house was enough to make them realize that petty theft was the least of their crimes. The living room ceiling was stained with blood and there were bullet holes here and there. In the master bedroom, the investigators found a collection of lingerie, much of it stained with blood. The mattress on the bed was also stained and electrical cords had been tied to the bedposts.

After searching the grounds, the investigators found ashes, teeth and human bones buried in a long trench. Because the act of cremation had made identification difficult, the authorities relied on other clues. For example, Lake had been trying to sell some furniture that belonged to his neighbours. He explained that the items had been left as payment for a debt when they had moved to Los Angeles. Yet, those same neighbours – Lonnie Bond, his girlfriend Brenda O'Connor and their baby – were nowhere to be found.

An impressive array of expensive video equipment was found in the house. It was traced back to Harvey and Deborah Dubs, a young couple who had disappeared from their San Francisco home in the previous year. Their 16-month-old son was also missing.

Among the victims that the police were able to positively identify was Donald Lake, Leonard's brother.

After two weeks, the police had discovered nine bodies and nearly 18 kg (40 lb) of charred teeth and bones. Though it was painstaking work, which involved dozens of people sifting through tons of soil, some progress had at least been made. The same could not be said about the hunt for Charles Ng. Like his many victims, he seemed to have vanished. Could it be that Ng, too, had taken his own life?

Jim Stenquist, Calaveras County information officer, reveals the secret entrance to the 'Operation Miranda' bunker.

130 CHAMBERS OF HORROR

FUGITIVE

In fact, Ng was very much alive. He had fled some 1,500 km (940 miles) to the north, where he had managed to cross the border into Canada. On 6 July 1985, after he had been on the run for more than a month, he was spotted shoplifting in a downtown Calgary department store. When he was approached by two male security guards, Ng pulled out a revolver and shot one of the men in the hand. Incredibly, the injured guard still managed to overpower the former Marine and keep him restrained until the police arrived.

It did not take the Canadian authorities long to identify Ng, but his extradition created a legal problem. Canada was a country that had abolished capital punishment, so the authorities were reluctant to send Ng back to California, where the death penalty was still in force. That is not to say that Ng was a free man. In December 1985 he was sentenced to four and a half years in prison for shooting the department store security guard. As Ng sat in a Canadian prison, American lawyers fought to have him returned to the United States. One of the arguments was that Canada risked becoming a safe haven for criminals who faced the death penalty at home.

Then on 26 August 1991, the Supreme Court of Canada ruled that Ng could be extradited. Minutes after the ruling, the murderer was on a flight back to the United States. Ng's trial did not begin until October 1998, more than 13 years after his last murder. Eight months later, he was found guilty of the murders of three women, six men and two babies. He was sentenced to death. In 1999, pending appeal, he took up residence on San Quentin Prison's death row.

Charles Ng enters court in Santa Ana, California, in 1985. He attempted to escape to Canada, but was caught in Calgary for shoplifting before being extradited back to the USA.

JOSEF FRITZL

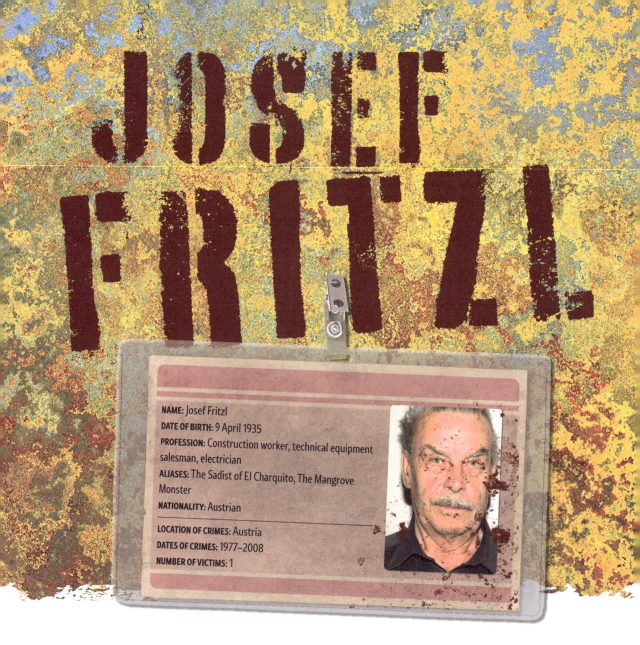

NAME: Josef Fritzl
DATE OF BIRTH: 9 April 1935
PROFESSION: Construction worker, technical equipment salesman, electrician
ALIASES: The Sadist of El Charquito, The Mangrove Monster
NATIONALITY: Austrian
LOCATION OF CRIMES: Austria
DATES OF CRIMES: 1977–2008
NUMBER OF VICTIMS: 1

Josef Fritzl told conflicting stories about his mother Maria. In some, she was 'the best woman in the world', in others she had been a cold, brutal being – almost inhuman. 'She used to beat me, hit me until I was lying in a pool of blood on the floor,' he once claimed. 'I never had a kiss from her.'

Later on, Fritzl claimed, his mother did not mellow with age. Instead, her harsh nature stayed with her, even into old age. When Fritzl was a senior citizen himself, he revealed that Maria's last years were spent in a locked room with a bricked-up window. Fritzl told concerned neighbours that his mother had died, when in reality she had been his captive. In ordinary circumstances, Fritzl's behaviour towards his mother would be shocking, but in the context of his other crimes the incident ranks as little more than a footnote.

DEATHLY PALE

The world knew nothing of Fritzl's crimes until the morning of Saturday 19 April 2008, when he telephoned for an ambulance. Seventeen-year-old Kerstin Fritzl was seriously ill at his home, number 40 Ybbsstrasse in the Austrian town of Amstetten.

The ambulance attendants were puzzled by the condition of their unconscious patient. Her symptoms were like nothing they had ever encountered. Deathly pale and missing many of her teeth,

Fritzl explained Elisabeth's disappearance by saying she had joined a cult.

Kerstin was close to death. She was transported immediately to the local hospital. A few hours later, Josef Fritzl turned up. Describing himself as her grandfather, he presented a letter from Kerstin's mother, Elisabeth:

'Please help her. Kerstin is very scared of strangers. She has never been in a hospital before. I've asked my father for help because he is the only person she knows.'

Josef Fritzl explained Elisabeth had run off to join a religious cult many years before, leaving the child with him. The police were called in as Kerstin lay close to death and a team of investigators began a search for Elisabeth Fritzl. The authorities wanted to question the mother about what they thought might be criminal neglect. Enquiries were made all over Austria and all sorts of databases were checked, yet nothing could be found on Elisabeth that was not at least a few decades old.

TELEVISED APPEAL

At the end of Kerstin's second day in hospital, the doctors made a televised appeal. They were struggling to diagnose Kerstin's condition and they thought that her mother might be able to help them. When Elisabeth failed to contact the hospital the police showed up at 40 Ybbsstrasse. They wanted to take DNA samples

JOSEF FRITZL 133

40 Ybbsstrasse, outwardly a normal house.

from the Fritzls. Josef's wife Rosemarie provided a sample, as did the other children that Elisabeth had previously abandoned. However, Josef himself was far too busy to give the authorities even a few minutes of his time.

One week after Kerstin had been taken to hospital, Rosemarie was surprised to see Elisabeth in her house. Her daughter had been away for nearly 24 years. Elisabeth was accompanied by two children, Stefan and Felix. Rosemarie had not been aware of their existence. Josef explained that their daughter had heard the doctors' appeals and had left the cult she had been with, so that she could see her seriously ill daughter.

When Elisabeth visited the hospital, the police were waiting. They wanted to know where the young woman had been during the previous two decades, and how it was that she had abandoned her children. Elisabeth was taken to the police station, where she was questioned for hours. As midnight approached, Elisabeth revealed that she had not joined a cult and she had not abandoned her children. Instead, she had been imprisoned by her father in the cellar at 40 Ybbsstrasse. Having broken her silence, Elisabeth told the police that she would reveal everything about the last 24 years of her life on condition that she never had to see her father again.

After the stunned investigators had acceded to her wishes, Elisabeth began a two-hour monologue in which she described in considerable detail the ordeal she had endured.

She told the police that her father had lured her into the cellar on 29 August 1984, where she had been sedated with ether and placed in a hidden bunker.

It seemed that the foundations of number 40 Ybbsstrasse were something of a maze. The oldest part of the house dated back to 1890 and numerous modifications had been made in the years that followed, including a 1978 addition that had been constructed by a builder.

For reasons of secrecy, however, Fritzl had built the bunker himself. It could only be reached by going down the cellar stairs, passing through a number of rooms and unlocking a series of eight doors. The final door was hidden behind a large shelving unit.

134 CHAMBERS OF HORROR

Elisabeth Fritzl, who now lives under an assumed name in an Austrian village known as 'Village X'.

The bunker itself consisted of a kitchen, a bathroom, a living area and two bedrooms. There was no source of natural light, and the air was stale and stagnant. The ceiling was very low – it was less than 2 m (6 ft 6 in) high at best. It had not been difficult for Fritzl to construct the bunker. As an electrical engineer, he had always been good with his hands.

GOOD PROVIDER

Born in Amstetten on 9 April 1935, Fritzl had been raised alone by his mother after his father had deserted his small family. Josef Fritzl Snr went on to fight as a Nazi stormtrooper and was killed during World War II. The younger Josef had been a good student with a notable aptitude for technical matters. He had just begun his career with a Linz steel company when he married 17-year-old Rosemarie at the age of 21. The couple had two sons and five daughters together, including the beautiful Elisabeth.

Fritzl was a very good provider, but he was also an unpleasant husband and father. In 1967 he was sentenced to 18 months in prison after having confessed to the rape of a 24-year-old woman. After his release he was employed by a construction firm and later on he travelled throughout Austria as a technical equipment salesman. Until April 2008, the electrical engineer had no further brushes with the law. That is not to say that he led an exemplary life. Among his neighbours he had a reputation as an unfriendly man, one who kept himself to himself and his family away from others. There was talk that he was very firm with his children and that absolute obedience was expected.

No matter how much Fritzl's neighbours gossiped about him, none of them had the faintest conception of what was taking place in his household. In 1977, Fritzl began sexually abusing Elisabeth. She was 11 years old at the time. Although she told no one, not even her close friend Christa Woldrich, it is easy to imagine what a devastating effect it must have had on her.

'I did get the impression that she felt more comfortable at school than at home,' Woldrich told one reporter. 'Sometimes she went quiet when it was time to go home again.'

A police van parked outside the back of the Fritzls' dwelling.

In January 1983, Elisabeth ran away from home, ending up in Vienna. She was then 16 years old. Even though she tried her best to hide, she only managed to remain free for three weeks before the police found her and returned her to her parents.

The authorities calculated that Fritzl was well into the construction of the bunker at this point. Eighteen months after the police had brought the girl back to number 40 Ybbsstrasse, Elisabeth's incarceration began.

Fritzl appeared to be very open about what had happened to his 18-year-old daughter.

He told everyone that she had been a drug-taking problem child who had gone off to join a religious cult. But there was no cult, of course. Fritzl backed up his story by forcing Elisabeth to write a letter in which she told everyone not to search for her because she was now happy.

Elisabeth was alone in the bunker until the birth of her first child. Her only visitor was her father, who would arrive every few days to bring her food. He would then rape her. The nightmare became greater still during Elisabeth's fourth year underground when she became pregnant for the first time, suffering a miscarriage. Elisabeth's second pregnancy led to the birth of Kerstin and Stefan arrived in the following year. There would be seven children in all, including Michael, who died when he was three days old. While Kerstin, Stefan and Felix, the youngest, lived in captivity, Fritzl arranged for the others to be taken care of by Rosemarie.

It had been difficult to explain the babies away. After all, Rosemarie knew nothing of the bunker. Like everyone else, she believed the troubled Elisabeth had achieved some sort of happiness as a member of a fictitious cult. However, Fritzl had already laid the groundwork by portraying Elisabeth as an unstable and irresponsible daughter. All that remained was to smuggle the babies upstairs in the middle of the night and then leave them on the front doorstep with a note from Elisabeth.

In May 1993, nine-month-old Lisa became the first of the grandchildren who would be cared for by Rosemarie. When Monika appeared in the following year, the press took note. 'What kind of mother would do such a thing?' asked one newspaper. After having raised seven of her own children, the neighbours took pity on Rosemarie. However, the senior citizen made no complaints and she proved to be devoted to her grandchildren. All three did well at school and they seemed happy and healthy, despite their incestuous background. Even the unfriendly Fritzl received a certain amount of respect and admiration for helping to raise three young children during the years in which one might rightly expect to take things easy.

For the children in the bunker, life could not have been more different. Kerstin, Stefan and Felix knew they had siblings living in the house above their heads. Indeed, Kerstin and Stefan could remember the babies being taken away.

To add insult to injury, Josef would bring videos that showed Lisa, Monika and Alexander enjoying a lifestyle that was vastly superior to their own.

Despite her suffering, Elisabeth did her best to provide Kerstin, Stefan and Felix with some semblance of a normal upbringing. She gave them regular lessons, in which they learned reading, writing and mathematics. All of the children, whether they were raised in the bunker by Elisabeth or upstairs by Rosemarie, ended up being intelligent, articulate and polite.

BUNKER MENTALITY

Fritzl has never explained why he took Lisa, Monika and Alexander upstairs, while keeping their siblings captive below. One possible explanation might have been lack of space. With a total area of around 35 m^2 (380 ft^2) the bunker was becoming increasingly cramped, particularly when the children grew bigger.

After the birth of Monika in 1993, Fritzl alleviated the problem somewhat by expanding the size of the bunker to 55 m^2 (600 ft^2).

On 27 April 2008, nine days after Fritzl had telephoned for an ambulance, a number of police officers arrived at the house of Josef and Rosemarie Fritzl. Josef Fritzl was taken into custody while Rosemarie and her grandchildren were taken to a psychiatric hospital, where they were reunited with Elisabeth.

On the day after his arrest, Fritzl confessed to keeping Elisabeth captive and fathering her children. He defended his actions by claiming that the sex had been consensual and that Elisabeth's incarceration had been necessary in order to rescue her from 'persons of questionable moral standards'. Elisabeth had refused to obey his rules ever since she had entered puberty, he said.

As Fritzl awaited trial for his crimes he became more and more enraged by the media coverage. Eventually, the electrical engineer released a letter through his lawyer in which he spoke of the kindness he had always shown his family. Fritzl pointed out that he could have killed them, but chose not to.

On 16 March 2009, the first day of his trial, Fritzl was charged with rape, incest, kidnapping, false imprisonment, slavery, grievous assault and the murder of baby Michael. He pleaded guilty to all of the charges with the exception of grievous assault and murder.

'I WAS BORN TO RAPE. I COULD HAVE BEHAVED A LOT WORSE THAN LOCKING UP MY DAUGHTER'.
- JOSEF FRITZL'S PLEA TO THE DEFENCE.

In keeping with the agreement she struck with the police on the day she finally emerged from the bunker, Elisabeth did not appear in court. Instead, the 42-year-old woman's testimony was presented in the form of an 11-hour video recording. The prosecution later revealed that Elisabeth had been watching the proceedings from the visitors' gallery. She had been heavily disguised to avoid being recognized.

The news caused Fritzl to break down. He changed his plea to guilty on all charges, thereby ending the court case. That same day he was sentenced to life imprisonment, with no possibility of parole for 15 years.

A forensic officer emerges from the Fritzls' front door.

GARY HEIDNIK

NAME: Gary Michael Heidnik
DATE OF BIRTH: 22 November 1943
PROFESSION: Psychiatric nurse, investor
ALIASES: Brother Bishop
NATIONALITY: American

LOCATION OF CRIMES: Pennsylvania, USA
DATES OF MURDERS: November 1986–March 1987
NUMBER OF VICTIMS: 2 killed + 4 kidnapped

Ellen Heidnik drank during her pregnancies. She drank a lot. Even at a time when the sight of a pregnant woman holding a wine glass was not unusual, Ellen stood out from the crowd. By the time her first child, Gary, was born – on 22 November 1943 in Eastlake, Ohio – Ellen's alcoholism had already begun to affect her marriage. Two years and one more son later, her husband filed for divorce.

The effects of the split overshadowed Gary's early years, as well as his brother Terry's.

Initially, the two boys stayed with their unstable, unreliable mother, but when she remarried they were sent to live with their father, Michael Heidnik, and his new wife.

MISSHAPEN HEAD

They were very unhappy times for Gary. He disliked his stepmother and he was brutalized by his disciplinarian of a father. He was often punished for wetting his bed and suffered even further when his father deliberately hung the stained sheets out of the second-floor bedroom window for all the neighbours to see. Horrendous as this experience was for Gary, it was nothing compared to the terror he felt when Michael dangled him by his ankles in place of the sheets.

School was no better. Gary was not only taunted for the bedwetting – he was also mocked because of his unusual appearance. As a young child he had fallen out of a tree, which had left him with a slightly misshapen head. Michael made his son's schooldays all

138 CHAMBERS OF HORROR

the worse by painting bull's-eyes on the seat of his trousers, thereby creating a target for the bullies. In spite of all of these drawbacks, Gary excelled in the classroom. He was invariably at the top of his class and his IQ was once measured at 130.

His intelligence, combined with his status as an outcast, might have contributed to his unusual ambitions. While so many of his male classmates dreamed of becoming baseball players and stars of football, 12-year-old Gary's twin aspirations were the achievement of great wealth and a career in the military. He made an early start by entering Virginia's Staunton Military Academy at the age of 14. Once again Gary proved to be an excellent student. However, unlike Barry Goldwater and John Dean, two of the school's illustrious alumni, Gary never graduated from the prestigious school. After two years of study he left the academy, returning to his father's house. He attempted to resume his studies at a couple of different high schools, but he felt that he was learning nothing, so at the age of 18 he dropped out of school and joined the army.

Though he made few friends amongst his comrades, Gary shone in the military. After completing basic training, he was sent to San Antonio in Texas, where he was to become a medical orderly. Now that his military career seemed well and truly on its way, Gary began pursuing his other long-held dream – to become wealthy. He supplemented his pay by making loans with interest to his fellow soldiers. Though his modest business would have been frowned upon by his superiors, Gary was otherwise an exemplary and intelligent military man. In 1962, while at a field hospital in West Germany, he achieved a near-perfect score in his high school equivalency examination.

A few months later it was all over.

In August, Gary began to complain of nausea, dizziness and blurred vision. The doctors who attended him identified two causes – stomach flu and 'schizoid personality disorder'. Before the year was up, he had been shipped back home. He was granted an honourable discharge and a disability pension. With one of his two dreams dashed into smithereens, Gary enrolled at the University of Pennsylvania. His chosen courses – chemistry, history, anthropology and biology – were so diverse in nature that it appeared that he was looking for direction. If so, Gary was unsuccessful. Using his army medical training, he worked for a time at two Philadelphia hospitals, but he proved to be a poor worker.

Gary Heidnik attended the prestigious Staunton Military Academy, but dropped out after two years.

Heidnik shot one of his tenants in the face with an unlicensed gun – yet police declined to investigate further.

Now without work and living on his pension his eccentricities grew, while his personal hygiene declined. Gary found a leather jacket, which he would wear regardless of the weather or the social situation. If he did not want to be disturbed, he would roll up one trouser leg as a signal to others. Then there were the suicide attempts – not just Gary's, but those of his brother and his mother, too. These were so frequent that they could be numbered in the dozens, but only Ellen was successful. In 1970, the four-times married alcoholic took her own life by drinking mercury.

Both Heidnik boys spent years moving in and out of mental institutions. Yet despite his many periods of confinement, Gary managed to begin amassing the wealth he had sought since he was a child. In 1971 he founded his own church, the United Church of the Ministers of God, and he ordained himself as its bishop. Although Gary had just four followers, they included two people who were close to him – his mentally retarded girlfriend and his brother.

OUT OF CONTROL

As a self-anointed minister, Gary began investing in earnest. He bought property and played the stock market, making a great deal of money when Hugh Hefner's Playboy empire went public in 1971. But all of the time he was spinning increasingly out of control. Gary became one of those individuals who is often described as 'known to the police'. There were any number of reasons for his notoriety. In 1976, for example, he used an unlicensed gun to shoot one of his tenants in the face. Incredibly, it was not until 1978 that he first went to jail. But the three- to seven-year sentence had nothing to do with the earlier shooting. Instead, Gary had been found

140 CHAMBERS OF HORROR

guilty of kidnapping, unlawful restraint, false imprisonment, rape, involuntary deviate sexual intercourse and interfering with the custody of a committed person.

All of this had come about because Gary had signed his girlfriend's sister out of a mental institution and had kept her confined to his basement. Not only had he raped the young woman but he had infected her with gonorrhoea. In the middle of what turned out to be four years of incarceration, he handed a prison guard a note explaining that he could no longer speak because Satan had shoved a cookie down his throat. Gary remained silent for over 27 months.

When he was finally released in April 1983, he returned to Philadelphia and resumed his role as a bishop with the United Church of the Ministers of God. Even though Gary's congregation had not grown much, from time to time it included mentally retarded women, whom he would impregnate.

It is hardly surprising that Betty Disto, Gary's first bride, was not immediately aware of his odd behaviour and poor hygiene because the couple had become engaged before they had even laid eyes on one another. The couple had met through a matrimonial service. They had been corresponding for two years when, in September of 1985, Betty flew from her address in the Philippines to the United States. Their October marriage lasted for just three months. Betty could not stand to see her groom in bed with other women, but she had no choice because Gary made her watch. Beaten, raped and threatened, a pregnant Betty fled home with the help of the local Filipino community.

Betty made her escape in the first few days of 1986, but Gary's life really began to fall apart towards the end of that year. On the evening of 26 November 1986, Gary abducted his first victim, a prostitute named Josefina Rivera. It all happened gradually.

She had been standing outside in the cold rain when Gary picked her up in his Cadillac Coupe De Ville. On the way, he stopped at McDonald's and bought her a coffee. She did not object when he took her to his home, a run-down house at 3520 North Marshall Street.

There was something surreal about it all. Gary's house had seen better days, as had the rest of the neighbourhood. Decades earlier, the area had housed working-class German immigrants. The streets had been spotless then, but now they were pockmarked and covered in litter. Drug dealers worked its streets selling crack cocaine and marijuana to passing motorists and poverty was everywhere, yet Gary had a Rolls-Royce in his garage.

The door to his home was like something from a children's movie. When it opened, Josefina noticed that Gary had glued thousands of pennies to the walls of his kitchen. As he led her upstairs to the bedroom, she realized that the hallway had been wallpapered with $5 bills. In many ways, the house was a reflection of its owner. Gary's gold jewellery and Rolex watch contrasted sharply with his worn and stained clothing.

Heidnik's flashy Rolex watch contrasted with his otherwise shabby appearance.

Like the rest of the house, the bedroom was sparsely furnished. There was nothing more than a waterbed, two chairs and a dresser. Gary gave Josefina the money they had agreed upon – $20 – and then he got undressed. The energetic and emotionless sex act was over in a matter of minutes. Josefina had felt a little uneasy about Gary, but what happened next took her by surprise. He grabbed her by the throat and choked her until she blacked out. Brief as it was, her loss of consciousness provided Gary with enough time to handcuff her.

Josefina was ordered to her feet and then she was marched downstairs to the basement. The unfinished room was cold, clammy and filthy, much like the old mattress that he made her sit on, and the floor was concrete, though some of the surface had been removed. After attaching metal clamps and chains to Josefina's ankles, Gary got down to digging the exposed earth.

He talked as he worked, telling the shackled woman that he had fathered four children by four different women, but it had all gone wrong. He had no contact with any of his offspring and yet he really wanted and deserved a family.

And with that bit of information, he raped her.

> 'SOCIETY OWES ME A WIFE AND A BIG FAMILY,' WAS HOW HE PUT IT. 'I WANT TO GET TEN WOMEN AND KEEP THEM HERE AND GET THEM ALL PREGNANT. THEN, WHEN THEY HAVE BABIES, I WANT TO RAISE THOSE CHILDREN HERE TOO. WE'LL BE LIKE ONE BIG HAPPY FAMILY.'

SCREAMING BLUE MURDER

Once she was alone, Josefina tried to escape. After freeing one of her ankles, she managed to prise open one of the basement windows and squeeze through it. Then she was out in the open. She crawled as far as the chain around her other ankle allowed her to and then she screamed at the top of her voice. But in Gary's neighbourhood screams like Josefina's were an everyday thing. The only person who paid any attention to the sound was Gary.

He ran downstairs, grabbed the chain and pulled her back into the basement. The filthy mattress was too good for her now. Dragging her across the cement floor, he threw her into the shallow pit. She was covered over with a sheet of plywood, upon which Gary placed heavy weights.

On her third day of captivity she was joined by a mentally retarded young woman named Sandra Lindsay. The girl seemed to have a very limited understanding of what was happening, so it was easy for Gary to get her to write a short note home.

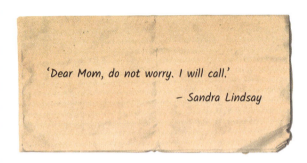

'Dear Mom, do not worry. I will call.'
– Sandra Lindsay

It was the last time Sandra's mother would ever hear from her daughter. Josefina and Sandra spent weeks together. Sometimes they were in the pit and sometimes they were chained to pipes in the basement. They endured repeated rapes, beatings and the ever-present cold.

On 22 December they were joined by 19-year-old Lisa Thomas, a third 'wife'. Gary lured the girl to 3520 North Marshall Street with offers of food and clothing and a trip to Atlantic City. In the end she only got the food and a spiked glass of wine. After she passed out, Gary raped her and then took her down to the basement.

On New Year's Day Gary abducted a fourth woman, but 23-year-old Deborah Dudley was totally unlike his other 'wives'. Ignoring the consequences, she fought back at nearly every opportunity. Her disobedience invariably led to the other three captives being beaten as well, which created disorder and tension within the group.

When Gary began to encourage the women to report on each other, Josefina saw an opportunity to gain Gary's trust. Though she continued to suffer at his hands, Gary came to believe that Josefina actually took pleasure in her circumstance.

Wife number five, 18-year-old Jacqueline Askins, arrived on 18 January. After raping and shackling the girl, Gary surprised his 'wives' with generous helpings of Chinese food and a bottle of champagne. After weeks of bread, water and stale hot dogs, it seemed like the most elaborate feast.

To what did they owe this unexpected treat? It was Josefina's birthday.

Philadelphia police investigate Heidnik's house. They found all manner of horrors lurking within.

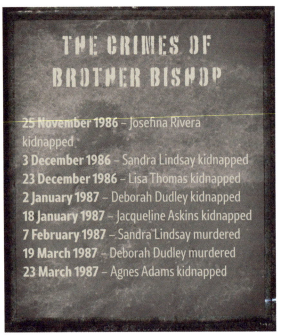

THE CRIMES OF BROTHER BISHOP

25 November 1986 – Josefina Rivera kidnapped
3 December 1986 – Sandra Lindsay kidnapped
23 December 1986 – Lisa Thomas kidnapped
2 January 1987 – Deborah Dudley kidnapped
18 January 1987 – Jacqueline Askins kidnapped
7 February 1987 – Sandra Lindsay murdered
19 March 1987 – Deborah Dudley murdered
23 March 1987 – Agnes Adams kidnapped

of his dogs entered the basement, tail wagging. In its mouth was a bone covered in fresh meat.

Within days, the house and the basement took on a foul odour. Gary was finding it hard to dispose of Sandra's remains. Using his food processor he ground up what he could, feeding the meat to his dogs and his wives – but some body parts were very difficult to deal with.

Sandra's severed head sat in a pot of boiling water for days, while her ribcage was broiled in the oven. The smell spread to some of the adjoining properties, which led to complaints from the neighbours. Although the police investigated they believed Gary's story that he had cooked some bad meat. Meanwhile, the torture endured by the women became even more intense. Gary began poking their ears with a screwdriver, in the belief that deaf wives would be easier to control. He also stripped the insulation from extension cords in order to shock his captives.

WICKED PUNISHMENT

However, any hopes that Gary might be softening were soon dashed. If anything, his abuse escalated. When he caught Sandra Lindsay trying to remove the plywood covering from the pit, she was forced to hang by one of her wrists from a ceiling beam.

She responded by going on hunger strike, but after a few days she appeared incapable of eating. When Gary tried to force food down her throat, she vomited.

By 7 February, Sandra had completely lost consciousness. At this point, Gary finally removed the handcuff that had kept her dangling and she fell into a heap on the concrete floor.

Kicking her into the pit, he assured his other wives that Sandra was faking. It was probably a matter of minutes later that Sandra died.

The women watched as Gary carried Sandra's body upstairs and then they heard the sound of a power saw. Later that day, one

Heidnik disposed of Sandra Lindsay's remains by grinding her up in a food processor.

Heidnik used a screwdriver to damage the ears of his victims, in the belief that they would be easier to control if deaf.

Josefina was not only spared these punishments, she became an administrator. On 18 March she helped with an elaborate method of torture. First of all the pit was flooded and then the other wives, still in chains, were forced into the water. After that the plywood covering was put in place and weighed down. Finally, the bare wire of the extension cord was pushed through a hole, thereby electrocuting the women.

The second of these shocks killed Deborah Dudley. Her death marked a significant change in Gary's relationship with Josefina.

In his eyes, her participation in the torture, combined with Deborah's death, meant she could be blackmailed. That made her trustworthy – or so he thought. For the first time in almost four months she was allowed to leave the basement. She shared Gary's bed, dined with him at restaurants and helped with his grocery shopping. Josefina even went so far as to accompany Gary to the country, where he disposed of Deborah's body.

On 24 March 1987, the day after she helped abduct a new woman, Agnes Adams, Josefina convinced Gary to let her visit her children. She promised him that she would return with yet another 'wife'. Gary dropped her off and waited in the car for her return. But Josefina did not visit her children – she had none. Instead, she sprinted to her boyfriend's apartment, where she poured out her bizarre and almost unbelievable story.

After the police arrived and noted the scarring that had been left by months of wearing heavy chains, they arrested Gary. His surviving 'wives' were rescued when the police converged on 3520 North Marshall Street on the following morning.

Gary's trial began on 20 June 1988. From the start, his defence lawyers attempted to prove that the one-time medical assistant was insane. They called a psychiatrist and a psychologist to the stand, but their efforts were in vain. Ten days later he was found guilty of two counts of first-degree murder, four counts of aggravated assault, five counts of rape, six counts of kidnapping and one count of involuntary deviate sexual intercourse. He was subsequently sentenced to death.

On the evening of 6 July 1999, 11 years after he had been sentenced, Gary Heidnik was executed by lethal injection. It is hardly surprising that his body was not claimed by the other members of his family.

Michael Heidnik, his father, had not seen him since the early 1960s. When he heard about the death sentence he made a brief statement to the press.

'I'm not interested. I don't care. It don't bother me a bit.'

Heidnik is escorted from his cell in prison.

JOHN REGINALD CHRISTIE

NAME: John Reginald Halliday Christie

DATE OF BIRTH: 8 April 1899

PROFESSION: Soldier, postman, driver

ALIASES: The Rillington Place Strangler, the Monster of Rillington Place

NATIONALITY: British

LOCATION OF CRIMES: England, UK

DATES OF MURDERS: 1943–53

NUMBER OF VICTIMS: 6+

Number 10 Rillington Place was located in a cul-de-sac in the Notting Hill area of London. The unremarkable three-storey house was run down and very grey, yet it came to rival 10 Downing Street as Britain's most famous address. While Sir Winston Churchill occupied the prime minister's residence, the other 'Number 10' was home to the most prolific British serial killer of the first half of the 20th century.

John Reginald Halliday Christie seemed such an ordinary man. Born in Halifax, West Yorkshire on 8 April 1899, he was the son of a carpet designer. The childhood he shared with his six siblings was strict and lacking in affection, but was not unusual for the late-Victorian and Edwardian period. For the most part the young Christie kept to himself, concentrating on his studies. His efforts were rewarded when he won a scholarship to Halifax Secondary School at the age of 11, where his favourite subject was mathematics. Though he was a promising student, Christie ended his studies four years later, after taking a job as an assistant film projectionist.

Christie enlisted in the army at the age of 17, shortly after World War I had entered its third year. In April 1918 he was sent to France, where he served as a signal officer. Two months later, he was badly injured in a mustard gas attack. Christie would claim that he had been blinded and rendered mute by the attack. While both claims were false, he spoke in a whisper for the remainder of his life.

Christie's relationships with women were hindered by his impotence. His condition was no secret, earning him the nicknames 'Reggie-No-Dick' and 'Can't-Do-It-Christie'. However, he discovered that he could perform with prostitutes, so he continued to use their services even after his May 1920 marriage to Ethel Waddington. Less than a year into the marriage, the young groom received the first of his many criminal convictions after stealing money orders while he was working for the Royal Mail. His earliest crimes only resulted in probation, but by 1924 he had begun moving in and out of prison.

ASSAULT ON A PROSTITUTE

Two of Christie's many early offences stand out. In May 1929, close to his ninth wedding anniversary, he was sentenced to six months' hard labour for striking a prostitute on the head with a cricket bat. Four years later, he was found guilty of stealing the car of a priest who had befriended him. Christie's early criminal activities seemed to come to a halt with this last crime, for which he served a three-month jail sentence.

Badly injured in a mustard gas attack, Christie spoke in a whisper for the rest of his life.

One of Christie's earlier attacks involved the use of a cricket bat.

As 1938 came to a close the Christies moved into 10 Rillington Place, a run-down building on a street that had seen better days, where they occupied the ground-floor flat and cellar. The house was a throwback to an earlier time. It consisted of three separate flats, one per storey, all without bathrooms. The tenants shared a single toilet, which was outside in the back garden. Nine months after moving in, Christie found a new job. World War II had just begun and the 40-year-old had been accepted into the Special Constabulary. It was a position of authority for which he was clearly unqualified, yet no one had bothered to check his background.

Christie was assigned to the Harrow Road police station. Despite his ongoing sexual dysfunction, he soon began having an affair with one of the women who worked in the canteen. The relationship continued until her husband returned from the war. Shortly afterwards, in August 1943, Christie committed his first murder. Taking advantage of the fact that his wife was out of town, he took Ruth Fuerst, a prostitute, back to the Rillington Place flat, where he strangled her during sex.

> 'I LEFT HER THERE IN THE BEDROOM. AFTER THAT, I BELIEVE I HAD A CUP OF TEA AND WENT TO BED.'

For a brief period of time Christie stored Ruth's body under the floorboards in the front room, eventually burying her in the garden.

Christie abruptly resigned from the Special Constabulary, though he gave no reason. Was it because he felt guilty after committing murder? Or did it have something to do with his affair with the woman in the canteen? Whatever the cause, Christie took another job, this time as a clerk at a radio factory.

His second victim was co-worker Muriel Eady, who met her end in October 1944. First of all Christie lured her to his apartment with the promise of a concoction that would cure her bronchitis and then he persuaded her to inhale from a jar containing Friar's Balsam. The pungent solution hid the smell that was created when Christie inserted a gas pipe into the jar. When Muriel lost consciousness she was raped and then strangled to death.

Five years passed before the next murders took place at 10 Rillington Place. But was Christie responsible? The bodies of Beryl Evans and her one-year-old daughter Geraldine, Christie's upstairs

The house at 10 Rillington Place, home of John Reginald Christie and the remains of his many victims.

A pipe-smoking man carries a parcel of human remains from 10 Rillington Place to a waiting police van.

neighbours, had been found in the garden's washhouse by grieving husband and father Timothy Evans. Or so he claimed. Evans then pointed an accusing finger at Christie. He said that his neighbour had killed his wife while attempting to perform an illegal abortion. Why the abortionist had killed Geraldine was a mystery to the young man.

Under intense questioning, Evans changed his story. This time he told the police that he was the one who had killed his wife and his daughter. He later withdrew his confession. Christie was the true murderer, he declared.

Evans was put on trial for the death of his daughter on 11 January 1950, while his wife's murder was left 'on file'. The prosecution's case relied heavily on the testimony of the crown's key witness – John Reginald Halliday Christie. Evans was found guilty and he was hanged on 9 March.

The next person to be murdered at 10 Rillington Place was Ethel Christie. She had been married to her husband for over 32 years when he strangled her on 14 December 1952. The event kick-started a three-month killing spree, during which three more women were murdered – Kathleen Maloney, Rita Nelson and

Christie covers his face as he appears at court on 4 April 1953.

THE MURDERS AT 10 RILLINGTON PLACE

24 August 1943 – Ruth Fuerst
7 October 1944 – Muriel Eady
8 November 1949 – Beryl Evans
8 November 1949 – Geraldine Evans
14 December 1952 – Ethel Christie
19 January 1953 – Rita Nelson
February 1953 – Kathleen Maloney
6 March 1953 – Hectorina Maclennan

Hectorina Maclennan. In all three cases Christie used gas to make each of his victims drowsy before raping them. He then strangled them with a piece of rope.

Christie kept the three bodies in his flat, hiding them in a kitchen alcove. From time to time, he would commit acts of necrophilia. He was very nearly exposed when one of his fellow tenants stole some produce from a local grocer and was chased back to 10 Rillington Place. After the man was arrested, a police inspector stood chatting to Christie:

'I said to him, "What a rotten smell there is in your house, Christie." And he said to me, "It's all those blooming tenants upstairs." I didn't realize at that time that I was standing in the front room with his mouldering wife underneath the floorboards where we were standing.'

Now 51 years old, Christie was unemployed and living off what he had taken from Ethel's bank account. He had even gone so far as to pawn her wedding ring and her few pieces of jewellery.

On 20 March he was desperate for cash, so he sublet his flat for roughly £8 a week and walked out of 10 Rillington Place for the last time. Though Christie had made little attempt to hide the bodies of his three final victims, four days passed before they were discovered.

While the police were investigating the property they found the bodies that Christie had buried in the garden, along with a Gold Leaf tobacco tin containing the pubic hair that he had clipped from his victims.

After a six-day manhunt, Christie was spotted on an embankment near Putney Bridge. When he was arrested, his only possessions were a few coins and some old newspaper clippings about Timothy Evans.

TERRIBLE CONFESSION

Christie admitted killing seven women, including Beryl Evans, but he never confessed to the murder of Geraldine Evans. In the end he was tried for only one murder, that of his wife Ethel. Standing in the very courtroom in which Timothy Evans had been sentenced to death, Christie pleaded insanity. However, the jury was not convinced and he was found guilty.

By the time he was hanged on 15 July 1953, plans were already in motion to erase 10 Rillington Place from the public memory. The house would remain standing, but the name of the cul-de-sac, with all of its hideous associations, would soon be changed to Ruston Close. In 1971, 18 years after the final murder, the squalid building was pulled down as part of a large-scale redevelopment of the area. Today, no building stands on the land that was once occupied by 10 Rillington Place.

ROBERT BERDELLA

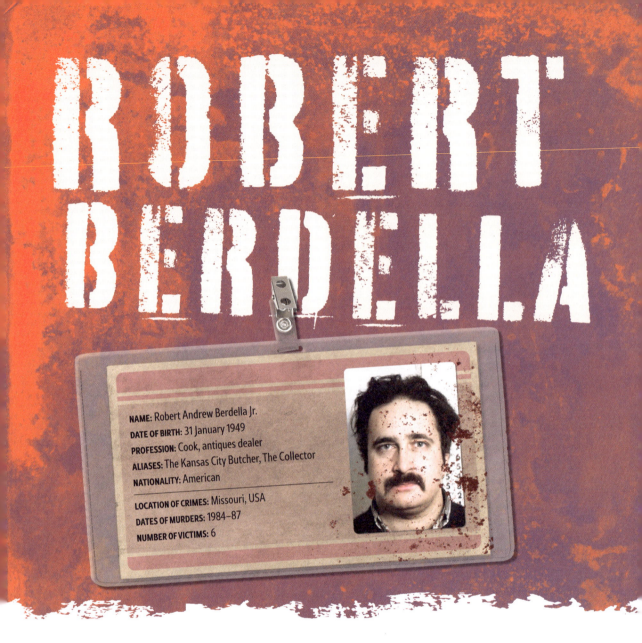

NAME: Robert Andrew Berdella Jr.
DATE OF BIRTH: 31 January 1949
PROFESSION: Cook, antiques dealer
ALIASES: The Kansas City Butcher, The Collector
NATIONALITY: American
LOCATION OF CRIMES: Missouri, USA
DATES OF MURDERS: 1984–87
NUMBER OF VICTIMS: 6

Robert ('Bob') Berdella told everybody about his time at the Kansas City Art Institute. It had been back in 1967, just as the Summer of Love was ending. He was 18 then, a young gay man who was away from his Ohio home for the first time. Berdella enjoyed his time at KCAI – he'd always been a good student – and he hoped that he would one day join the faculty as a professor. But he was to be disappointed. Although he had a significant talent it never quite matched up to his aspirations, so he became a chef. It was not the best-paying job, so he supplemented his income by dealing in drugs on the side. He was twice arrested for possession, but he escaped a jail sentence on each occasion.

Berdella never left Kansas City. Indeed, he put down roots by purchasing a house at 4315 Charlotte Street. It was quite large for an unattached man living alone, but Berdella fancied himself as something of a collector. Books, art and anything else that took his fancy were gathered up and crammed into his three-storey woodframe house. Most of what he collected, however, was simply junk. His house became increasingly cluttered and when he stopped cleaning up after his dogs it began to stink.

In view of the insanitary conditions at home, it was just as well that Berdella gave up being a chef. He opened a shop, Bob's Bizarre Bazaar, in which he sold drug paraphernalia, folk art, lava

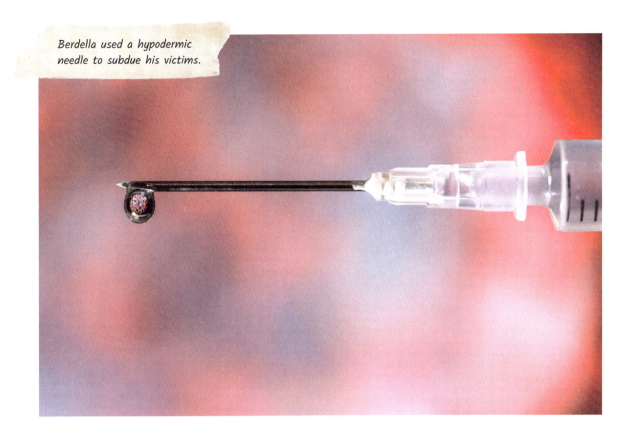

Berdella used a hypodermic needle to subdue his victims.

lamps and occult items. The people on Charlotte Street saw him as a good neighbour, though they weren't too happy about the declining state of his house. It was clear that Berdella was not interested in maintaining his property. On the other hand, he appeared to be keen on gardening. He was always working in his back yard, often after dark.

Berdella always seemed ready to give something back to the community. He was an active participant in the local neighbourhood watch scheme and he was willing to open his doors to troubled young men who had nowhere to stay. These acts of charity attracted some unwanted attention in 1985, when police investigators contacted Berdella concerning two missing men.

The first of these was Jerry Howell, who was just 19 years old when he vanished on 5 July 1984. The other missing man was 25-year-old James Ferris, who had gone missing on 26 September 1985. Both men had been seen in Berdella's company. How did the investigators know this? They had been told by a third young man, Todd Stoops. Although Berdella admitted that he knew the two missing men, he denied being involved in their disappearances. The Kansas City Police Department kept Berdella under surveillance for a time, before moving on to other investigations.

Almost a year later, in June 1986, Todd Stoops disappeared too.

On the evening of 29 March 1988, Berdella was driving through a part of Kansas City that was known for male prostitutes when he spotted a good-looking 22-year-old named Chris Bryson.

It was all too easy to get the young, married man into his brown Toyota Tercel. All he needed to do was pass on an invitation to a 'party'. In fact, it seemed as if the party had already begun. As he drove to his Charlotte Street home, Berdella drank one beer after another.

INJECTED IN THE NECK

Bryson was not put off by the smell or the junk inside Berdella's home, nor was he frightened of the overweight man who had picked him up. When Berdella suggested that they should go upstairs to get away from his three chow chow dogs, Bryson agreed. As Bryson reached the top landing, he was struck on the back of his head. Berdella then jabbed a hypodermic needle into his neck and he slumped down. Bryson had seconds to reconsider his host before losing consciousness.

DRUGGED AND GAGGED

Berdella dragged his latest catch into the bedroom and stripped off his clothing. Over the next few hours he played around with the unconscious man, taking photographs all the while. Berdella was always careful to document his activities with his victims. When Bryson came round he found himself tied up in spread-eagle fashion, with a pillowcase over his head. When it was removed, the captive man knew from his blurred vision that he had been drugged. Roughly seven hours had passed since Berdella had knocked him out. Though he was gagged Bryson did his best to communicate, but his unintelligible pleas for mercy had the opposite effect on his captor.

Then Berdella began to torture the young man. For whatever sick reason, he concentrated his violence on Bryson's eyes, poking them with his fingers and applying an unknown liquid that caused a stinging sensation. He then sat on his sex slave, before hitting the young man's bound hands with an iron bar. Not content with that, he attached wires to Bryson's genitals and thighs and then ran an electric current through them. After a few more photographs, Berdella gave Bryson another two injections.

It was when the young man regained consciousness for a second time that his captor explained his situation to him. Bryson was told that he was now Berdella's sex toy and his punishments were designed to reinforce the fact. Should Bryson refuse to accept his new position in life, his suffering would only worsen. In fact, he might 'end up in the trash', like the others before him. Bryson did his best to follow Berdella's wishes but the torture continued, despite his subservience. He endured electric shocks and rape and at one point Berdella injected drain cleaner into his throat.

All the while, the captive man was looking for an opportunity to escape. But was escape possible? Berdella made a point of showing him pictures of his discarded sex toys: the men in the photographs appeared to be dead. Although little is known about what happened to Berdella's other captives, Chris Bryson's experiences are well documented.

The reason is quite simple: he lived to tell the world about his ordeal. On 4 April 1988, five days into Bryson's nightmare, Berdella made a mistake that would ultimately cost him his freedom. Before leaving 4315 Charlotte Street that day he made certain to tie Bryson up as usual. But this time he altered his routine by binding his victim's hands in front of him, instead of tying them to the bed. Fortunately, Bryson was clear-headed enough to pick up some

Chris Bryson eventually escaped wearing nothing but a dog collar and leash. It took some time before he was able to articulate what had happened to him.

matches, light them and then methodically burn through the ropes that secured his wrists.

When he had managed to free himself, Bryson rushed for the open window and jumped through it. He fell two storeys to the ground. Wearing nothing but a dog collar and a leash, he then started running. Terrified and disorientated, Bryson acted very much like an escaped animal. He sprinted through Berdella's neighbourhood without seeking help. It was obvious that he had no destination in mind. He just wanted to run and keep running.

Bryson's headlong progress was halted when he was cornered by two police cars. After noting the collar and leash, the officers in attendance thought he had been a willing participant in a sex game that had gone wrong. At first, Bryson could not tell them otherwise because the mental and physical torture had rendered him barely capable of speech. Eventually, he was able to identify himself and communicate just some of the horrors he had endured.

Bryson was in the hospital when Berdella returned home, but by then the police had a good description of him – and they had his address. The overweight 39-year-old was arrested outside his home on a charge of sexual assault. Defiant to the end, he did not allow the investigators to enter his Charlotte Street house, so they were forced to wait for a search warrant. There was one other obstacle: Berdella's chow chows. When the warrant came through, the police officers were accompanied by animal control specialists.

INCRIMINATING PHOTOGRAPHS

After the dogs had been led away, the detectives moved to the second floor where they discovered the room in which Bryson had been held. Its contents were much as the victimized man had described. They found the burned rope, the syringes and the sinister electrical device that had been used to administer shocks. Moving to the next room, the investigators found a box of photographs. Some were of Bryson, but the remainder featured other victims. All of the men had been bound and gagged and they were obviously in distress.

Even so, the police officers still entertained the suspicion that Berdella's victims had been his willing lovers. Any such thoughts quickly vanished when they entered the third upstairs room, which was the master bedroom. It contained two skulls, two envelopes full of teeth and Berdella's detailed records of the torture he had meted out to each victim. The more the authorities looked, the more they turned up. In one bedroom closet they discovered a bag filled with

Berdella took hundreds of photographs of his crimes.

human vertebrae. There was also a wallet that had belonged to a man who had been reported missing.

Berdella was arraigned on the day of his arrest. The first charges against him were confined to the offences that he had committed against Chris Bryson. There was one count of felonious restraint and another of first-degree assault, followed by seven counts of sodomy. By this time, however, the investigators were sure that the shop owner had committed far more serious crimes in the past.

A mechanical digger was taken to the yard in which Berdella had done his night-time gardening. The machine's shovel only had to enter the soft earth twice before it came up with a human skull.

The investigation was not limited to Berdella's house. Detectives combed the streets worked by male prostitutes, looking for anyone who would talk. They soon discovered that Berdella had something of a reputation. In fact, he was considered to be dangerous. After shuffling through hundreds of photographs Berdella had taken, the police officers identified roughly 20 men. However, it was nearly impossible to establish just how many people had been murdered by the former chef.

Meanwhile, the forensic examiners were beginning to come up with some names. One of the skulls in Berdella's bedroom was found to belong to Robert Sheldon, an 18-year-old who had disappeared in April 1985. The skull that had been dug up in Berdella's garden belonged to 20-year-old Larry Pearson, who had been missing since 9 July 1987.

Armed with Berdella's photographs, and a 58-page journal in which he had detailed his crimes, the prosecutors began to lay further charges against the degenerate sex offender. As they did so, the suspect surprised both the police and the prosecutors by offering a full confession in exchange for a life sentence. With the threat of the death penalty out of the way he had nothing to lose. On 13 December 1988 he began the first of what would be three days of testimony.

Berdella told the hearing that his first victim had been Jerry Howell, whose disappearance had been investigated three years earlier. The murderer said that his physical relationship with Howell had soured when he had refused to pay back money he owed. In retaliation, Berdella tortured Howell before finally killing him. The next thing was to dispose of the corpse. Before he dismembered the body, he hung it upside down so the blood would drain from it. The sight excited him so much that he felt the need to take photographs. Eventually he cut the corpse up, using kitchen knives and a chainsaw. He then placed the pieces into a number of plastic bags, in time for the weekly refuse collection.

Berdella's second victim was Robert Sheldon, an 18-year-old who had stayed at the Charlotte Street house on several occasions. Sheldon's ordeal began on 19 April 1985, when he was subjected to a torture regime that was similar to that which had been meted out to Howell. Berdella admitted that he had intended to keep the teenager for a significant length of time. To this end, he injected Drano (a drain-cleaning product) into Sheldon's left eyeball, thinking that blindness would make the young man even more subservient. And yet Berdella killed Sheldon after only four days because he feared that his captive might be discovered by another visitor.

Berdella disposed of the teenager's body by cutting it up in his bath. He put the remains out with the rubbish – except for the head,

Berdella cut up the bodies of his victims with a chainsaw before sending them out in plastic bags for the weekly refuse collection.

158 CHAMBERS OF HORROR

The authorities dug deep: the skull in the garden belonged to 20-year-old Larry Pearson.

which he buried in his garden.

The murderer's experiments with electrocution began two months later when he claimed his third victim, Mark Wallace. After only a few days, the 20-year-old man was killed, dismembered and put out on the kerb for collection by the dustmen.

TERRIBLE DEATHS

Berdella's fourth victim, Walter Ferris, signed his own death warrant in September 1985 when he made the mistake of asking the shop owner whether he could stay at his house for a while. Berdella claimed that his death was an accident, the result of a lethal combination of drugs, and yet there was evidence of torture.

Todd Stoops, the young man who had informed the police about Berdella, was the next person to die. He had been advised to keep his distance from the suspect, but he had not listened. Berdella took Stoops captive on 17 June 1986 and he died two weeks later, perhaps because of the injuries he suffered when Berdella pushed his fist up the young man's rectum.

More than a year passed before Berdella killed again. Larry Pearson, a 20-year-old male prostitute, was the last victim to die. More submissive than the others, he became Berdella's sex toy for about six weeks. Then quite unexpectedly he began to fight back, so he was killed.

On 19 December 1988 Berdella appeared in court. He pleaded guilty to one count of first-degree murder and four counts of second-degree murder. Having fulfilled his part of the deal with the state he would be spared the death penalty.

Although Bob Berdella would spend the rest of his life in prison, his sentence would be a short one. Less than four years later, on 8 October 1992, he died of a heart attack.

CHAPTER 5

ANGELS OF DEATH

Angels of death are some of the most disturbing of all serial killers. These are the murderers who, on the face of it, seem to be the carers in our society: housewives, grandmothers, nurses, doctors – in short, pillars of the community. They are well-respected family men and women who spend their lives taking care of others. They seem such unlikely perpetrators of murder that their evil crimes often go undetected for years, leaving them to kill dozens, even hundreds, of victims.

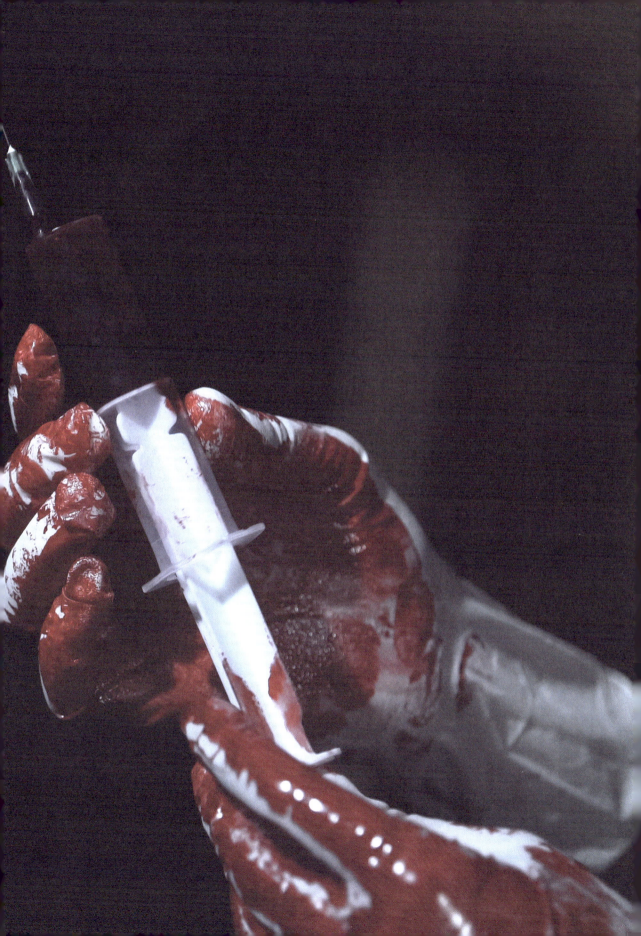

HAROLD SHIPMAN

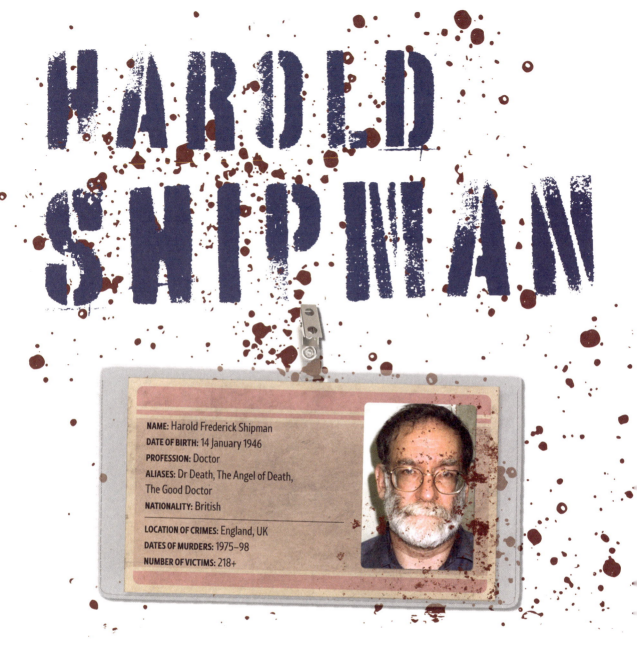

NAME: Harold Frederick Shipman
DATE OF BIRTH: 14 January 1946
PROFESSION: Doctor
ALIASES: Dr Death, The Angel of Death, The Good Doctor
NATIONALITY: British

LOCATION OF CRIMES: England, UK
DATES OF MURDERS: 1975–98
NUMBER OF VICTIMS: 218+

With a total of **over 200** suspected murders to his name, Harold Shipman is the most prolific serial killer of modern times. His grisly tally of victims puts him well ahead of Pedro Lopez, the 'monster of the Andes', who was convicted of 57 murders in 1980. (Lopez claimed to have killed many more, but the exact number of deaths was never verified.) Until Shipman's crimes came to light, Lopez had the dubious distinction of topping the serial killer league; at present, however, it is a British family doctor, rather than a penniless Colombian vagrant, who has become the world's number one murderer.

MOTHER'S FAVOURITE

The sorry tale begins in 1946, when Harold Frederick Shipman was born into a working-class family in Nottingham. Known as Fred, the boy had an unusual childhood. He had a brother and sister, but it was clear that he was his mother's favourite. She felt that Fred was destined for great things, and taught him that he was superior to his contemporaries, even though he was not especially clever and had to work hard to achieve academic success. During his schooldays, he formed few friendships with other children, a situation that was exacerbated when his mother became seriously ill with lung

Harold Shipman appeared to be a good man to his neighbours, though his colleagues glimpsed a darker side lurking beneath his pleasant exterior.

cancer. The young Shipman took on the role of carer to his mother, spending time with her after school waiting for visits from the family doctor, who would inject her with morphine to relieve her from pain. It is possible that the stress of this experience during his formative years may have pushed him into mental illness, causing him to re-enact the role of carer and doctor in the macabre fashion that he later did.

By the time Shipman was 17, his mother had died of cancer, after a long and painful illness. He enrolled at medical school, despite having to resit his entry exams. Although he was good at sport, he made little effort to make friends. However, at this time he met and married his future wife Primrose; the pair went on to have four children, as Shipman began his career as a doctor in general practice. To many, he seemed kind and pleasant, but colleagues complained of his superior attitude and rudeness. Then he began to suffer from blackouts, which he attributed to epilepsy. However, disturbing evidence emerged that he was in fact taking large amounts of pethidine, on the pretext of prescribing the drug to patients. He was dismissed from the practice but, surprisingly, within two years he was once again working as a doctor, this time in a different town.

PILLAR OF THE COMMUNITY

In his new job, the hard-working Shipman soon earned the respect of his colleagues and patients. However, it was during his time at Hyde, over a 24-year period, that he is estimated to have killed at least 236 patients. His status as a pillar of the community, not to mention his kindly bedside manner, for many years masked the fact that the death toll among Shipman's patients was astoundingly high.

Over the years a number of people, including relatives of the deceased and local undertakers, had raised concerns about the deaths of Shipman's patients. His victims always died suddenly, often with no previous record of terminal illness; and they were usually found sitting in a chair, fully clothed, rather than in bed. The police had been alerted and had examined the doctor's records, but nothing was found. It later became clear that Shipman had falsified patient records, but at this stage the doctor's calm air of authority was still protecting him against closer scrutiny.

Then Shipman made a fatal mistake. In 1998 Kathleen Grundy, a healthy, active 81-year-old ex-mayor with a reputation for community service, died suddenly at home. Shipman was called and pronounced her dead; he also said that a post-mortem was

Harold Shipman worked in Hyde, Manchester for 24 years, in which time he killed hundreds of his patients.

unnecessary, since he had paid her a visit shortly before her death. When her funeral was over, her daughter Angela Woodruff received a badly typed copy of Mrs Grundy's will leaving Shipman a large sum of money. A solicitor herself, Mrs Woodruff knew immediately that this was a fake. She contacted the police, who took the unusual step of exhuming Mrs Grundy's body. They found that she had been administered a lethal dose of morphine.

Surprisingly, in murdering Mrs Grundy, Shipman had made little effort to cover his tracks: either to forge the will carefully or to kill his victim with a less easily traceable drug. Whether this was through sheer arrogance and stupidity, or through a latent desire to be discovered, no one knows. However, once the true nature of Mrs Grundy's death was uncovered, more graves were opened, and more murders came to light.

During his trial, Shipman showed no remorse for the 15 murders he was accused of. (There were known to be others, but

Shipman was imprisoned at HMP Wakefield, where he committed suicide four years after his conviction.

these alone were more than enough to ensure a life sentence.) He was contemptuous of the police and the court, and continued to protest his innocence to the end. He was convicted of the murders and imprisoned. Four years later, without warning, he hanged himself in his prison cell.

Today, the case of Harold Shipman remains mystifying: there was no sexual motive in his killings and, until the end, no profit motive. His murders did not fit the usual pattern of a serial killer. In most cases, his victims seem to have died in comfort, at peace. It may be, as several commentators have pointed out, that he enjoyed the sense of having control over life and death, and that over the years he became addicted to this sense of power.

What is clear is that, in finally taking his own life, Harold Shipman ensured ultimate control: no one would ever fully understand why he did what he did.

DONALD HARVEY

NAME: Donald Harvey
DATE OF BIRTH: 15 April 1952
PROFESSION: Hospital orderly
ALIASES: Angel of Death
NATIONALITY: American
LOCATION OF CRIMES: Ohio and Kentucky, USA
DATES OF MURDERS: 1970–87
NUMBER OF VICTIMS: 87

Claiming some 87 victims, Donald Harvey is possibly America's most prolific serial killer. Working as a hospital orderly, he murdered patients in what he claimed were mercy killings. However, he also let his murderous ways spill out into his personal life.

On the surface there was little clue in his early life that Harvey would turn out a serial killer. His mother said that he had 'always been a good boy' and the principal of his elementary school said: 'He was always clean and well dressed with his hair trimmed. He was a happy child, very sociable and well-liked by the other children. He was a handsome boy with big brown eyes and dark curly hair… he always had a smile for me. There was never any indication of any abnormality.'

However, it appears that his parents had an abusive relationship. His father dropped him on his head when he was just six months old, before the soft spot had closed. He suffered another head injury at the age of five when he fell off the running board of a truck. Although he did not lose consciousness, there was a cut 10–13 cm (4–5 in) long on the back of his head.

From the age of four he was sexually abused by his Uncle Wayne. A neighbour also sexually abused him, but Harvey did not mind this as the old man gave him money.

At high school, his classmates saw him as a teachers' pet who would rather have his nose stuck in a book than play sports. He did well academically, initially. But learning came too easily. He

168 ANGELS OF DEATH

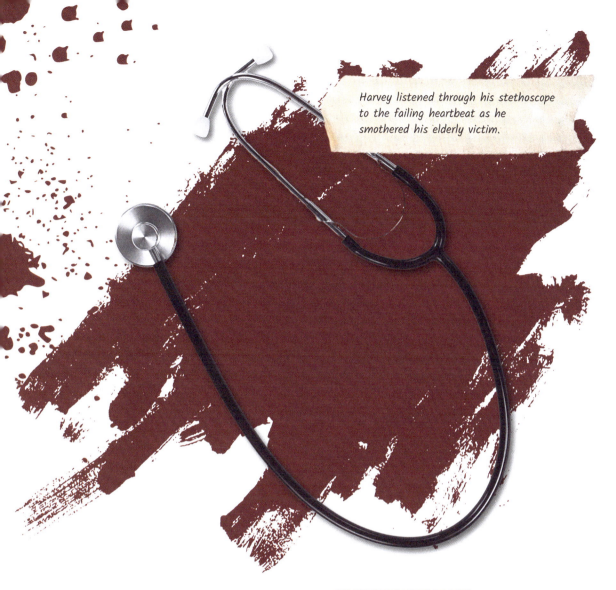

Harvey listened through his stethoscope to the failing heartbeat as he smothered his elderly victim.

grew bored and dropped out. He had his first consensual sexual encounter when he was 16. The following year he began an on-off sexual relationship with James Peluso that lasted for 15 years.

With little direction in life, Harvey left Booneville, Kentucky, and moved to Cincinnati, where he got a job in a factory. In 1970, he was laid off. His mother asked him to visit his ailing grandfather who was in Marymount Hospital in London, Kentucky. Spending time there, he got to know the staff.

One of them asked Harvey if he wanted a job as an orderly. Unemployed at the time, he jumped at the chance. Though he had no medical training, his duties included passing out medication, inserting catheters and changing bedpans. The job meant he spent time alone with patients. Around that period, he claimed he was raped by his roommate.

AN ANGRY YOUNG MAN

While Harvey made out that he was a mercy killer, his first murder was motivated by anger. He later told Dan Horn of the *Cincinnati Post* that when he went to check on 88-year-old stroke victim Logan Evans in his private room, the patient rubbed faeces in his face. Harvey lost control.

'THE NEXT THING I KNEW, I'D SMOTHERED HIM,' HE SAID. 'IT WAS LIKE IT WAS THE LAST STRAW. I JUST LOST IT. I WENT IN TO HELP THE MAN AND HE WANTS TO RUB THAT IN MY FACE.'

Harvey put a sheet of blue plastic and a pillow over the old man's face and listened to his heartbeat with a stethoscope until he was dead. He disposed of the plastic and cleaned him up, dressing Evans in a fresh hospital gown. Then he had a shower before notifying the nurse on duty of Evans' death. Harvey had no fear of getting caught.

'No one ever questioned it,' he said.

The following day he said he accidentally killed 69-year-old James Tyree when he used the wrong-sized catheter on him. When Tyree yelled at him to take it out, Harvey silenced him with the heel of his hand. Tyree then vomited blood and died.

Three weeks later came the first of what could be considered mercy killings. Forty-two-year-old Elizabeth Wyatt told him she wanted to die, so he turned down her oxygen supply. Four hours later, a nurse found her dead.

The following month, he killed 43-year-old Eugene McQueen by turning him on his stomach when he knew he wasn't supposed to. McQueen drowned in his own fluids. Harvey told the nurse merely that McQueen looked bad and she told him to continue with his duties. Consequently, Harvey gave McQueen a bath even though he was already dead. For as long as he worked at Marymount, the staff teased Harvey for bathing a dead man.

He accidently killed 82-year-old Harvey Williams when a gas tank proved faulty. But the next death at his hands was premeditated murder. Eighty-one-year-old Ben Gilbert knocked him out with a bedpan and poured its contents over him, saying that he thought Harvey was a burglar. Harvey retaliated by catheterizing Gilbert with a female-sized 20-gauge catheter instead of the smaller 18-gauge used for men. He then straightened out a coat hanger and shoved the wire through the catheter, puncturing Gilbert's bladder and bowel. Gilbert went into shock and fell into a coma. Harvey disposed of the wire and replaced the 20-gauge catheter with an 18-gauge. Ben Gilbert died four days later.

Harvey began a seven-month relationship with Vernon Midden, a married man who had children. He was an undertaker who taught Harvey the tricks of the trade and introduced him to the occult. When the relationship went sour the following January, Harvey fantasized about embalming him alive.

KILLING AS AN ACT OF KINDNESS?

Maude Nichols had been so neglected that her bedsores crawled with maggots. When she arrived at Marymount, Harvey fixed her up with a faulty oxygen tank. He simply neglected to turn on the oxygen for 58-year-old William Bowling, who had difficulty breathing and subsequently died of a heart attack.

A faulty oxygen tank also did for 63-year-old Viola Reed Wyan after his attempt to smother her was interrupted. She had leukaemia and Harvey complained that she smelt bad. Ninety-one-year-old Margaret Harrison was despatched with an overdose of Demerol, morphine and codeine that was intended for another patient.

Harvey decided that 80-year-old Sam Carroll had suffered enough and he was given a faulty oxygen tank. Maggie Rawlins was smothered with a plastic bag. Both 62-year-old Silas Butner and 68-year-old John V. Combs were killed with faulty oxygen tanks after attempts to smother them had failed. Ninety-year-old Milton Bryant Sasser was killed with an overdose of morphine which Harvey had stolen from the nurse's station. Harvey tried to dispose of the syringe by flushing it down the lavatory, where it was found by a maintenance man. Harvey left Marymount Hospital soon after. He was still only 18.

Harvey then had his first heterosexual encounter. He got drunk

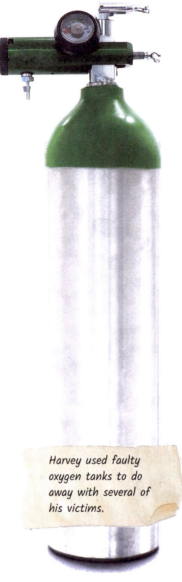

Harvey used faulty oxygen tanks to do away with several of his victims.

170 ANGELS OF DEATH

Donald Harvey suffered a couple of serious head injuries when he was young. He was also sexually abused by his Uncle Wayne.

with the daughter of the family he was staying with and they ended up naked. Nine months later she had a child, naming Harvey as the father, though he rejected any responsibility.

Depressed, Harvey tried to kill himself by setting fire to the bathroom of an empty apartment. He was arrested and fined $50. Then he was arrested on suspicion of burglary, though the police really wanted to question him about his involvement with the occult. During the interview, he admitted killing 15 people at Marymount Hospital, but they did not believe him.

He briefly enlisted in the US Air Force, but was discharged after trying to commit suicide. A further suicide attempt landed him in a Veterans' Administration Hospital after his parents would not take him in.

In 1972, he started work at the Cardinal Hill Convalescent Hospital in Lexington, Kentucky. It is not thought he killed anyone there. For ten months he lived with Russell Addison. This was followed by a five-year relationship with Ken Estes.

In September 1975, he became a nursing assistant at the VA Hospital in Lexington. He tampered with the oxygen supply for Joseph Harris, possibly resulting in his death. Harvey also claimed he had a hand in the deaths of James Twitty, James Ritter, Harry Rhodes and Sterling Moore.

To be initiated into the local occult group, Harvey had to hook up with a woman, so they could then swap partners with another couple. This resulted in the conception of another child, though Harvey denied any responsibility once again. He also acquired a spirit guide named Duncan, a doctor during his lifetime, who now directed him to kill from beyond the grave.

POISONOUS RELATIONSHIP

In 1980, Harvey began dating Doug Hill. When they fell out, Harvey attempted to poison him by putting arsenic in his ice cream. In August, he moved in with Carl Hoeweler. When he found Carl was fooling around with other men, he put small doses of arsenic in his food to prevent him going out. Fearing that Carl's 'fag hag' friend Diane Alexander was trying to split them up, he gave her hepatitis-B serum stolen from the hospital. He also tried unsuccessfully to infect her with AIDS.

His 63-year-old neighbour Helen Metzger was also considered a threat and murdered with arsenic in her food, though Harvey contended he did not mean to give her a lethal dose. Her family got sick from leftovers served at the funeral. Carl's 82-year-old father Henry was also despatched by arsenic. Carl's brother-in-law Howard Vetter was killed accidentally, Harvey claimed, when he left wood alcohol in a vodka bottle. Harvey also murdered another neighbour, Edward Wilson, who he thought was a threat to his relationship with Carl Hoeweler. Wilson was despatched with arsenic in his Pepto-Bismol bottle.

Harvey killed Hiram Profitt accidentally, giving him the wrong dose of heparin. Former boyfriend James Peluso, then 65, asked Harvey to help him out if ever he could not take care of himself. Harvey put arsenic in his daiquiri.

After he joined the neo-Nazi National Socialist Party, Harvey was fired from the VA Hospital in 1985 for carrying a gun in his gym bag. Body parts which he intended to use in occult practices were also found. The following year, he started a new job at Daniel Drake Memorial Hospital in Cincinnati.

After six weeks, he smothered 65-year-old Nathan J. Watson with a bin bag after several thwarted attempts. Watson was semi-comatose and was fed through a gastric tube and Harvey said he didn't think anyone should live that way. He also believed Watson to have been a rapist.

Four days later, 64-year-old Leon Nelson was despatched the same way. A week after that 81-year-old Virgil Weddle was killed with rat poison. Cookies stolen from him were used in rites for Duncan. Rat poison was also used to kill Lawrence Berndsen the next day.

Harvey put cyanide in 65-year-old Doris Nally's apple juice. Sixty-three-year-old Edward Schreibesis got arsenic in his soup, though arsenic failed to kill Willie Johnson. Eighty-year-old Robert Crockett succumbed to cyanide in his IV. Sixty-one-year-old Donald Barney had cyanide injected in his buttocks, while 65-year-old James T. Wood was given cyanide in his gastric tube. Eighty-five-year-old Ernst C. Frey got arsenic the same way.

Eighty-five-year-old Milton Canter got cyanide in a nasal tube. Seventy-four-year-old Roger Evans ingested it in his gastric tube. Sixty-four-year-old Clayborn Kendrick got it the same way. More cyanide was injected into his testes.

Cyanide was given to 86-year-old Albert Buehlmann in a cup of water and to 85-year-old William Collins in orange juice. Seventy-eight-year-old Henry Cody had it fed through his gastric tube.

Following his break-up with Carl, Harvey was treated for depression and tried to kill himself by driving off a mountain road, injuring his head. Sixty-five-year-old Mose Thompson and 72-year-old Odas Day were despatched with solutions of cyanide, while 67-year-old Cleo Fish got it in her cranberry juice. Two other patients were given arsenic but survived, while 47-year-old Leo Parker succumbed to cyanide in his feed bag.

Eighty-year-old Margaret Kuckro got it in her orange juice, as did 76-year-old Stella Lemon. Sixty-eight-year-old Joseph M. Pike and 82-year-old Hilda Leitz were despatched with the adhesive remover Detachol. Forty-four-year-old John W. Powell was killed with cyanide in his gastric feeding tube. An autopsy was performed and the pathologist smelt bitter almonds – the characteristic aroma of cyanide. Three laboratories confirmed its presence and the Cincinnati Police Department was notified.

Harvey came under suspicion because of his sacking from the VA Hospital. He called in sick the day that staff were given polygraph tests. When questioned, he admitted killing Powell, saying he felt sorry for him, but denied killing anyone else.

Pat Minarcin, then an anchor at WCPO-TV in Cincinnati, figured that if he had killed once he might have done it on other occasions. Digging into Harvey's past, he managed to link him to 24 murders, filling a half-hour special report.

Court-appointed defence attorney Bill Whalen cut a plea bargain. If the death penalty was taken off the table, he said, Harvey would confess to all the murders. In August 1987 in Ohio, Donald Harvey pleaded guilty to 24 counts of murder and was sentenced to three concurrent terms of life. That November in Kentucky he pleaded guilty to another nine murders, giving him another life sentence plus 20 years. In the end, the self-styled Angel of Death pleaded guilty to 37 murders.

Incarcerated in Toledo Correctional Institution, he was found badly battered in his cell on 28 March 2017 and died two days later. Fellow inmate James Elliott was charged with his murder.

Harvey is led to jail, 1987.

THE LAINZ ANGELS OF DEATH

NAMES: Waltraud Wagner, Maria Gruber, Irene Leidolf and Stephanija Mayer
YEARS OF BIRTH: 1940 (Mayer) 1960 (Wagner), 1962 (Leidolf), 1964 (Gruber)
PROFESSION: Nurse
ALIASES: The Lainz Angels of Death
NATIONALITY: Austrian
LOCATION OF CRIMES: Austria
DATES OF MURDERS: 1983–89
NUMBER OF VICTIMS: 49–200

In court: (from left to right) Stephanija Mayer, Maria Gruber, Irene Leidolf and Waltraud Wagner. They claimed they had killed elderly parents out of pity, but did they enjoy their power too much?

In **Lainz General Hospital** in Vienna four nurses murdered as many as 200 elderly and infirm patients who annoyed them. Beverley Allitt's murderous spree went on for a matter of weeks, but the Lainz Angels of Death managed to stay under the radar for six years.

In 1982, 23-year-old Waltraud Wagner began work as a nurse's aide at Lainz General Hospital's Pavilion Five, which housed elderly patients, many of whom were terminally ill. Initially, she sought to make her patients comfortable and ease their pain and suffering, then in the spring of 1983 a 70-year-old woman patient repeatedly begged Wagner to put her out of her misery. Wagner refused, but while she was off duty she reflected on the woman's appeals.

Plainly her death was inevitable, for no one recovered in Pavilion Five, and Wagner began to think that perhaps it was more humane to accede to the patient's request. So the next time the old woman begged for death Wagner gave her an overdose of morphine and watched the pained expression on her face turn to one of bliss.

Wagner had no regrets about what she had done. She was pleased that she had relieved someone whose life had run its course and when other patients begged her to end their suffering she obliged. Soon she got used to playing God.

Over the years, Wagner was joined on the graveyard shift in Pavilion Five by 19-year-old Maria Gruber, a single mother and nursing-school dropout, and 21-year-old Irene Leidolf, who had a husband at home but preferred hanging out with the other women after work. Like Wagner, they came from large families in rural Austria with little higher education. While drinking in a bar near the hospital it was natural for them to discuss their patients and Wagner suggested to them that, in some cases, patients should be put out of their misery. It was the compassionate thing to do. The other two agreed. It upset them to see their patients suffering so much.

Wagner taught them how to administer the right amount of morphine that would be lethal but not arouse suspicion. They saw this as mercy killing and felt no guilt. Later the deadly team was completed by Stephanija Mayer, a divorced grandmother who had emigrated from Yugoslavia. She was 20 years older than Wagner but despite her seeming maturity she was happy to go along with the terminal procedures the others had established.

'THE WATER CURE'

Until 1987 they despatched only the most severely ill, but then the termination rate accelerated. They began to kill any patient they found annoying. These included patients who made a complaint, summoned the nurse during the night, snored loudly, soiled the sheets or refused their medication. These minor infractions would result in a death sentence, with Wagner joking that the patient concerned had booked 'a ticket to God' or had 'a meeting with the undertaker'.

To avoid questions about the amount of morphine that was being used, they began to despatch patients using insulin and Rohypnol. Then to cover their tracks more completely, Wagner introduced what she called 'the water cure'. Patients' heads would be tipped back, with their tongues depressed and their nostrils pinched, and then a jug full of water would be poured down their throats, filling their lungs. They would then drown. It was a slow and agonizing death, though virtually undetectable. Elderly patients frequently had fluid in their lungs when they died and the killing went on unimpeded.

NURSES LAUGH ABOUT KILLINGS

By 1988, rumours were rife that a murderer was at work in Pavilion Five, but the head of the ward Dr Franz Xavier Pesendorfer made no effort to investigate. The Angels of Death were eventually betrayed by their own hubris. In February 1989, while having a drink after work, they were discussing the death of elderly patient Julia Drapal. She had been given the water cure for refusing her medication and calling Wagner a slut, so clearly she deserved to die. A doctor seated nearby heard them laughing about it and reported the matter to the police. The four women were suspended while the bodies of those who had died on the ward were exhumed. Many were found with water in their lungs, which proved nothing, but others were found with high levels of morphine, insulin or Rohypnol in their bodies. After a six-week investigation, Wagner, Gruber, Leidolf and Mayer were arrested and charged with murder.

LIKE NAZI EUTHANASIA PROGRAMME

News of the killings stunned Austria. They brought to mind Nazi medical experiments at Auschwitz and other Nazi death camps. The mayor of Vienna called the four nurses the 'death angels'. They were seen as sadists, like the women who had guarded the concentration camps, which were still fresh in the memory of many Austrians.

Between them, the four women admitted killing 49 patients who were too demanding or troublesome. Wagner alone admitted 39 murders. But later they retracted substantial parts of their confessions, claiming that they had killed only a handful of patients who were terminally ill, to alleviate their pain. Wagner admitted only ten assisted deaths and they were mercy killings, she insisted.

More bodies were exhumed and they were charged with the 42 counts of murder. However, the state prosecutor said that the number of victims was much higher and would probably never be known. Some estimates put the number as high as 200.

In the month-long trial, the state prosecutor Ernst Kloyber evoked Austria's Nazi past. He told the jury:

'This was no mercy killing, but cold-blooded murder of helpless people, which reminds us of a period in Austrian history none of us likes to remember … It is a small step from killing the terminally ill to the killing of insolent, burdensome patients, and from there to what was known under the Third Reich as euthanasia. It is a door that must never be opened again.'

The judge dismissed Wagner's claim that they were alleviating pain, pointing to her use of the 'water cure'.

'These patients were gasping for breath for up to half a day before they died,' he said. 'You cannot call that pain relief.'

Wagner was convicted of 15 counts of murder, 17 counts of attempted murder and two counts of physical assault. She was sentenced to life imprisonment. Leidolf was convicted of five murders and also sentenced to life. Both immediately appealed. Mayer was sentenced to 20 years and Gruber to 15 for manslaughter and attempted murder. It had been the biggest murder trial in Austria since World War II.

YOUTH CULTURE BLAMED

Dr Pesendorfer had been suspended when the four nurses were arrested in April 1989 and he was found culpable of failing to pursue rumours of mass killings in his department that had been circulating for at least a year. He defended his actions, saying he had alerted the authorities, doctors and supervisory nurses and had ordered post-mortems as soon as suspicions were raised.

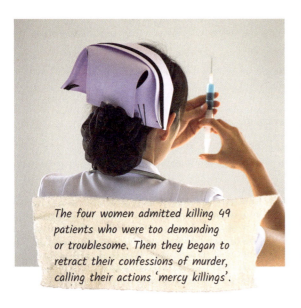

The four women admitted killing 49 patients who were too demanding or troublesome. Then they began to retract their confessions of murder, calling their actions 'mercy killings'.

ANGELS OF DEATH

'What more could I have done?' he said. 'The dead were not victims of the system but victims of crimes that could not have been anticipated and prevented.'

Other criticisms were levelled at the health service. Hildegard Fach, the head of the National Union of Nurses, said that the four women were merely nurses' aides and were not qualified to give injections. She said that regulations were routinely violated in Austrian hospitals, with nurses' aides allowed to give medication intravenously when their duties were supposed to be limited to cleaning, feeding and assisting patients. As a result, innocent nurses had been abused by the public. One even said she had been spat upon.

Commentators pointed out that the case spoke volumes about post-war society, which had become increasingly obsessed with youth and material well-being at the expense of any sensitivity towards the aged and infirm. A survey showed that 25 per cent of those questioned thought that euthanasia was justifiable in some circumstances.

GIVEN NEW IDENTITIES

Gruber and Mayer, convicted on lesser charges, were discreetly released in the 1990s and given new identities by the Austrian government, but in 2008 the release of Wagner and Leidolf caused outrage. The Austrian newspaper *Heute* carried the headline: 'The death angels are getting out.'

Even before their release, they had been let out to go shopping or visit a hairdresser. It was explained that this was part of a pre-release programme preparing them for life outside prison. They would have been released soon anyway, as in Austria those sentenced to life only serve 15 years. They too were given new identities, so they could resume life anonymously.

'It's inhumane and immoral to execute a killer,' said one Viennese citizen, 'but it's not fair to their victims' loved ones when a killer can look forward to a nice life outside prison.'

DIE PRESSE

The most recent investigation into what is 'holy' to the Austrians showed it quite clearly: Their own health is most important to the individual, but the general protection of human life – in the narrow, as well as the broadest sense – ranked behind protecting material goods. To damage an auto appears to be much worse than visiting injustice or harm on one's fellow man.

Waltraud Wagner is brought to court. She admitted to 39 murders, but later claimed that her crimes were mercy killings.

BEVERLEY ALLITT

NAME: Beverley Gail Allitt
DATE OF BIRTH: 4 October 1968
PROFESSION: Nurse
ALIASES: The Angel of Death
NATIONALITY: British
LOCATION OF CRIMES: England, UK
DATES OF MURDERS: February–April 1991
NUMBER OF VICTIMS: 13

On **23 February 1991**, just two days after Beverley Allitt had started work as a nurse on Children's Ward Four at Grantham and Kesteven Hospital in Lincolnshire, seven-week-old Liam Taylor was brought in with a chest infection.

His doctor did not think his condition was serious but in hospital it could be properly monitored. The staff nurse said that newly enrolled state nurse Allitt would take good care of him, but when they returned two hours later they were told that he had taken a turn for the worse.

'I was feeding him and he suddenly threw up,' said Allitt. 'It went all over me. I had to go and change my uniform.'

The child was so sick, she said, that he had stopped breathing for a moment.

'He was choking on his vomit,' she said. 'If he'd been at home, you'd probably have lost him.'

The couple were upset but took an instant liking to the young nurse who was so frank with them and they were relieved and grateful when Allitt volunteered for an extra night shift to look after him. However, early in the morning Allitt called for an emergency

Beverley Allitt had been to Grantham College of Further Education with Sue Phillips. Allitt told Phillips she would look after her daughter Katie. 'She will be all right with me.'

resuscitation team as Liam had stopped breathing. The doctors managed to revive him, but there was bad news. The specialist told Liam's parents that, if their child survived, he would have severe brain damage.

'Normally, in children who have respiratory failure, their condition can be stabilized in a matter of minutes,' Dr Charith Nanayakkara said. 'In Liam's case, it took an hour and 15 minutes.'

The chaplain was called to christen the child. Liam's parents then agreed to switch off the life support system, but Liam did not die – not immediately anyway. His parents took turns holding him until he finally perished seven and a half hours later.

The doctors could not understand how he had died. A post-mortem concluded that Liam had suffered an 'infarction' of the heart – that is, the muscles of the heart had died. This usually happened in patients in middle age or beyond, after a lifetime of heavy smoking or drinking, so the pathologist could not explain how it had happened to a tiny child.

INSULIN IN BLOOD

Then on 5 March, just three days after Liam had been buried, 11-year-old Timothy Hardwick was admitted to Ward Four. He had been born with cerebral palsy and had suffered an epileptic fit. Again Allitt seemed to lavish care on the child and initially the doctors were pleased with his progress. Suddenly, when the ward was particularly busy, Timothy unexpectedly died. Given his chronic condition, no further investigation was made and no one called the police.

In the same bed just five days later, 14-month-old Kayley Desmond stopped breathing while in the care of Allitt. Then her heart stopped beating. She was revived and rushed to the intensive care unit at the Queen's Medical Centre in Nottingham, amid concern that she might have suffered brain damage when starved of oxygen. It was assumed that this had occurred when, as a bad feeder, she had inhaled milk and stopped breathing. No one spotted that under her right armpit there was a needle puncture with a small bubble of air behind it, as if someone had injected her ineptly. It was only seen when her X-rays were re-examined later. Nevertheless, Kayley made a full recovery.

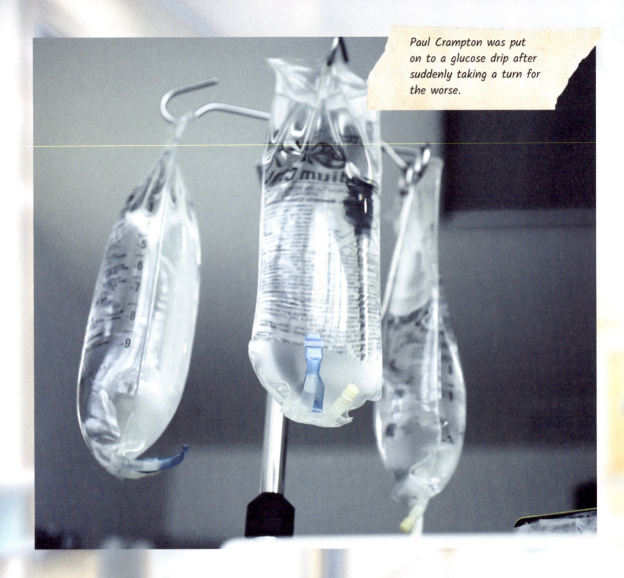

Paul Crampton was put on to a glucose drip after suddenly taking a turn for the worse.

Another ten days passed before five-month-old Paul Crampton was admitted to the ward with mild bronchitis. Responding well to treatment, he was due to be discharged four days later when suddenly he took a turn for the worse.

Sue Phillips, the mother of Becky and Katie Phillips, who were also on the ward, said: 'I heard Bev Allitt say: "I think I know what's wrong with him. He's hypoglycaemic."'

Paul was put on a glucose drip and quickly recovered.

'I thought how clever the nurse was to have realized what was wrong with him so quickly,' Sue Phillips said.

He had two more unexplained attacks of hypoglycaemia, a critical lack of sugar in his body. After the third attack, he was rushed to the Queen's Medical Centre, with Allitt in the ambulance, where the lab discovered that he had a high level of insulin in his blood.

PARENTS' GRATITUDE

The following day five-year-old Bradley Gibson was admitted suffering from pneumonia and during the night he complained of pain in the arm where his antibiotic drip was attached. He was attended by Allitt. On the second occasion, he suffered a cardiac arrest. For half an hour, the emergency resuscitation team battled to save him – successfully – and he too was taken to the Queen's. His parents went to the local newspaper, the *Grantham Journal*, to praise the doctors and nurses who had saved their son and the paper ran the story under the headline 'Our Miracle'. Three national newspapers picked up on it.

The day after that, two-year-old Yik Hung 'Henry' Chan was admitted after he had plunged from a bedroom window on to the patio below, suffering a fractured skull. Although he was dizzy and complaining of bad headaches, his condition quickly improved and the doctors were thinking about sending him home. However, when attended by Allitt the child started vomiting. Other staff saw he was blue, so the emergency team were called and he was revived with oxygen. When this happened a second time, Henry, too, was rushed to the Queen's.

Four days later, it was the turn of identical twins Becky and Katie Phillips. Becky had been admitted for observation after suffering from acute gastroenteritis. She was untroubled for the first two days because Allitt had been off duty. When she returned, Becky's mother Sue Phillips recognized her immediately, because they had been to Grantham College of Further Education together. Strangely, though, Allitt did not acknowledge her.

When Becky returned home she fell ill again and was taken back to hospital. The doctors suspected that the problem was with the milk the twins were being fed. Whereas the hospital used ready-mixed baby's milk, Sue mixed her own from powder. That evening Becky screamed and her eyes rolled in her head. Allitt did not want Sue to take Becky home but nevertheless she was discharged. However, despite a midnight rush to A&E, she died in the night. No reason could be found, though the doctor in A&E thought she might have contracted meningitis. The death certificate said 'infant death syndrome' – cot death.

As a precaution, Katie was sent to hospital for observation, only to be cared for by Allitt, who now offered Sue seemingly genuine words of comfort. Seeing Sue was tired, Allitt told her to go home and get some rest.

'You go. I will look after her,' said Allitt. 'She will be all right with me.'

Within half an hour of reaching home, Sue got a call saying Katie was having trouble breathing. She suffered a cardiac arrest, but Allitt was on hand to call for 'resus'. Emergency treatment saved Katie's life, but the same thing happened again two days later. Rushed to the Queen's, she was found to have suffered brain damage. She had cerebral palsy, paralysis of the right side and damage to her eyesight and hearing. What's more, five of her ribs were broken. This was put down to frantic efforts to resuscitate her. But Katie's mother Sue was so grateful to Allitt for saving her daughter's life that she asked her to be her godmother. As it was, the hospital's chaplain became Katie's godparent.

QUESTIONS RAISED

A few days later, six-year-old Michael Davidson was admitted after being accidentally shot with an airgun. After minor surgery to remove the pellet, Allitt helped prepare an intravenous antibiotic. When it was administered, the child stopped breathing. His face turned black and his back arched. CPR from Dr Nanayakkara had him breathing again before the emergency team arrived and after being resuscitated he recovered and was eventually discharged.

That same day two-month-old Christopher Peasgood was admitted with breathing difficulties. While he was put in an oxygen tent, Allitt suggested that his parents, who had lost a child to cot death two years earlier, should go and have a cup of tea. When they returned they found the emergency team in action. The boy was blue. A nurse had discovered that the alarm indicating he had stopped breathing had been turned off. Nevertheless, Allitt assured Christopher's parents that he would be all right, but he suffered another cardiac arrest during the night. Fearing that he was dying, the child was christened. The doctors wanted to send him to the Queen's but feared he might not survive the journey. However, Christopher's parents agreed to the move, deciding they had nothing to lose, and in the intensive care unit there he quickly recovered.

Christopher King was a month old when he was admitted for an operation, but he became inexplicably ill before going to surgery and had to be revived with oxygen. The operation was a success, but he had to be resuscitated four more times before he was sent to the Queen's. His mother Belinda was a nurse and she swore that she would never take Christopher back to Ward Four.

Seven-week-old Patrick Elstone had been playing and laughing when his parents had dropped him off for a check-up, but in Allitt's care he had stopped breathing – twice. He was rushed to the Queen's, but not before he had suffered brain damage. By then, the doctors at the Queen's were beginning to ask the question: Why were so many children coming into their care from Ward Four?

LIGNOCAINE FOUND

Asthmatic 15-month-old Claire Peck had been admitted to the ward on 18 April. She was put on a nebulizer that cleared her airways and she was discharged two days later, but after a coughing fit she returned on 22 April. Her mother Susan found Nurse Allitt unfriendly, even hostile, and the Pecks had been ushered away while their daughter was being treated. Left alone with the child, Allitt suddenly cried out: 'Arrest! Arrest!'

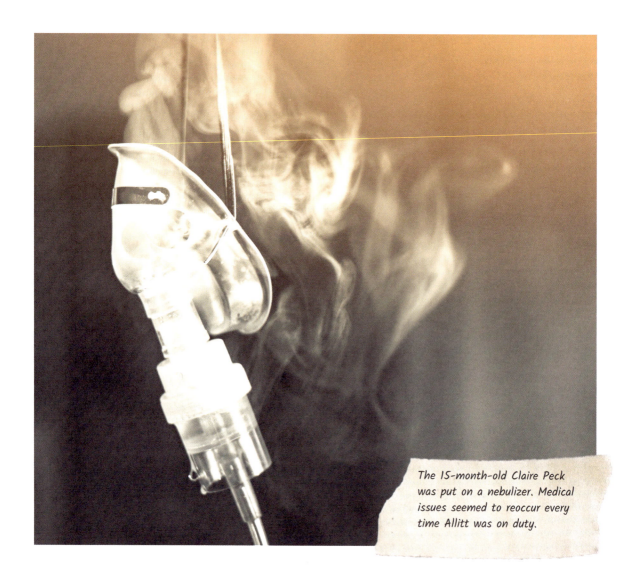

The 15-month-old Claire Peck was put on a nebulizer. Medical issues seemed to reoccur every time Allitt was on duty.

Doctors came running and revived the child, but as soon as she was left alone with Allitt the same thing happened again. This time the doctors could not save her. Susan Peck, holding the dead child, noticed that everyone else was upset but Allitt just sat there staring.

The authorities at first suspected that legionnaires' disease was responsible, so although no virus was found the ward was meticulously scrubbed. Initially a post-mortem showed that Claire had died from natural causes, but Dr Nelson Porter, a consultant at the hospital, was unhappy with the number of heart cases that had occurred in Ward Four over the previous eight weeks and ordered further tests. Lignocaine, a drug that was used to treat adults suffering from cardiac arrest, was found in Claire's body. It was never given to babies.

The police were called in and it was discovered, by checking the rotas, that Allitt was the only person who was present every time there was a medical emergency. Also, notes covering Paul Crampton's stay were missing. Allitt was suspended, but the parents of the Phillips twins had so much faith in her that they hired a private detective to clear her name.

MUNCHAUSEN'S SYNDROME

After Allitt's arrest a missing ward diary was found in her home. She was charged with four counts of murder and 11 counts of attempted murder, to which she pleaded not guilty at Nottingham Crown Court on 15 February 1993. In the court case, which lasted two months, the prosecution easily showed that Allitt had the means and

In less than two months at Grantham and Kesteven Hospital, Allitt had attempted to kill 23 children.

the opportunity to commit the crimes – but what of the motive? Consultant paediatrician Professor Roy Meadow told the court that Allitt exhibited all the symptoms of Munchausen's Syndrome and Munchausen's Syndrome by Proxy. In the first condition, the sufferer seeks attention by self-harm or faking complaints. Allitt's extensive medical record confirmed that. Even while she had been out on bail she had been admitted to hospital complaining of an enlarged right breast. It was discovered that she had been injecting herself with water. She attended the court for just 16 days, absenting herself for the rest of the time due to mysterious illnesses.

The second condition is usually exhibited by mothers, where they seek medical attention by complaining that their offspring is suffering from fictitious complaints or by inflicting actual abuse.

Professor Meadow said that to suffer from both Munchausen's Syndrome and Munchausen's Syndrome by Proxy was extremely rare, but he came across around 40 cases of the proxy condition a year.

Allitt was found guilty on all charges. In Children's Ward Four at Grantham and Kesteven Hospital in Lincolnshire, she had administered potentially lethal injections or attempted to suffocate 23 children in her charge, killing four and leaving a further nine irreparably damaged – all in just 59 days.

DANGER SIGNS SINCE CHILDHOOD

In court, it became clear that Beverley Allitt should never have been allowed to become a nurse because she had shown disturbing symptoms of a mental disorder from an early age. One of four children, she sought attention by wearing dressings and casts over supposed wounds that she would allow no one to examine. Growing overweight as an adolescent, her attention-seeking became aggressive and her parents regularly had to take her to hospital for treatment for fictitious ailments. These included pain in her gall bladder, headaches, urinary infections, uncontrolled vomiting, blurred vision, minor injuries, back trouble, ulcers and appendicitis, resulting in the removal of a perfectly healthy appendix. The scar was slow to heal as she kept picking at the wound.

While training as a nurse she had a poor attendance record, frequently being absent with supposed illnesses. She was also suspected of odd behaviour, including smearing faeces on the walls of the nurses' home. Her boyfriend accused her of being aggressive, manipulative and deceptive. She falsely claimed to be pregnant and told people he had AIDS and she had accused a friend of his of rape, though she did not go to the police.

When Allitt returned to the dock for sentencing, the judge told her:

You have been found guilty of the most terrible crimes. You killed, tried to kill or seriously harmed 13 children, many of them tiny babies. They had been entrusted to your care. You have brought grief to their families. You have sown a seed of doubt in those who should have faith in the integrity of care their children receive in hospital. Hopefully, the grief felt by the families will become easier to bear, but it will always be there. You are seriously disturbed. You are cunning and manipulative and you have shown no remorse for the trail of destruction you have left behind you. I accept it is all the result of the severe personality disorder you have. But you are and remain a very serious danger to others.

He gave her 13 concurrent terms of life imprisonment, which meant she would serve a minimum of 30 years and would only be released if she was considered to be no danger to the public. Committed to Rampton Secure Hospital, she admitted three of the murders and six of the attempted murders.

Beverley Allitt arrives at court.

CHAPTER 6

MASS MURDERERS

As with serial killings, most acts of mass murder by individuals have taken place in recent decades. Shootings at schools and workplaces have increased dramatically and are some of the most shocking and terrifying crimes imaginable. These killers, motivated by rage against society and often believing they have a higher purpose, engage in an orgy of violence against their targets and the killing only stops when they either end their own lives or are stopped by the authorities.

ANDERS BREIVIK

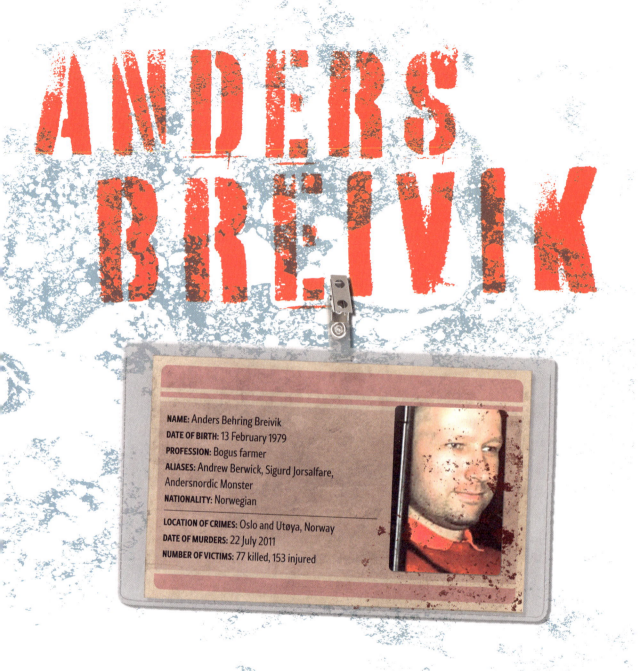

NAME: Anders Behring Breivik
DATE OF BIRTH: 13 February 1979
PROFESSION: Bogus farmer
ALIASES: Andrew Berwick, Sigurd Jorsalfare, Andersnordic Monster
NATIONALITY: Norwegian

LOCATION OF CRIMES: Oslo and Utøya, Norway
DATE OF MURDERS: 22 July 2011
NUMBER OF VICTIMS: 77 killed, 153 injured

On the afternoon of 22 July 2011, a curious compendium titled *2083 – A European Declaration of Independence* was emailed to over a thousand recipients around the globe. Its author was a complete unknown, but by the end of the day he would be famous – not for his writing, but as the worst spree killer in world history.

Anders Behring Breivik was born on 13 February 1979 in Oslo, but lived most of his earliest days in London, where his father, an economist, worked as a diplomat for the Royal Norwegian Embassy.

At the age of one, his parents divorced, setting off a custody battle that his father lost. Still an infant, Breivik returned with his mother, a nurse, to Oslo. Although she was soon remarried, to a Norwegian Army officer, Breivik would later criticize what he perceived as an absence of the masculine in his childhood home. In his writings, he disparages his mother for his 'matriarchal upbringing', adding 'it completely lacked discipline and has contributed to feminizing me to a certain degree.'

Anecdotal evidence shows Breivik to have been an intelligent,

188 MASS MURDERERS

caring boy, one who was quick to defend others against bullying. However, his behaviour changed markedly in adolescence. Over a two-year period, so Breivik claims, he engaged in a one-man 'war' against Oslo's public transit company, causing £700,000 in property damage. His evenings were spent running around the city with friends, committing acts of vandalism. At the age of 16, Breivik was caught spray-painting graffiti on the exterior wall of a building, an act that brought an end to his relationship with his father. The two have had no contact since.

Though the stepson of an army officer, Breivik was declared 'unfit for service' in Norway's mandatory conscription assessment. The reason for this surprising judgement has yet to be disclosed; Breivik told friends a story that he'd received an exemption to care for his sickly mother. However, a possible explanation is his use of anabolic steroids, a drug that he'd been taking since his teenage years in an effort to bulk up. Breivik was a man obsessed with his appearance.

In 2000, at the age of 21, he flew off to the United States to have cosmetic surgery on his forehead, nose and chin. Unmarried at 32, Breivik considered himself a most desirable bachelor, and boasted frequently of his conquests, yet not one of his acquaintances can remember him ever having had a girlfriend.

The operation he referred to was part of a nine-year plan that culminated on that horrible day in July 2011. According to Breivik, work began in 2002 with the establishment of a computer programming business that was intended to raise funds. Instead, the company went bankrupt, forcing him to move back to his mother's house. This humiliating setback seems to have brought on a period of relative inactivity. By 2009, however, Breivik was back in business. He set up a company, Breivik Geofarm, which was nothing more than a cover so that he might buy large quantities of fertilizer and other chemicals used in bomb-making without raising suspicion. The next year, after a failed attempt at buying illegal weapons in Prague, he purchased a semi-automatic Glock pistol and a Ruger Mini-14 semi-automatic carbine through legal channels.

Breivik murdered with these guns, but his first victims on 22 July 2011 were killed with a car bomb planted in his Volkswagen Crafter. That afternoon, he drove the automobile into the government quarter of Oslo, taking care to park it in front of the building housing

'When it comes to girls, I'm tempted – especially these days, after training and I'm feeling fantastic. But I try to avoid entanglements, because they may complicate my plans and put the whole operation in jeopardy.'

A fascistic image of Breivik from his personal website.

ANDERS BREIVIK **189**

Utoya Island was Breivik's ultimate destination.

the Office of the Prime Minister, the Minister of Justice and Police and several other high-ranking government ministers. At 3.22 pm, the car bomb exploded, shattering windows, and setting the ground floor of the building on fire. Though Labour Prime Minister Jens Stoltenberg, thought to have been a chief target of the attack, survived without a scratch, the explosion killed eight people and left 11 more with critical injuries.

Things could have been much worse. It's curious that through all Breivik's years of planning, he'd never taken into account the fact that July is the month Norwegians go on holiday. What's more, he'd chosen to carry out his attack late on a Friday afternoon, a time when most government employees had already left for the weekend.

During the mayhem in downtown Oslo, Breivik changed into a fake police uniform, made his way some 40 km (25 miles) to the shores of Lake Tyrifjorden, and caught a ferry to the island of Utoya. His destination was a summer camp that was held annually by the youth wing of the Norwegian Labour Party. By the time he arrived – 4.45, one hour and 23 minutes after the Oslo blast – news of the tragedy had already been announced to the camp staff and roughly 600 teenagers on the island. Breivik appeared as he presented himself: a police officer who had come to ensure that the 26-acre island was secure. After first asking people to gather around so that he could speak with them, Breivik opened fire. He shot indiscriminately, apparently intent on killing as many people as possible. Breivik's bullets struck people as they took to the lake, hoping to swim to safety.

It wasn't until 32 minutes after the shooting began that police on the mainland were aware of something taking place on Utoya Island. Their delayed response is a matter of investigation. They waited until the Beredskapstropen, a special counter-terrorism unit, arrived from Oslo, before making the crossing. The boat that they sailed on was so overloaded that it nearly sank before reaching the island. Even before they left shore, Breivik placed a phone call to surrender, only to change his mind. The killing continued until 6.26 pm – one hour and 24 minutes after it had begun – when the gunman made a second call. He was apprehended by the Beredskapstropen eight minutes later.

In all, Breivik killed 69 people on Utoya Island and in its surrounding waters. Many of the survivors escaped with their lives by swimming to areas that were only accessible from the lake, while others hid in a schoolhouse, which the gunman chose not to enter. Some survivors played dead, even after being shot for a second time. Still others were rescued by vacationers and others with boats, who risked coming under fire from the shore.

Breivik claimed a total of 77 lives with his two attacks; a further 153 people were injured. The dead ranged in age from 14 to 61, with a median age of just 18 years. He'd killed 55 teenagers.

Anders Breivik has acknowledged that he committed the bombing in Oslo and the shootings on Utoya, but has denied guilt. In his words, both events involved 'atrocious but necessary actions'. These four words came from his lawyer. Much of the gunman's motivation can be gleaned through *2083 – A European Declaration of Independence*, the 1,513-page document that he released to the world just 90 minutes before setting off the Oslo bomb. In this collection of writings, much of it plagiarized from others, Breivik argues against feminism and for a return to a patriarchy that he felt was lacking in his own upbringing. The murderer rails against multiculturalism and what he sees as opening the door to the Islamization of Europe. Portraying himself as a knight, Breivik calls on other white Europeans to wage a religious war against Muslims and Marxists. His ultimate goal, as

A photo taken from a helicopter showing Breivik next to several bodies.

reflected in the title of the document, was the deportation of all followers of Islam from Europe by 2083.

> 'A MAJORITY OF THE PEOPLE I KNOW SUPPORT MY VIEWS, THEY ARE JUST APATHETIC. THEY KNOW THAT THERE WILL BE A CONFRONTATION ONE DAY, BUT THEY DON'T CARE BECAUSE IT WILL MOST LIKELY NOT HAPPEN WITHIN THE NEXT TWO DECADES.'

Breivik appeared in Oslo District Court three days after the attack. Facing charges of terrorism, the accused entered a not guilty plea, adding that he did not recognize the system under which he would be tried. The arraignment was held on camera, due to fears that he might somehow use the venue to communicate with compatriots. Following his trial in August 2012, Breivik was found guilty and given a sentence of containment, a penalty that allows a felon to be incarcerated for up to 21 years – the maximum sentence allowed in Norwegian law.

Breivik revisits the scene of his crime to provide police with evidence.

ERIC HARRIS AND DYLAN KLEBOLD

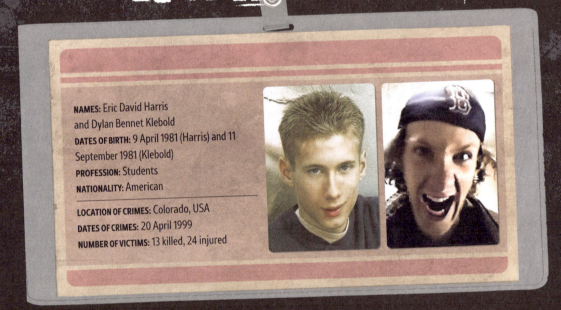

NAMES: Eric David Harris and Dylan Bennet Klebold
DATES OF BIRTH: 9 April 1981 (Harris) and 11 September 1981 (Klebold)
PROFESSION: Students
NATIONALITY: American

LOCATION OF CRIMES: Colorado, USA
DATES OF CRIMES: 20 April 1999
NUMBER OF VICTIMS: 13 killed, 24 injured

Together Eric Harris and Dylan Klebold had many dreams. They wrote of elaborate plans for a major explosion on a par with the Oklahoma City bombing. Another scheme involved hijacking a plane at Denver International Airport, flying 2,600 km (1,600 miles), and crashing into a building in New York. Ultimately, they chose as their target a public building they knew better than any other: their own high school. Had everything gone according to plan, their rampage, known as the Columbine High School Massacre, would have been the worst school shooting in history.

Eric David Harris was born on 9 April 1981 in Wichita, Kansas, the second son of a part-time caterer and a United States Air Force transport pilot. In July 1993, the family relocated to Littleton, Colorado. They lived in rented accommodation for three years, eventually buying a house in an upper-middle-class neighbourhood close to Columbine High School.

Dylan Bennet Klebold, a native of Colorado, was born in Lakewood on 11 September 1981, 20 years to the day before the events of 9/11. His mother was an employment counsellor and his father had a small, home-based real estate business.

Harris and Klebold met as boys while attending middle school.

Eric Harris was cited as 'a very bright individual likely to succeed in life' after an anger management course.

They had much in common. In 1996, Harris set up a website devoted to *Doom*, a violent computer game in which players must kill demons and zombies to reach higher levels of play. Also posted on the site were jokes and brief entries concerning his parents, friends and school. It wasn't long before Harris began to add instructions on how to make explosives, and records of the trouble he and Klebold were causing. The site had few visitors and attracted little attention until late 1997 when the parents of Harris' former friend, Brooks Brown, discovered that it contained death threats aimed against their son. Further investigation by the sheriff's office revealed other threats directed at the students and teachers of Columbine High School, where Harris and Klebold were students. Harris had posted remarks concerning his hatred of society and the desire he had to kill.

A few months into the investigation of the website, in January 1998, Harris and Klebold were caught in the act of stealing computer equipment from a van. They attended a joint court hearing, where it was decided that they both needed psychiatric help. The pair avoided prosecution by participating in a programme that involved three months of counselling and community service. Although both expressed regret publicly, in his journal Harris wrote of his cleverness in deceiving the judge.

Not long after the court hearing, Harris removed the section of his website in which he'd posted his thoughts and threats. However, as the date of the massacre drew near, he added a new section in which he kept a record of his gun collection and bomb-making activities. Also included was a 'hit list' of those he wished to target. The sheriff's office wrote a draft affidavit for a search warrant of the Harris house, but this was never filed.

Exactly when Harris and Klebold began planning their massacre has been a matter of some debate. However, what can be said with

Dylan Klebold attended his high school prom with a date only three days before the shooting spree.

certainty is that their actions were not the result of a whim. Over the course of several months, Harris and Klebold had built their bombs and gathered their ammunition. Well aware that they would be made famous by their actions, Harris left behind a collection of videos in which the two discuss their motivations. Harris recalled that as a member of a military family he had had to move from town to town, always having to start afresh. He also expressed resentment of his brother Byron, who was extremely popular and an accomplished athlete. Parents excepted, Klebold spoke about the grievances he had with his family, who he felt always treated him as their inferior.

The pair relished the place they would stake in history through their actions. Hollywood, they were certain, would fight over the rights to their story. The two discussed who might make the better film – Steven Spielberg or Quentin Tarantino?

They were so dedicated to the documentation of their designs that they made a tape just prior to their departure for the high school. Klebold, the first to speak, announces, 'It's a half-hour before our Judgement Day.' After saying goodbye to his parents, he adds, 'I don't like life very much... Just know I'm going to a much better place than here.'

Harris' farewell is much more rushed. 'I know my mom and dad will be in shock and disbelief,' he says. 'I can't help it.'

'It's what we had to do,' Klebold adds. They spend some time creating something of a video will, listing various belongings that they want to go to friends. When Klebold determines that it is time to go, Harris concludes, 'That's it. Sorry. Goodbye.'

What followed did not go according to plan. Everything had been mapped out in such great detail, and yet the events that took place on that sunny Tuesday in April were largely the result of improvisation.

Harris and Klebold planned the massacre to begin in the late morning of 20 April 1999. Their first step was planting a firebomb in a field not far from the school. Set to explode just prior to the start of their assault on the school, it is assumed to have been placed as a diversion for emergency personnel.

The bomb did detonate, though only partially. The small fire it caused was easily extinguished by the local fire department.

The pair arrived at the school in separate cars and parked in different parking areas. Klebold walked over to where Harris had parked. There they armed two 9 kg (20 lb) propane bombs, enough to destroy the cafeteria and bring down the library above as well. With five minutes to detonation, they carried duffel bags containing the bombs into the cafeteria, left them on the floor, and returned to their respective cars. En route to his car, Harris encountered Brooks Brown, and warned him: 'Brooks, I like you. Now get out of here. Go home.'

Harris and Klebold's plan was to wait and fire upon students fleeing the explosion. However, when both bombs failed to detonate, Klebold went back to Harris' car. Carrying duffel bags containing a 9 mm semi-automatic rifle, a 9 mm semi-automatic pistol, two sawn-off 12-gauge shotguns and a number of explosive devices, they walked together towards the cafeteria entrance, and stopped on the outdoor steps.

At 11.19, the pair pulled out their shotguns and began firing at the students. Their first shots were directed at two students eating lunch on the lawn. One of the two, a girl, became the first fatality. Although Klebold entered the cafeteria briefly, presumably to determine why the bombs had not detonated, the pair focused for the first minutes on the outside of the high school. While shooting, they began to throw pipe bombs on the lawn, the roof and into the car park. Like the cafeteria bombs, these all proved to be duds.

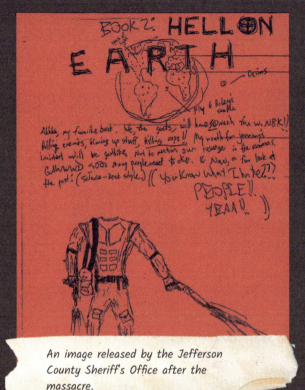

An image released by the Jefferson County Sheriff's Office after the massacre.

Five minutes after the first shot was fired, a sheriff's deputy who happened to be at the campus began exchanging fire with the gunmen. While this was happening Dave Sanders, a teacher, managed to evacuate the cafeteria through a staircase leading up to the second floor.

Harris and Klebold ran into the school and proceeded down two corridors, shooting and throwing pipe bombs. They eventually entered the library, where they shot out the windows and began to fire at the police officers outside. The gunmen then turned around and set their sights on students who had been hiding under tables. In the next seven minutes, Harris and Klebold killed ten people and injured 12 others.

When the gunmen left the library, they proceeded to the science area, firing indiscriminately. Coming across locked classroom doors, they would peer inside at the students, but make no attempt to gain entry.

The gunmen returned to the cafeteria, where Harris attempted without success to detonate one of the failed propane bombs.

The gunmen drank from cups students had left behind on the tables and looked out of the windows, watching as emergency vehicles arrived. They then left and wandered around the school's main corridors. Again, they looked at students through the windows of locked classroom doors, but never attempted to enter the rooms. They paused outside a washroom entrance, taunting the students inside by saying that they were about to enter and kill whomever they found. However, the pair did not go in; rather they continued to wander, seemingly without aim.

At 12.05, nearly half an hour after they'd left, Harris and Klebold re-entered the library to find it nearly empty. All but two survivors had managed to get away – one pretended to be dead and the other, Patrick Ireland, was unconscious. The gunmen attempted to shoot at police officers through the windows, without success. After setting a Molotov cocktail alight, Klebold watched as Harris killed himself; seconds later he took his own life.

Two and a half hours later, Ireland regained consciousness. He crawled out through the window, where he was picked up by SWAT team members. It would be nearly another hour before the police officers finally entered the library. By this time, Harris and Klebold had been dead for just under three and a half hours. It was estimated that nearly 800 police officers circled the school that day – but not one of them entered the building while the two gunmen were still alive.

Harris and Klebold's shooting spree lasted approximately 49 minutes; all those killed or injured were shot during the first 16 minutes. Witnesses report that after they'd killed their final victim both gunmen remarked that the thrill had gone out of shooting people.

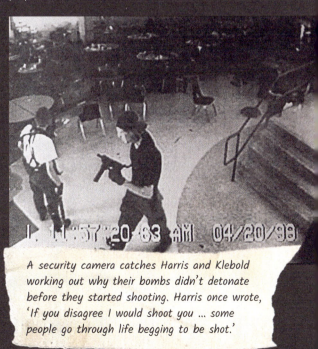

A security camera catches Harris and Klebold working out why their bombs didn't detonate before they started shooting. Harris once wrote, 'If you disagree I would shoot you ... some people go through life begging to be shot.'

TED KACZYNSKI

NAME: Theodore John Kaczynski
DATE OF BIRTH: 22 May 1942
PROFESSION: Mathematician
ALIASES: The Unabomber
NATIONALITY: American

LOCATION OF CRIMES: USA
DATES OF MURDERS: 1978–95
NUMBER OF VICTIMS: 3 killed, 23 injured

Ted Kaczynski, also known as 'The Unabomber', was a highly intelligent, educated man who nevertheless organized a series of crude bombings that killed and maimed a number of people. He apparently carried out the crimes in the belief that he was helping to cause the downfall of civilized society and halt the progress of technology; but it also emerged that, although he had a brilliant academic mind, he was mentally unbalanced.

He was born Theodore John Kaczynski in Chicago on 22 May 1942. He grew up in Evergreen Park, a working-class area in the suburbs of Chicago. While still a baby, he had a strong allergic reaction to some medicine he was given, and had to be taken to hospital. He was kept there for several weeks, separated from his parents, who were only allowed to visit occasionally. His mother attests that, having been a happy baby before the incident, he then became withdrawn and turned away from human contact. It is thought that this separation may have caused him mental health problems later in life.

MATHEMATICS GENIUS
Despite this early setback, Ted showed very high intelligence as a young child, and was clearly very gifted. However, he entirely

Ted Kaczynski at the University of California, Berkeley. He was an accomplished mathematician and seemed well on his way to a successful academic career before his abrupt resignation in 1969.

lacked social skills, and was disinclined to play with other children or to engage with adults. He did well academically, graduating from high school early after skipping several grades. He went on to study mathematics at Harvard, earning his degree there, and then gaining a master's degree and a PhD from Ann Arbor University, Michigan. He astounded his professors with his ability to solve problems they could not, and in a short time reached a level in the subject that only a handful of people in the country would have been able to comprehend. Not surprisingly, he was offered a fellowship and teaching work, and spent three years as a lecturer in Michigan, also publishing papers on mathematics in several learned journals.

Kaczynski was then offered a post at the University of California, Berkeley. He spent two years there as an assistant professor in mathematics, before abruptly resigning from the job in 1969. It was unclear why such a brilliant mathematician, who could have reached the top of his profession in a very short time, suddenly quit the academic scene.

KILLER MAIL BOMBS

Kaczynski no longer had a permanent source of income, other than the occasional odd jobs he did for local people. His family also helped him out, lending him money. However, he was now extremely poor, and lived in a small cabin in the countryside, isolated from the community and becoming more and more eccentric.

In the late 1970s, Kaczynski began to send bombs through the mail. His first target was a university professor who became suspicious and had the package opened by a campus police officer. It exploded, but fortunately the officer was only slightly injured. Next, Kaczynski began to target airlines, sending bombs designed to explode in airports and on aeroplanes. The bombs were home-made, and not very efficient, so initially little damage was done.

However, Kaczynski then stepped up his campaign with bombs that, while still primitive, were now lethal. In 1985, he sent one to the University of California, which resulted in a student losing four of his fingers and the sight in one eye. In the same year, Kaczynski

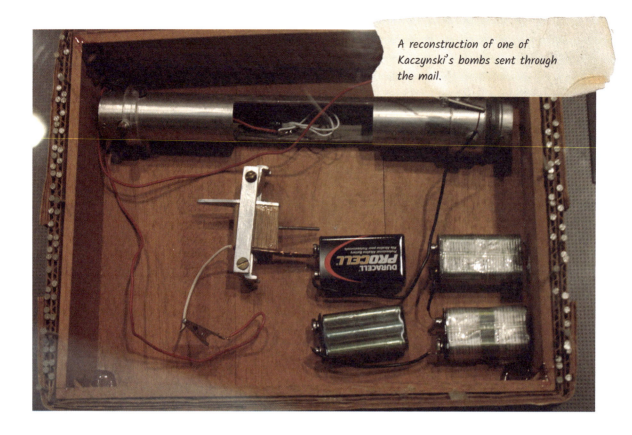

A reconstruction of one of Kaczynski's bombs sent through the mail.

began to target computer stores, leaving nail bombs in the parking lots outside these stores. In one case, the store owner was killed outright.

THE UNABOMBER MANIFESTO

After this atrocity, Kaczynski's activities ceased for a while. However, in 1993 his next target was a computer science professor at Yale University, David Gelernter, who thankfully survived the bomb Kaczynski mailed to him. Another academic, geneticist Charles Epstein, was not so lucky. He was maimed by one of Kaczynski's bombs in the same year. The following year, Kaczynski targeted an advertising executive, and the year after, the president of the California Forestry Association.

Kaczynski now began to write letters to the papers, and in some cases to his former victims, claiming responsibility for the attacks, on behalf of his 'anarchist group' Freedom Club (FC). He demanded that a manifesto he had written be printed in one of the US's major newspapers and claimed that he would then end his bombing campaign. In order to try to resolve the situation, *The New York Times* printed it, which became known as 'The Unabomber Manifesto'. A great deal of controversy surrounded this decision; in some quarters, it was felt that this was pandering to the murderer. However, the newspaper argued that printing the manifesto might help to solve the mystery of who the Unabomber was, and track the culprit down.

The manifesto was a rant, though at times an intelligent and informed one, against the evils of modern technology. It argued that human beings suffer from the 'progress' of technology, which harms the majority of people on the planet and causes immense environmental damage. Its author believed that the only way forward was through halting technological progress, and returning to the simple life, living close to nature. Kaczynski also criticized 'leftists' for allowing an advanced, complex society to develop to the detriment of humanity.

CLOSING IN ON KACZYNSKI

When the manifesto was published, Kaczynski's brother David recognized it as putting forward Ted's ideas in the writing style he knew only too well. At one time, David had admired his brother greatly, and followed his ideas. In fact, he had bought a plot of land with Ted outside Lincoln in western Montana. Ted now lived there, in a 3 m x 3.6 m (10 ft x 12 ft) cabin without electricity or running water, and led a reclusive life, rarely going out, as his neighbours later reported, except to buy food that he could not grow in his garden. David had baled out from this way of life early on and decided to adopt a more mainstream approach.

Realizing that his brother was responsible for the bombing campaign, David contacted the police and told them where Ted was living. Officers arrested Ted Kaczynski at his cabin in Montana in April 1996. The FBI had assured David that they would not tell his brother who had turned him in, but sadly, his identity was later leaked. David used the reward money he received to pay his legal expenses, but also to recompense the families of his brother's victims.

When the case came to trial, the most obvious defence for Ted Kaczynski was insanity, but Kaczynski rejected this. Instead, a court psychiatrist diagnosed him as fit to stand trial, though suffering from schizophrenia. Kaczynski pleaded guilty to the bombings, but later withdrew his plea. The withdrawal was not accepted, and Kaczynski was given a life sentence with no parole. Kaczynski died in North Carolina in 2023.

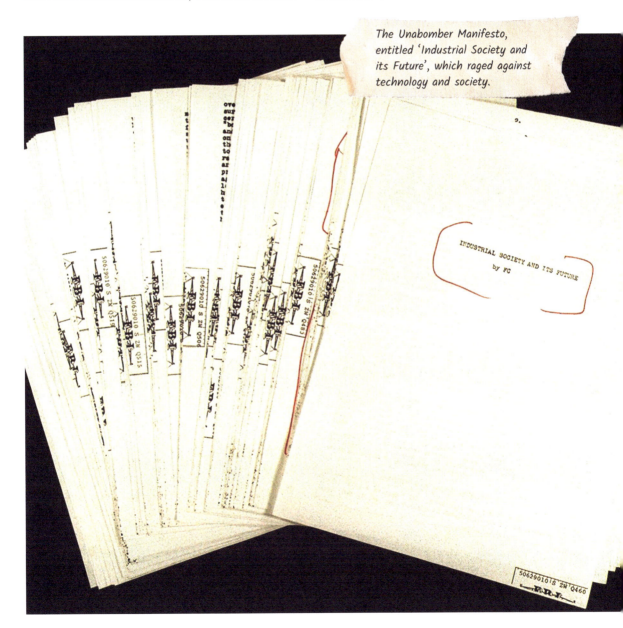

The Unabomber Manifesto, entitled 'Industrial Society and its Future', which raged against technology and society.

ADAM LANZA

NAME: Adam Peter Lanza
DATE OF BIRTH: 22 April 1992
PROFESSION: Student
NATIONALITY: American
LOCATION OF CRIMES: Connecticut, USA
DATE OF MURDERS: 14 December 2012
NUMBER OF VICTIMS: 27 killed, 2 injured

Newtown is a small sleepy town of 27,000 residents in Connecticut. It was the last place anyone would think of as the setting for a crime that would shock the world. On 14 December 2012, 20-year-old Adam Lanza changed everything. He shot his mother in the head before returning to his old school, Sandy Hook Elementary, in Newtown. Then, armed with a semi-automatic, military-style rifle, he burst into the school spraying bullets everywhere. Terrified teachers tried to calm their students as the nightmare unfolded. By the time the ordeal was over, Lanza's bullets had claimed the lives of 20 children, aged between six and seven, and six adults.

Adam Lanza lived most of his life in Newtown. To friends and neighbours, his parents Nancy and Peter appeared to be a loving, caring couple who did their best to provide their son with a good upbringing. But beneath the surface there were tensions.

In 2001 his parents separated. This was when things really

Adam Lanza pictured in 2005 when he would have been 12 or 13.

started to turn sour. Lanza's relationship with his mother grew increasingly strained. Nancy was a gun enthusiast. She collected guns, kept them well stocked with ammunition and subscribed to a gun magazine. There were always lots of paper targets lying around the house. The family often went to the shooting range.

A disturbing family photo shows Adam Lanza as a toddler decked out in camouflage, wearing an ammunition belt and holding a gun to his mouth.

JEALOUSY

Lanza attended Sandy Hook Elementary School briefly as a child. His mother volunteered there between 1998 and 2012. This caused tension between them. He became jealous, believing that his mother showed more affection towards her students than she ever did towards him. By this time, he had moved on to Newtown High School. Though an honours student, he was taken out of school to be home-schooled by his parents, and attended Western Connecticut State University in 2008 and 2009. Lanza had trouble socializing and making friends. He disliked anything that forced him into contact with other people – he hated birthdays, Christmas and holidays with a passion.

As a teenager he was diagnosed with Asperger syndrome. Lanza also suffered from obsessive compulsive disorder; he refused to touch doorknobs with his bare hands and changed his socks 20 times a day. He was prescribed drugs to help with his autism and other behavioural disorders but refused to take them. He grew increasingly angry at being forced to go for psychiatric tests at Yale. A nurse there, who saw him between 2006 and 2007, described him as 'emotionally paralyzed'.

When he was about ten years old he wrote a story with another boy entitled 'The Big Book of Granny'. The story is about an old woman who kills people indiscriminately with the gun in her cane. In one chapter, there's a game called Hide and Go Die. In it, one character stated rather chillingly, 'I like hurting people… especially children.'

OBSESSED WITH MASS MURDER

Like many boys, Lanza was fascinated by conflict and guns. But it didn't stop there. He became obsessed by the mass shootings at Columbine High School in 1999 and at Northern Illinois University in 2008. The Newtown report, released in November 2013, noted

Lanza became increasingly cut off and was clearly beginning to contemplate his own gun massacre.

he had 'hundreds of documents, images, videos pertaining to the Columbine H.S. massacre, including what appears to be a complete copy of the investigation'.

In his bedroom he kept a collection of newspaper cuttings on school shootings and there was a game called *School Shooting* on his computer. On the wall was a huge spreadsheet featuring the top 500 mass murders of all time, which he had created himself, and he had also written a document listing the prerequisites for mass murder. But no one ever came into his room to find out what was going on.

Increasingly, Lanza began to cut himself off from the outside world. His mother may have been trying too hard to protect him. She didn't insist that he take the medication he had been prescribed. She also cancelled follow-up trips with mental health professionals. After 2008, he stopped having any treatment at all. Nancy Lanza struggled to accept the fact that her son had disabilities. She repeatedly described him as 'gifted' when his intellectual abilities were really quite average.

As he grew older, his parents struggled to break through the barriers he put up. Despite living in the same house as his mother, he only contacted her by email. At one point, he didn't speak to her for three months. The windows of his room were covered with black garbage bags and he let no one else in. At the time of the killings, he hadn't seen his father for two years.

There was only one friend Lanza felt able to connect with. He remains anonymous and his testimony has only come out with the publication of the Sandy Hook Report. The two friends used to meet to play the video game *Dance Dance Revolution* and they talked about everything from Japanese techno music to paedophilia to chimp society. Lanza spent so much time playing *Dance Dance Revolution* that he acquired the nickname the 'DDR guy'.

In June 2012 the friends had a falling-out over a movie. Just months before the shooting, Lanza had thus lost his only buddy and became more and more isolated. He spent the three months before the shooting playing video games, studying previous mass murders and interacting online with a community of murder enthusiasts.

Lanza had developed his own theory of mass murder. As he saw it, they always occurred 'in contexts which involve some permutation of alienation'. His view of society was a gloomy one. He talked of the 'rape of civilization' and he railed against 'enculturing human children'. He put up post after post on online forums, explaining his philosophy, obsessing over mass killings and egging on others to bloodthirsty acts. No one ever intervened.

ANOREXIC

He was a scrawny teenager who suffered from anorexia. His eating habits were unhealthy. He would add salt to his drinking water. At the time of his death he was 1.83 m (6 ft) tall but weighed only 51 kg (112 lb). In retrospect, the chief medical examiner suggested that malnutrition might have caused damage to his brain.

Nancy Lanza was only too aware that her son had a violent streak. Just a week before the shooting, she told a friend that she was afraid that he was getting worse. He kept burning himself with a lighter, but Nancy was afraid that he might try to commit suicide. Nancy had health issues herself. She had recently been diagnosed with MS.

On 10 December 2012 Nancy Lanza made a fateful decision which might have precipitated the killings. She decided to try an 'experiment'. She would leave Lanza on his own for a few days while she made a trip to New Hampshire. A few hours after she left, there were signs that her 'experiment' wasn't going too well. Adam had bumped his head and was bleeding.

On the evening of 13 December, she returned home for the last time. At 9.00 am the next day, Nancy Lanza was sleeping peacefully in her bed when her son entered and shot her in the head with her own gun. He took her guns, a Bushmaker XM15-E2S rifle, a civilian version of the semi-automatic weapon used by the US Army in Afghanistan and Iraq, and two handguns, a Glock pistol and a Sig Sauer, and left the house. Armed to the teeth, he climbed into his mother's car and drove to his old school, Sandy Hook Elementary.

The doors to the school were locked, so Lanza shot his way in through a nearby glass panel. Dressed in black clothing, sunglasses and a green utility vest, he struck a terrifying figure. The first shots fired were heard over the school intercom. The head janitor saw Lanza and yelled at him: 'Put the gun down!' Lanza ignored him and proceeded to kill the school's principal, Dawn Hochsprung, and the school psychologist, Mary Sherlach.

Lanza moved on to Lauren Rousseau's first-grade classroom. Rousseau had sent her children to the back of the room and was trying to hide them in a bathroom as Lanza entered. Soon Rousseau, Rachel D'Avino, a behavioural therapist, and 14 children were dead. A six-year-old girl was the only survivor of the attack. She managed to phone her mother: 'Mommy, I'm okay, but all my friends are dead.'

Kaitlin Roig-DeBellis hid her students in a tiny 1 m x 1.2 m (3 ft x 4 ft) bathroom. She told them: 'If we're going to live, we have to find a hiding place … Evil is coming for us and there's nowhere to go.'

Many thought Lanza was harmless, but his obsession with school shootings kept growing.

Town volunteers of the Sandy Hook Fire and Rescue Department were some of the first people on the scene after the shooting. Here, they hug during a minute of silence held on 21 December 2012.

Roig-DeBellis instructed her students to remain silent, and barricaded the door. One of them told her, 'I don't want to die before Christmas.' Eventually, the police arrived and knocked loudly. Terrified, she demanded some ID before she opened up. A badge slid under the door and she flung it open in relief.

Some teachers read stories to their children and others quietly sang Christmas carols. Twenty-seven-year-old Victoria Soto died shielding a child from Lanza's gunfire.

Yvonne Cech and Maryann Jacob hid their students in the library and pushed a filing cabinet against the door when they could not get the lock to work. Lanza tried to enter and, when it proved too much work, he moved on to easier prey.

It was only five minutes from the sound of the first gunshots to the welcome whine of police sirens, but it was already too late. Over 100 rounds had already been fired. Police officers encountered a horrific scene. Bullet-ridden corpses of children and teachers alike were strewn across the school. Trauma teams were assembled ready to deal with any casualties and the emergency room of the nearest hospital was prepared to receive an influx of visitors. In the end only three victims reached the hospital. The others were already dead. The final shot was fired at 9.40 am – it was Lanza taking his own life.

For the survivors, the memory of this terrible day never goes away. Kaitlin Roig-Debellis remembers it 'every second of every minute of every single day'. The community of Newtown, Connecticut, still struggles to come to terms with the horrific event.

One of the teacher's daughters still cannot believe it happened. According to Ashley Cech, 'If you know Newtown, if you know Sandy Hook, you just had this idea that nothing wrong could happen there.'

Sadly, Adam Lanza proved otherwise.

A touching memorial to the 26 victims, young and old, of Adam Lanza: Newtown will never be able to forget the terrible day that they were gunned down in cold blood.

INDEX

Abotsway, Serena 93
Adams, Agnes 144, 146
Agisheff, Amina 10
Alexander, Diane 172
Allen, Cathleen 129
Allen, Harry 57
Allitt, Beverley 178–85
Anderson, Lilian 51
Anderson, Mylette 51
Angel, Ron 51
Askins, Jacqueline 142, 144
Askren, Jeffrey 129

Baker, Sherry 106
Barbosa, Daniel Camargo 28–31
Barbosa, Theresa 28
Barney, Donald 172
Bates, William 49, 51
Berdella, Robert 154–9
Berndsen, Lawrence 172
Bintanja, Henk 46
Bockova, Blanka 77, 78
Bodnarchuk family 19, 21
Bollivar, Jennie 46
Bond family 129
Bonner, Debra 10, 12
Bowling, William 170
Bozhinoski, Radoslav 70
Breivik, Anders 188–91
Briceño, Daniel Camargo 28
Bright, Kathryn 106, 109, 113
Bright, William 106
Bronzich, Connie Jo 47
Brown, Margaret 54
Bryson, Chris 155–7, 158
Buehlmann, Albert 172
Bundy, Carol 40–3
Bundy, Ted 17
Butner, Silas 170

Cameron, Lord 56
Cameron, Stevie 92
Campbell, Charles Eugene 51
Canter, Milton 172
Carr, Carswell 49, 51
Carr, Mandy 49, 51
Carrière, Laurent 47
Carroll, Michael 129

Carroll, Sam 170
Carrou, Charmaine 46
Castillo, Alcira 29
Cech, Yvonne 204
Chan, Yik Hung 'Henry' 181
Chapman, Marcia Faye 10, 12
Chikatilo, Andrei 84, 85
Chillington, John 98
Christensen, Carol Ann 12, 16
Christie, Ethel 149, 152, 153
Christie, John 148–53
Clark, Douglas 40–3
Clark, Franklin 40
Cleave, Kelly Van 116–18, 120, 122, 123
Cody, Henry 172
Coffield, Wendy Lee 10, 12
Collier, Peter 54
Collins, William 172
Collison, Helen 54
Columbine High School massacre 192–5
Combs, John 170
Comer, Marnette 43
Constanzo, Adolfo de Jesus 34
Conway, Bill 36, 37
Cooke, Isabelle 54–5, 56
Cosner, Paul 129
Crampton, Paul 180, 182
Crawford, Betty 33
Crey, Dawn 92
Crockett, Robert 172
Curtis, Alice 48, 51

Darreau, Alphonse 45
Davidson, Michael 181
D'Avino, Rachel 203
Davis, Dolores 109, 112, 113, 114
Dawson, Ann 49, 51
Day, Odas 172
d'Escogne, Felix 45
Desmond, Kayley 179–80
Dolinin, Tamara 21
Dowdy, Bernard 32
Drusinova, Tatyana 85
Dubbs, Sandra 38
Dubchak family 19, 21
Dubs family 129
Dudley, Deborah 142, 144, 146
Dunn, Sydney 54, 57

Duparr, Laddie 46, 47

Eady, Muriel 150, 153
Elliott, James 172
Elstone, Patrick 181
Epstein, Charles 198
Estes, Debra 12
Evans, Beryl 150, 152, 1153
Evans, Geraldine 150, 152, 153
Evans, Logan 169–70
Evans, Roger 172
Evans, Timothy 152

Fager family 112
Fawkes, Sandy 48, 50
Fernández, Dioselina 28–9
Ferris, James 155
Fox, Nancy 104, 107–8, 109, 110, 113, 114
Frey, Ernest 172
Fritzl, Alexander 137
Fritzl, Elisabeth 134, 135–6, 137
Fritzl, Felix 136, 137
Fritzl, Josef 132–7
Fritzl, Kerstin 132–4, 136, 137
Fritzl, Lisa 136, 137
Fritzl, Maria 132
Fritzl, Michael 136
Fritzl, Monica 137
Fritzl, Rosemarie 134, 135, 136, 137
Fritzl, Stefan 136, 137
Fuerst, Ruth 150, 153

Gabbert, Sandra 15–16
Galbraith, Russell 57
Garmash, Sergei 21
Gelernter, David 198
Gerald, Jeff 129
Gibson, Bradley 180–1
Gilbert, Ben 170
Giulietti, Donald 129
Goldberg, Richard 57
Granger, Don 105
Greer, Gary 91–2
Gruber, Maria 174–7
Grundy, Kathleen 164, 166
Gryshchenko, Galina 21
Gudz, Victor 21
Gunnar, Charles 129
Guno, Rebecca 91

Hakim, Vitali 46
Hardwick, Timothy 179
Harris, Byron 194
Harris, Eric 192–5
Harris, Joseph 171
Harrison, Margaret 170
Harvey, Donald 168–73
Hedge, Marine 109, 111–12, 113
Heidnik, Betty 141
Heidnik, Ellen 138, 140
Heidnik, Gary 138–47
Heidnik, Michael 138–9, 146
Hemker, Cornelia 'Cocky' 46
Hendy, Cindy 116–23
Hicks, Ebon Charylnn 50
Hill, Doug 172
Hinds, Cynthia Jean 10, 12
Hiscox, Bill 92
Hochsprung, Dawn 203
Hoeweler, Carl 172
Horn, Dan 169
Houston, Sam 108
Hovey, Doris 49, 51
Howe, Marjorie 51

Jacob, Avoni 46
Jacob, Maryann 204
Jaramillo, Giovanny Arcesio Noguera 31
Johnson, Emmett 50
Johnson, Lois 50
Johnson, Randy 129
Johnson, Willie 172
Jones, Karen 43
Jones, Richard 16

Kaczynski, David 198–9
Kaczynski, Ted 196–9
Kasayev, Victor 21
Kellett, David 97, 98
Kendrick, Clayborn 172
King, Christopher 181
King, Sara 16
Klebold, Dylan 192–5
Klimova, Tamara 87
Kneilands, Anne 53
Knight, Katherine 96–101
Knowles, Paul 48–51
Kochergina, Nadezhda 21

Kondzela, Galina 21
Kryuchkov family 21
Kuckro, Margaret 172
Kulyazhov, Valery 85

Lake, Donald 129, 130
Lake, Leonard 126–31
Lanza, Adam 200–5
Lanza, Nancy 200, 202, 203
Lanza, Peter 200, 202
Leclerc, Marie 45
Lee, Earl 51
Lee, Kasee Ann 10
Leidolf, Irene 174–7
Leitz, Hilda 172
Lemon, Stella 172
Ličoska, Duko 70
Ličoska, Lubica 69, 70–1
Lindsay, Sandra 142, 144
López, Pedro 31, 162
Lucas, Henry Lee 32–9

Mackenzie, Susan 50
Maclennan, Hectorina 153
Malinowski, Mikhail 21
Maloney, Kathleen 152, 153
Malvar, Marie 11–12
Manuel, Peter 52–7
Marrero, Rebecca 17
Marusina family 21
Masser, Brunhilde 77, 78
Mawson, Judith 11
McGinniss, Kelly Kay 11
McLaughlan, Mary 52–3
McMahon, George 25
McMunn, Mr and Mrs 55
McQueen, Eugene 170
Meadow, Roy 183
Melnik, Oleg and Ludmila 21
Meteric, Don 34
Metzger, Helen 172
Meyer, James 51
Meyer, Stephanija 174–7
Midden, Vernon 170
Milligan, Terry Rene 10
Mills, Opal Charmaine 10, 12
Minarcin, Pat 172
Mirceski, Igor 70
Montano, Angie 119–20, 123
Moore, Reuben 35, 36

Moore, Sterling 171
Mortyakova, Svetlana 85
Moskalyova, Marina 86
Mrak, Bianca 79
Murray, John 42, 43

Nally, Doris 172
Nelson, Leon 172
Nelson, Rita 152, 153
Ng, Charles 126–31
Nicol, Allan 52
Nolan, Dan 13
Novosad family 21

Odintsov, Sergei 21
Onoprienko, Anatoly 18–21, 82
Otero family 104–5, 109, 110

Panzram, Carl 22–7
Parashchuk, Maria 21
Parenteau, Clifford 129
Parker, Leo 172
Parker, Marie 118, 122–3
Pavelski, Gorica 71
Pearson, Larry 159
Peasgood, Christopher 181
Peck, Claire 181–2
Peck, Susan 181–2
Peluso, James 172
Perkins, Patricia Gay 92
Pesendorfer, Franz Xaver 176–7
Phillips, Becky and Katie 180, 181
Phillips, Sue 180, 181
Pichushkin, Alexander 84–7
Pickton, Robert 90–5
Pierce, Kathie 49, 51
Pike, Joseph 172
Pilat family 19, 21
Podolyak family 21
Porter, Nelson 182
Powell, Becky 34, 35, 36, 37, 39
Powell, Frank 34
Powell, John W. 172
Price, John 96, 98–101
Profitt, Hiram 172

Rader, Dennis 102–15
Rail, Sheryl 91
Rawlins, Maggie 170
Ray, David Parker 116–23

Ray, Jesse 117, 118
Reichert, Dave 10
Relford, Shirley Van 109
Rhodes, Harry 171
Rich, Kate 34, 36, 37
Ridgway, Gary 10–17
Risteski, Ante 70
Ritter, James 171
Rivera, Josefina 141–2, 144, 146
Rogozin, Sergei 18
Roig-DeBellis, Kaitlin 203–4
Rossmo, Kim 91
Rousseau, Lauren 203
Rule, Linda 16
Ryan, Phil 37
Rybalko, Alexander 21

Sandy Hook shootings 200–5
Sasser, Milton Bryant 170
Saunders, Dave 98
Savitsky, Anatoly 21
Schäfer, Margaret 74–5, 77–8
Schenner, August 77–8
Schreibesis, Edward 172
Schrempf, Elfriede 77, 78
Service, Robert 90
Sheldon, Robert 158–9
Sherlach, Mary 203
Shipman, Harold 162–7
Shipman, Primrose 164
Simjanoska, Mitra 69–70, 71, 73
Smart, Doris 55, 56
Smart, Mrs 34–5
Smart, Peter 55, 56
Smith, Harold 57
Sobhraj, Andre 45
Sobhraj, Charles 44–7
Sonenberg, George 39
Stenquist, Jim 130
Stoltenberg, Jens 190
Stoops, Todd 155, 159
Svetlovsky, Alexander 21
Syomin, Yury 87

Taneski, Vlado 68–73
Taylor, Liam 178–9
Temelkoska, Živana 69, 71, 73
Thomas, Lisa 142, 144
Thompson, Mose 172
Tkach, Serhiy 80–3

Toole, Druscilla 34
Toole, Ottis 32, 33–4, 38, 39
Tremont, Annabella 46, 47
Trpkovski, Goce 71, 73
Tsalk, Boris 21
Twitty, James 171
Tyree, James 170

Unabomber 196–9
Unterweger, Jack 74–9
Uszacke, Alexander 26

Vasylyuk, Victor and Anna 21
Vian, Shirley 106–7, 110, 113
Vigil, Cynthia 120–1, 123
Viricheva, Maria 85–6
Voloshko, Serhiy 83

Wagner, Waltraud 174–7
Wallace, Mark 159
Walsh, Adam 38
Warnke, Robert 26
Watson, Nathan J. 172
Watt, Marion 54
Watt, Vivienne 54
Watt, William 56
Weaver, Joe Dan 37
Weddle, Virgil 172
Wegerle, Vicki 104, 109, 112, 113, 114
Whalen, James 172
Wilcox, Leann 10
Williams, Anna 111, 113
Williams, Harvey 170
Williams, James 95
Wilson, Edward 172
Wilson, Exxie 43
Wilson, Mona 93
Wine, Dawn 51
Wine, Karen 51
Woldrich, Christa 135–6
Wood, James T. 172
Woodruff, Angela 166
Wyan, Viola Reed 170
Wyatt, Elizabeth 170

Yancy, Roy 118, 122

Zaghranichny, Sergei 21
Zaichenko family 19, 21
Zakharko, Stepan 21

INDEX **207**

PICTURE CREDITS

t = top, b = bottom, l = left, r = right

Alamy: 12, 17, 32, 33, 35, 45, 49, 52, 54, 55, 56, 79, 95, 102, 103, 105, 112, 115, 143, 147, 151, 153, 162, 168, 173, 174, 175, 177, 185

Associated Press: 48, 126 (x2),

Barrington Barber: 22

Corbis: 13, 16, 26, 27, 44, 47, 74, 76, 90, 92, 94, 97, 116r, 129, 132, 136, 137, 138, 148, 149, 152, 163, 188, 190, 191 (x2), 192(x2), 193, 194, 195b

FBI: 120

Getty Images: 15, 39, 50, 84, 108, 131, 171, 201, 204

Press Association: 121b, 122, 134, 178, 179, 189, 195t

Public Domain: 25, 68, 80, 91, 96, 99, 100, 107, 135, 154, 159, 200, 203

Rex Features: 18, 127

Shutterstock: 4, 6, 8, 11, 19b, 21, 23, 24, 29, 30, 31, 36 (x2), 37, 38, 42, 46, 58, 61, 63t, 64, 65, 66, 67, 70, 72, 73, 78, 83, 85, 86, 88, 93, 98, 101, 104, 109, 111, 119, 124, 133, 140, 141, 144, 145, 150, 155, 156, 157, 158 (x2), 160, 165, 166, 169, 170, 176, 180, 182, 183, 186, 202, 205

Shutterstock Editorial: 20

Topfoto: 41, 53

Washington Post: 60, 63b

Wikimedia Commons: 10, 19t, 28, 34, 40 (x2), 71, 75, 81, 82, 117, 118, 128, 139, 196, 197, 198, 199

Zuma Press: 116l, 121t, 123, 130

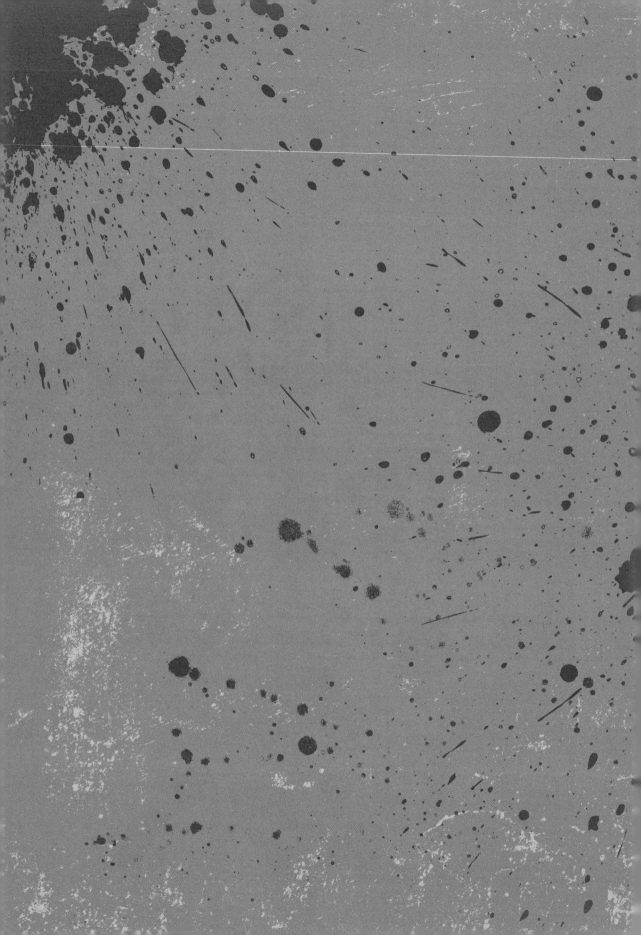